RECORD

RETREAT

REPORT

Also by Łukasz Marek Sielski

Should You Become a Software Developer? A book you should read before you decide to learn to code

The Not-So-Fun Ride to School

RECORD
RETREAT
REPORT

How hundreds of thousands fought road crime

Łukasz Marek Sielski

First published in Great Britain in 2024 by SIELAY Ltd.

Copyright © 2024 Łukasz Marek Sielski

Revision 1 – July 1sth 2024

The right of Łukasz Marek Sielski to be identified as the Author of the Work has been asserted by him in accordance with the Copyright, Designs and Patents Act 1988.

All rights reserved. No part of this publication may be reproduced, stored in a retrieval system, or transmitted in any form or by any means without the prior written permission of the publisher, nor may it be otherwise circulated in any form of binding or cover other than that in which it is published and without a similar condition being imposed on the subsequent purchaser.

Proofreading and inline-editing Martin Ouvry.

A CIP catalogue record for this title is available from the British Library.
Amazon Kindle ASIN B0D6DP9KHX
EBOOK Draft2Digital ISBN 979 8 227 35303 0
Amazon Paperback ISBN 979 8 853 97773 0
Amazon Hardcover ISBN 979 8 325 43796 0
www.sielay.com
www.phonekills.com

Printed and distributed by Amazon.

Please subscribe to the author newsletter at https://sielay.com

Some think using the phone while driving, speeding, or parking on zigzags is a victimless crime. They are frustrated that a driver caught doing these things can lose their driving licence and sometimes, as a result, their job. But the law wouldn't be in place if there weren't some tragedies resulting from such behaviour. And some motorists ignore that fact and takes the risk. Still more are likely to blame someone who has reported their behaviour. Blaming a witness is like blaming the tree that was in the way of a drunk driver who lost control of their vehicle.

To all victims of road crime

"The death of one man is a tragedy; the death of millions is a statistic"[i]. A pedestrian killed by a cyclist is a breaking story. One thousand seven hundred people killed by motorists is just a number.

Contents

Let's clean the path 11
A land of snitches 15
Pioneers 23
    In the beginning, there was a camera 25
    The platform 27
    Magnatom 29
    Not the only one 37
The mainstream 41
    Neighbour 45
    Broadcaster bullying of cyclists 51
    Traffic Droid 55
    Sherry 61
Jeremy 67
    Attack 75
    A voice of concern 81
    Q and A 87
    The Battle of Kensington 91
The force 97
    Disruptors 101
    Successful trial 109
    From 0 to 15 thousand 113
    Fix the justice system 117
    An envious cop 131
    Record, retreat, report 133
The masses 137
    When the feedback works 139
    Granny 143
    Adolescent boys hate women on bikes 149

Prove you're not a camel	157
Too many to mention	163
The unspeakable	165
The Bush and the Corner	169
Snakes and Turtles	181
The language	187
Behind the wall	195
Is there Hope?	199
Acknowledgements	203
Figures	205
Index	207
Endnotes	216

Let's clean the path

Let's clean the path

Is it cliché to claim that writing a book was a life-changing journey? Well, I will say it anyway. It transformed me. This book is deeply personal, even though I have tried to keep my distance and objectivity. Yet, while working on it, I found that I was not that unique at all. My experiences, observations and feelings are surprisingly common. Millions of people in the UK are victimised, bullied and harassed by motorists' entitlement and road crime. Tens – if not hundreds – of thousands have resolved to resist, in the form of *third-party reporting* – the main topic of this book.

In these pages, you will have a chance to meet people who influenced that phenomenon. But you may notice that it exists in its own right. It doesn't depend on any one of those people. Nothing would change if Mikey, Lewis or Jeremy put their cameras down tomorrow. There will still be an unfathomable number of others uploading videos of dangerous drivers to the police. It has reached a critical mass, and it cannot be stopped, no matter how many salty crocodile tears might flow down offenders' cheeks.

The research wasn't too challenging. On the contrary, it was more difficult to filter sources and stick to the main topic. To achieve that, we must clarify several things:

First, this book is purely about *third-party reporting*. We may touch on the topics of active travel, car dependency, climate change, or fifteen-minute cities, or any other headline-worthy theme. But it won't be a full study of those issues. It would be a disservice to investigate them without proper attention and distraction from the main mission of the book.

Secondly, cycling will not be our primary interest, and neither would I claim to portray everyone who chooses to travel on two wheels, drive or walk. Bikes are central to this story because the media have built a narrative about this vehicle. The story would be different if we had the same uproar about drivers using dashcams. But as it affects our topic, we will dive a bit into what seems to be an engineered hate towards cyclists, who nowadays seem to be the only group that can be publicly dehumanised and harassed without severe consequences. However, it will be a generalised survey of the issue, and will focus mainly on the link to *third-party reporting*.

Let's clean the path

Thirdly, I hope some of you do *not* agree with me and my guests. Presenting their perspective is in itself a success to me. Even if you do not change your mind about these things, it will at least mean you are open to a dialogue rather than further hate and "footballisation". We may need to debunk typical cliches like road tax, red light jumping, riding in the middle of the road and the benefits of hi-viz and helmets – but we will do it briefly. Some indeed require clarification. To tackle the first of these, I had to send an FOI[2] request to HM Treasury to disprove the claim that there is a hypothecated[3] road tax. There is no such thing.

The **fourth** thing I shall move out of our way is the personal views of my guests. They were chosen because of their value to the story. Some of them hold very controversial positions on other topics. Reaching out to several resulted in an uproar on social media. Perhaps it was for valid reasons, but what sort of study would it be without the core influencers? A car driver crashing into a pedestrian rarely has the luxury of asking them who they vote for or what they think about identity politics.

The **Fifth** and last thing is me. It may seem incredible to be immersed in the story and be both a narrator and an extra (surely not a lead). I will share my tale with you, but it only matters because I'm involved in the reporting. Anything else is just a distraction. I knew that my position would be both a blessing and a curse. Writing under my real name was tough, but controlling the information was simpler than containing the spillage. I learned that the hard way. And I will come back to that; I promise.

Let's clarify: I have skin in the game on all fronts. I am a cyclist, riding with a video camera and with close to a thousand reports of traffic offences. I am vocal about road travel. I wear an *Evil Cycling Lobby* jumper in the office and support colleagues who commute on the bike: "That's Lukasz from the bike shed. He's famous!" one reporter said the other day when we met in the pub, causing consternation for my colleagues.

At the same time, I am a driver with a few decades' experience of being behind the steering wheel. I understand the value of some motor usage. I am also an immigrant – and yes, this argument is used against me regularly – assimilated, tax-paying, and owning a black passport (it is not blue, is it?).

I work in the media, and that fact triggered many people to cancel me on Twitter in the early days. Being a *journo* is an excellent reason to be blocked. But I am not a reporter. I am an engineer. But okay, I get it. The media in the UK needs a better track record regarding the topic being discussed. Even the *Evening Standard* with Ross Lydall and the *Guardian* with Peter Walker, both with massive contributions to road safety, can publish jaw-droppingly wrong, click-bait titles fuelling further aggression towards cyclists or ignorance of the damage caused by drivers. What matters to me is that I can voice my beliefs as long I stay professional. Trust me, I have been to places where alternative opinions were not welcome.

As the path is clear now, I shall make the tone less formal with more contractions and tend to the story. I hope you'll enjoy it.

Let's clean the path

A land of snitches

In the eyes of *Telegraph* columnist Celia Walden, the United Kingdom has become a country of snitches.[4] Writing in the context of the 2020 lockdown, she ridiculed people reporting barbecues, sleepovers, or laughs. Then she moved to Mike van Erp's[5] video that landed Guy Ritchie a six-month driving ban. When she wrote, "There's one thing I loathe more", I couldn't work out if she meant dangerous drivers or those who report them. Perhaps, as a non-native speaker, I missed the subtlety of her statement. However, the ambiguity raised a crucial question. What do we despise more, wrongdoing or standing up to offenders? Does it depend on one's role in the event? Is it about our history, background, or pre-existing affiliations? Would we report a burglar? What about a drunk driver? What about someone who passes a cyclist close enough to scare them but does not kill?

I sat on a crowded bus in central Warsaw and realised that Walden might have been onto something. On the Warsaw streets were a greater number of drivers glued to their screens than in London. In 2021, in Poland, there were almost twice as many road deaths per million inhabitants as in the UK (Poland 2,245[6] per 38 million – 59; UK 1,158[7] per 63 million – 24). It is such a frightening fact that it has been used as the opening to the fantastic book *Watching the English* by Kate Fox.[8] She remembered a day when she drove with her husband to a wedding. At first, she noticed drivers pulling onto the hard shoulder to let others overtake them. She thought that was extremely polite and considerate. Her spouse quickly pointed to the number of crosses and shrines left on the roadside. Each marked a fatal collision. Yet, third-party reporting doesn't exist in that country.

If you look at the media headlines and figures, the UK is a world leader in third-party reporting – where the public forwards the evidence of crime or offence to the police. Why is it so? Why not the United States or China, where most of the technology used in our cameras is developed? Why not Australia, where, some say, the first headcam cyclists appeared? Why not the Netherlands,

Denmark, Germany, or France, which have a much larger number of commuter cyclists, so there is a greater chance for tension as well?

Is *snitching* a profoundly British thing? Is it a fault or a national virtue? It may originate from the values and institutions of the country and its legal system.

"The police are the public, and the public are the police."[9]

We could consider plenty of factors, but Peel's *Nine Principles of Policing by Consent*, the pillars of British law enforcement, could be the most important. The common understanding is that this model regards police officers simply as citizens in uniform – nothing more. That fact alone changes the dynamics of society. Bobbies are not untouchable demigods like in other countries. The second fundamental change suggested by Peel was that a force's success is measured not by the number of arrests but by the absence of crime. Last but not least, principles require the police to seek public approval and cooperation and actively encourage it. That is a reason for third-party reporting to exist.

The method is rare. Except for the UK, it's applied only in Ireland, Canada, Australia and New Zealand. While Peel is credited for the principles, they seem to have different authors. Historians suggest that they were created by joint commissioners of the newly formed Metropolitan Police, Charles Rowan and Richard Mayne, who were inspired by Peel's speeches.

British people have a unique relationship with law enforcers. It's unlike the rest of the world. At least it used to be, as some authors claim,[10] forces have more recently turned into paramilitary organisations far from the cherished *bobbies-on-the-beat*.[11] In what other country can one approach an officer and challenge them without being arrested (or shot)? Nothing stops us from approaching a police van and saying, "Sir, can you please turn off the engine while parked?" Many officers don't know it's illegal to keep the engine idling. You can check that in the Highway Code, rule 123,[12] and associated legislation.[13,14]

One can file Freedom of Information (FOI) requests to scrutinise a local force or prove that drivers are the biggest group of third-party evidence submitters. We have a community speed watch. Many patrols involve special constables.[15] Except in airports, embassies, and a few other places, you won't see police carrying firearms.

Diplomatic units are particularly bad with traffic law. They had a habit of parking in front of my office, on the double yellow lines, blocking the visibility of the junction and pedestrian crossing ahead. After months of chasing them on social media, they finally stopped doing that. Can one achieve such a result anywhere else?

Let's not forget that police commissioners are elected by the people as well. That is, except in Scotland. The power the public has over law enforcement seems unprecedented, yet very few Brits know or value that fact. On the contrary, many still see cooperation with the force as collaboration with a fascist regime. Such over-dramatised narrative often has very high-profile sources: Jeremy Clarkson dwelled on the topic with a level of fashion fetish: "Like the Stasi never went away. It even comes with a sinister uniform. Black shorts over black tights, a lemon-green shirt, and a surveillance camera on your head. It's like the Stasi never went away",[16] he wrote in his *Sun* column. Katie Hopkins, in a post after visiting imprisoned ex-BBC presenter Alex Benfield, convicted of four accounts of stalking,[17] wrapped up her tweet with the *#bikenonce* hashtag.[18] It was received as a reference to one of the stalker's victims – Jeremy Vine. It is no surprise that following such name-calling pornography, some people feel entitled to call concerned citizens a *snitch, nonce, grass, squealer* or *rat* – all of it prison slang.

We have to put up with tirades of hate from jail-inspired minorities. Despite that, people are still willing to spend their time and energy on third-party reporting. But why? It cannot be only because they can, right? What motivates them? There is something specific about the setting – our roads.

And no, it's not about the way they are built. Neither is it because we drive on the left.[19] Except for strange experiments like Stevenage, we don't have wide alleys like Central or Eastern Europe – nor even wider multi-lane roads as in the US. There is much less space to put cycle lanes or widen the pavements.

Our streets are narrow and clogged with parked cars, overgrown hedges, wheelie bins and other things, primarily SUVs, struggling to pass. As for their layout, British high streets look more like those in the Netherlands or Denmark. They also have hills, and wind, and the rain is worse over there. Car ownership is as significant, yet they chose a different approach. If it's not about the roads as such, perhaps it's about how we (do not) share them?

Many drivers don't comply with, or know, for that matter, about recent changes to road hierarchy.[20] Good luck using the new H2 rule when crossing a side street in Kensington. You'll likely end up on a cab's bonnet if you're not filming. During one of my road crossings early in January 2024, I was centimetres from being mown down by a van driver. I tried to cross a side street and instead of letting me go, he sped up. That was the third event like that in a week, so I decided to cross with a camera turned on. Video from the event gathered 1.5M views on X before it was taken down as the Met decided to prosecute the driver. My manner of crossing was rightly criticised – including by Daniel ShenSmith, a.k.a the Black Belt Barrister.[21] I agreed with that, in a follow-up recording describing infrastructural issues at the junction.[22] Yet the event was far from uncommon to the local authorities – who, to my understanding, choose to ignore it. In private chats with the local police, when asked about the crossing's safety, the only answer I got was a shrug and a mention of "no resources".

In many developing countries, a car still symbolises social status. In the UK, it's an outdated symbol of freedom. One can remember only two situations in recent history when so many people tried to shield their rights as laid down in the Magna Carta: during the 2020 lockdown and when the update to the Highway Code was introduced. The H2 rule wasn't changing anything but making rules 170[23] and 180[24] more transparent to the drivers. Not complying with them means failing the driving test. Yet, from behind the steering wheel, everyone seems to be in your way, an obstruction, a nuisance. Even the legal system seems to see it this way. Collecting 78 penalty points (most sources state 68, but even the original article contains both figures[25]) and still holding a driving licence is possible.[26] According to the *Sun*, over 10,000 drivers with over 12 points on their licence were spared the ban in 2019. *Exceptional hardship* is being used as a get-out-of-jail-free card, and causing death by dangerous driving may often end with a suspended or no sentence. Cycling UK research in 2021 revealed that more than 8,000 drivers escaped the ban by using that argument.[27] Between 2017 and 2021, the total number was 35,569. That is one in five (142,275 who received the ban).[28] It doesn't make *exceptional hardship* very *exceptional*, does it? In recent UK history, every single person who killed someone while cycling was found and jailed – I will talk about the exception in the chapter "Fix the justice system". But there were 7,708 hit-and-run collisions in 2021 in London alone, in which at least 167 people died.[29] Many of those events end up without the culprit being found or named. Even the person who drove their Land Rover into a primary school in Wimbledon, killing two girls and seriously injuring others, is unknown to the public today.[30] It feels like murder or manslaughter is legal in the UK as long as a car is the weapon.[31]

London may be the safest place to cycle in the whole of Europe. Yet the lack of consistent infrastructure throws cyclists into heavy traffic or onto the pavements. And the legality of pavement cycling is more complex than it may seem, with the Highway Code and various memoranda contradicting each other. Women are exceptionally at risk. One woman died on the day I edited this chapter. In rural settings it's even worse, with relatively narrow and bendy roads, often with hedges limiting visibility and with high speeds allowed.[32] Who sticks to the speed limit anyway? Almost half the drivers surveyed by the RAC admitted ignoring it.[33] Even former Home Secretary Suella Braverman made headlines for allegedly trying to dodge points for speeding by arranging a private awareness course.[34]

The problem is broader than cycling vs driving. Being a pedestrian in the UK is stressful and plain dangerous. On the one hand, there are no jaywalking laws,[35] but there are also very few safe crossings. A dropped curb or pedestrian aisle aren't legally a crossing. Each zebra requires a Belisha beacon, so drivers understand what the crossing means. That massively increases their cost and is something rather tricky to comprehend for a driver from the continent. Pavement parking is endemic, and parents with prams or people with disabilities must often enter the road to pass. That ends in tragedies. Try to ask a driver to give you more space and prepare for a saucy response or an assault. Funnily enough, pavement parking is illegal in London, but the law is hardly ever enforced. Scotland introduced a pavement parking ban recently, but we are still to see it working in practice. And we have only mentioned situations where the pedestrian must enter the road. Trevor Bird, 52 was walking with his 24-year-old son from the local social club, when the driver of a blue BMW mounted the pavement and hit them. The father died on the spot, while the son was taken to hospital with severe head injuries.[36] Between 2005 and 2018, 548 pedestrians were killed by vehicles on the pavements: that's 40 a year. Out of 548, six of them were killed by cyclists.[37]

In such a vile environment, given the legal and practical tools, it was only a question of when, not if, people would take things into their own hands. And they did. Only recently has third-party reporting been focused on drivers using mobile phones. It all started with close passes, near hits, cutting in front of the rider, and pulling out without checking.

The media picked the term *vigilante* to label people using this system. But it's not what that word means. At least not if you check in the dictionary.

> *vigilante – a person who tries in an unofficial way to prevent crime or to catch and punish someone who has committed a crime, especially because they do not think that official organisations, such as the police, are controlling crime effectively. Vigilantes usually join together to form groups.*[38]

A vigilante enforces justice. But that's not what reporting is. It's the act of being a witness. Police, the Court Prosecution Service (CPS), and courts enforce the law. If Mike van Erp, David Brennan or Dave Sherry were vigilantes, they'd go full-blown Judge Dredd, knocking mirrors and windscreens. It is just another label, the same as *lycra louts, cycle zealots, bike nonce,* etc. Dehumanising and slurring. At the same time, people who demolish public property instead of common criminals can be called *blade-runners*![39] Do they know Harrison Ford is an *avid cyclist*?[40] This othering is going hand in hand with driver entitlement. It boils down to and comes back to us as real-life direct attacks, harassment or assaults. Some of the stories I'm about to tell you seem surreal, yet they happened. What was the trigger? The mere fact that the person dared to ride a bike on a road.

If all of that was not enough for people to fight back, then what is? Of course, we can raise the question of those who confront drivers or start looking out for offenders. I've been there. I know how it feels and the toll it takes. But is it a root problem, a symptom, or a cry for help? Desperation is a last resort when the state and society do not do enough to protect the vulnerable.

Cycling has become more inclusive, and the average cyclist in the capital no longer fits the image of the 20-30-year-old white male. This is the same for third-party reporting. The reasons that most known and popular reporters match the old stereotype is that ladies, ethnic minorities and LGBTQ+ people experience far more violence and abuse. They prefer to stay unnoticed. Most people using third-party reporting services are in fact drivers,[41] yet the cyclists get the beating. You're unlikely to risk more of that if you're already targeted.

It's easy to smear someone by calling them a *grass*. It's simple to play whataboutery, referring to *red light jumping* and not wearing a helmet. It's more challenging to take responsibility for one's actions or inaction. It's harder to admit that we may be part of the problem. Our lack of patience or empathy can cause not only someone else's anxiety, but it can also kill them. And killing is one of the things motoring does best.

What we, and Walden, should hate are not those *snitches* but the bullies many people turn into when they sit down behind the wheel.

A land of snitches

Pioneers

It was January of 2023. A few months earlier, my first book had come out, and I started to think about what to do next. While it was just a indie publication, it was a great lesson. It quickly taught me what I had done wrong, from ignoring promotion to not investing enough time and effort in quality. My thoughts were racing back and forth between the book, work, family and my third-party reports. There weren't many in the previous year, just 35. Almost ten times fewer than in 2019. The process wore me down and I desperately wanted to change something. I tried to commute safely and to have a clear conscience that I was still doing something whilst not stealing precious time from my closest family and friends.

It was some random argument on X that did it: "Loads of drivers on phones. Won't be able to report all captured. But the guy who later parked on zigzags suggested he can stab me for sure."[42] In a typical comment from a football-themed profile, Mac Bennet asked, "Do you have a job and/or a life? Genuinely curious."[43] It irritated me: "I work as a senior level manager and engineer. Have friends, family, and life. Many hobbies. Wrote a book. Enough?" "Pleasantly surprised", he replied. I was astonished. I'd expect some further rant, but Mac left it there. He left me with a thought. It's all his fault ;-)

The rest of the evening I spent googling for any previous publications on the topics of headcam cyclists and third-party reporting. No luck. That was my next challenge. That was a story I wanted to tell. A format I had never tried to write in my adult life,[44] it required research on a new scale. Finally, I had a way of channelling my selfish inner desire to have a positive impact.

If we had to define the mission of this book – even if I fail to deliver – we could say it's to answer the question of why people resolve to third-party reports. Is it useful? Is that correct? Does it make a difference? Does it save lives? Is it a growing or a declining phenomenon? Is there an alternative? What's the point? Can I even answer those questions? Or at least suggest some ideas?

To arrive there, we must start from a different angle: How? How did it begin? How and why did people decide to take things into their own hands? How is it possible for the police to delegate some of their responsibilities to the public? Who was the first to use a camera to defend themselves against dangerous drivers? Whose video was the first that resulted in actual prosecution?

Understanding how we got there could help us arrive at plausible reasoning. On a personal level, I might understand better why I joined the cause. Why can't so many of us leave our homes without a camera now?

The idea was not to draw any specific outline before at least half of the planned interviews were concluded. At best, I knew I wanted to tell the story chronologically. Who was there first?

It turned out that it was the camera.

In the beginning, there was a camera

Third-party reporting, as we know, requires evidence in the form of a photo or a video. To capture that footage, we need a device. Nowadays, we are spoiled with choices, from expensive GoPro and Insta360 to affordable ChilliTech or *no-names* from Alibaba or eBay. Plenty of pedestrians use their mobile phones to record events. Drivers equip their cars with NextBase, Vantrue, Garmin, Thinkware, or other competitive solutions. Many modern cars have them built in by default.

Where do the famous headcams used by many cyclists come from? That topic was presented in detail in an article by Zach in Pelvy,[45] so I'll sum it up: In the early 1960s, skydiver Bob Sinclair attached his gyro-stabilized camera to a football helmet and shot his jumps for the *Ripcord* show. Not much later, NASA modified the Hasselblad 500c and used them in space. F1 driver Jackie Stewart started putting his Nikon camera on his helmet to get stills from his drives. Later, he had a full-blown camera bound to one side of his head and a massive battery on the other.

The technological breakthrough came in the 1980s with the Canon Ci-10 pocket-size camera, which, with an inventive connectivity hack by Aerial Video Systems, allowed first-person broadcasting on air for the first time. For bikes, Mark Schulze mixed up a heavy VHS cam and a VCR set-up in his backpack. Later experiments involved a high-frame-rate CritterCam by Greg Marshall.

The real change came with the introduction of the GoPro camera. To this day, it's synonymous with recording cycle rides. In the early 2000s, Nicholas "Nick" Woodman, during his adventurous, adrenaline-seeking trips to Australia and Indonesia, formed an idea of a light, waterproof action camera that could also be affordable. He found a proper base for his prototype, arranged manufacturing in China, and went on a selling spree for his first mechanical, analogue, waterproof photo camera. His success in 2005 allowed his team to launch the first digital recorder the very next year. It was simple, rudimentary, and limited.

The tool found its purpose in 2006. They might not have been the first to record dangerous driving, but they will be the earliest history will remember. I'll come back to it shortly.

Since then, modern commuters have been spoilt for choice. It's still a niche digital market, and the key players don't change often. Outside GoPro, others worth mentioning are Insta360, ChilliTech, Drift, Cycliq, Technalogic, Akaso, and Garmin. They vary greatly in terms of resolution, battery lifetime, durability, price, and more.

The platform

Since 2006, more and more people have had access to light, portable cameras. Their videos have to go somewhere. Initially, the clips weren't about road danger; instead, they were made to show the fun side of rides. In the UK, the place that first gathered enthusiasts was the Cycling Plus forum. Eventually, videos started to land on YouTube, where they were accessible to the broader public.

The YouTube platform was founded in 2005 by three ex-PayPal employees: Chad Hurley, Steve Chen, and Jawed Karim – and was bought by Google sixteen months later. It was the birthplace of many phenomena, and bike-ride clips were just one of them. More and more viewers were attracted by footage of deadly situations from roads worldwide, with Russian dashcam footage becoming a gold standard of horror. Bike rides were still a tiny drop in the ocean, yet they attracted constantly growing audiences. YouTube, though, wasn't a suitable medium for general communication and virtual hanging out. Twitter[46] took on that role, gathering everyone interested in the abundance of topics and playing a prominent role in scaling awareness. It attracted the haters and trolls as well. After Twitter's massive success in the United States, the platform became important in the UK. It was the place where everyone had to be. Institutions and media followed. So did the headcam cyclists.

The Croydon Cyclist maintained a list of riders with cameras from all over YouTube.[47] By 2012, it included 473 British helmet-camera users, and also:

- American (86)
- Australian (33)
- Canadian (15)
- Dutch (12)
- German (10)
- Others (725 in total, 43 unassigned).

The oldest still online is "A Ride through Clyde Tunnel",[48] recorded by Magnatom[49] on June 29th 2006. Afterwards, Penticle uploaded "French recumbent ride"[50] on July 10th. The third was "Commute to work – new helmet cam"[51] by Andrew Bennet[52] on August 27th.

It did not take long for those leisure rides to be replaced by close calls: "Almost doored",[53] October 6th 2006, when Andy Bennet was inches from being taken out by an SUV driver who did not check the road before opening the door, and "Bus vs camera",[54] February 6th 2007, when Magnatom was tailgated and pushed by a local bus driver – the event which landed him in the local papers.

No matter who I asked, those names popped up each time. Who was the first? David Brennan and Andrew Bennet. I failed to contact Andrew, despite trying to reach every Andy, Andrew, Andrei, and Andrey Bennet I could find on X. After documenting the new cycle infrastructure in Vauxhall in 2015, he stopped posting bike rides and replaced them with diving footage. On the other hand, David remained active and eager to help me tell this story.

As the hills wrapped the Firth of Forth when I rolled towards his home, David Brennan's homeland became a bracket for this tale.

Magnatom

When I approached interviewees for this book, David was the first to respond, eager to share his experiences. Yet he remained humble throughout. The day after my memo, he replied with a lengthy letter outlining his journey through the years using the camera on his rides and beyond. David doesn't claim to be the first, and points at Andy instead. When it came to prominence, he left himself far behind other pioneers and has put far more limelight on Mike van Erp – the famous Cycling Mikey. They both began simultaneously on the Cycling Plus forum, sharing and discussing their footage. "Mikey always seemed to have a better camera than me!" David observed.

In both his writing and in person, there is something remarkable about David's spirit. Brennan strikes you as having outstanding drive, pushing himself towards new goals, usually for the greater good. The first article mentioning his name, in 2004, described how, while at Glasgow Southern General Hospital, the young scientist co-ran research debunking the common misogynistic belief that women are worse than men at reading maps.[55] At least, that's what the editorial spin was. In fact, his team confirmed that both sexes used the same regions of the brain linked to map-reading ability. That instinct took this bright lad into a battle one-on-one with road violence and grew into an idea for a national movement (literally) under the name "Pedal on Parliament". He managed to materialise that idea with the help of six friends. It may be, as he says, his "scientific brain" or "strong sense of justice".

It was on the commute to his place of work that he experienced the brutality of the roads. And it didn't make it any better that they led through picturesque Scottish landscapes.

On one occasion, he was passed by a van driver extremely close. He decided not to let it slip away but called the police, providing the plates. "They were decent enough and spoke to the driver," he said, but they couldn't do anything more without witnesses or evidence. A a light bulb in Dr Brennan's brain lit up. "A camera was the answer."

It was a remarkable coincidence that Oregon Scientific released a "cheap camera", as David called it. Yet it took him some time to collect funds to afford the purchase. Would that stop him? Not at all. He strapped his mobile phone to his backpack and recorded the ride through the Clyde Tunnel – the first YouTube uploaded. When asked about what he felt back then, he said: "It felt wrong that I could be placed in danger on the roads with absolutely no recourse if something happened."

The camera was helpful not only when dealing with the police but also when the footage was shared on the forum. David received a lot of feedback. "Much of it was positive and supportive, some of it was negative. Not abusive at that time, at least not initially, but some people would scrutinise every single detail of the situation and question my cycling. Whilst that was surprising to me, it was actually informative. It taught me to always question my actions and my motivations. It taught me to realise that, yes, sometimes I was in the wrong and to learn from that and try and improve. So, I've always been willing to listen to criticism so long as it was genuine and not abusive."

In the beginning, David's actions started to offer a lot of hope. After several scary incidents with bus drivers, First, a local bus operator, agreed to his suggestion to run a safety campaign. In an interview for *Metro*, Glasgow Edition, David said,[56] "I've got a camera in my helmet and, after an incident this year, I sent the video to First with suggestions they should start a drivers' campaign. I was amazed when First contacted me to say it would agree to the campaign." It was called "Give Cyclists Room" and was supposed to involve stickers inside the cabins of thousands of buses reminding drivers to give cyclists room and to enforce the message at safety briefings. It was a success with a sour aftertaste. The bus drivers did not appreciate being scrutinised. The hate campaign started to stem from their informal forum BloodBus, where conspiracy theories began. Most – like an accusation that David cycles because of losing his licence through drunk driving – were very quickly debunked and shut down.

The tension was great enough to throw Magnatom into the pages yet again. The *Sun* named him a "Tapped Crusader"[57] and suggested that his reports led to several bus drivers being sacked. David was approached by STV and managed to pass on his message after the *Sun* went on a three-day spree about him. "I am not out to antagonise anybody. I am trying to convey the message that all road users should be equal and that there should be more respect on the roads. As a cyclist, you get a lot of abuse on the roads. It's about mutual respect, and road users need to integrate better."[58] On the last day, the paper columnist John Smeaton tried his worst to trivialise David, calling him "Ped-Al Qaeda"[59] and listing a series of nonsensical myths about cyclists. To the claim that third-party reporting causes hatred towards cyclists, this is my riposte: It doesn't. That hate was already there.

Magnatom wasn't alone in his sentiments about road safety. The same week, when the *Scottish Sun* released their tirade, Fiona Russell recollected her experience in the pages of the Guardian.[60] She presented a fairer image of David and mentioned other successes of headcam use in the UK. Winchester-based Paul McNeil[61] pursued his claims after a collision on his way to work. He was one of hundreds already wearing a camera. As Russell reported, Action Cameras, one of the UK's leading sellers, experienced a threefold rise in sales in 2008. That meant an average of 50 per week for commuters.

With the rising popularity of Twitter, abuse multiplied. These weren't just insults. On one occasion, someone complained to David's employers about tweets being sent during work time. While he learned a painful lesson from it, the complainer was sloppy enough to leave tracks to be named and shamed, and eventually apologised. And the worst part? They used their own work computer to send abusive messages to David. It wasn't an easy journey for Brennan, but he persisted and, over time, focused more on promoting active travel and safe infrastructure in Scotland.

The most bizarre event happened in 2020.[62] David was cycling to work, carefully filtering through dead-slow traffic. When the lane widened and the driver in front of him kept close to the centre, Magnatom filtered past him and moved into the space ahead. The driver was triggered because the cyclist had navigated the traffic faster, and drove very close to him. David shouted in an apparent adrenaline rush, asking the motorist what he was doing. He reacted to the shock of the proximity of the vehicle by slapping its bonnet. The infuriated petrol-head jumped out of the car and came to hit David in the face. Any sensible person would expect such footage, once submitted to the police, to result in a charge of assault for the driver. But that wasn't the case. As the *Scottish Sun* reported, the driver ended up with a warning after David complained to the police about their poor response, and David was charged with a breach of peace as he had caused "fear and alarm" by swearing after he was abused and hit. Any reasonable person seeing the video, which is still online, would think that officers were either delusional or prejudiced. David later had the charge dropped and had five separate complaints against the police upheld.

Many months after getting David's letter, I packed my bike on a train to Edinburgh. I planned to cycle back to London and collect funds for RoadPeace, a charity supporting road crash victims. The main point of that trip was a detour to meet David in his home in the suburbs of Glasgow. I was afraid of visiting after day-long pedalling in the heat, but he insisted that his house was open and that he was used to visitors who were "tired and sweaty after a long bike trip or horse ride". And so, it was – open, though not smelly. I was welcomed by a tall cheerful man accompanied by a positivity-beaming family. They greeted me with a fuelling dinner and a Guinness cake (ace!). At the table, when listening to their children, you could feel the passion of the father and the piercing and inquiring intelligence of their mother. Curious and astonished, I munched through the plates as more and more layers of the hero unravelled in front of my eyes. Afterwards, we sat alone and thought about where the story might lead. After reading a detailed letter from David and digging through his media coverage, I didn't have much to add. Yet he still felt obliged to assist. Crushed by the carbohydrate rush in my head, I resolved to steal Steven Bartlett's question: Are you alright?

"At this moment, I've reached the stage when I've lost the energy to report things anymore," he said. On the still youthful face of a fit Scottish lad, you could see the emotional toll. His spirit was high, but his eyes hid a strain of sadness. "There is a case at the moment I reported back in November 2019. I actually went to the court back in April last year [2022], and it's still not completed. It will be almost four years before anything happens, and it was just a close pass." It wasn't the first time someone told me about reporting problems in Scotland. Along with Northern Ireland, it has no third-party reporting framework and a completely different legal system. Indeed, a week earlier, I had spoken about it with Deacon Thurston, another headline-reaching headcam cyclist from there.

When I asked David to think about the deeper meaning of what he had started and what kept him going, he said: "Over the years, for me, it just got really, really frustrating. But I was always happy to share my experience and do all that sort of stuff. I was never somebody to hide who I was. I had problems at work when somebody made a complaint about me. It has been a long journey. I always had an absolute belief that we should have a system where we shouldn't have to feel the need to get helmet cameras. I want to be able to go on a cycle lane and not feel any need to wear it. But essentially, we're in a situation when, certainly, for me, I cannot go on a ride without sticking one on. Because if something happens, I have absolutely no protection."

You could feel the stress in his voice, as though, in those few sentences, he had lost all his previous happiness. Yet, like it helped him release some tension, he grasped a deep breath and continued: "The problem with the police is that even if you've got a camera, you never know whether you're going to get any sort of protection anyway. As a result of my helmet camera use and publicity, I had people throw rocks at our house and car." He pointed at the windows. "They left tacks on the path to my front door. There was a case when a threatening letter was sent to my neighbours. Someone was threatening to throw poison into their gardens, with the aim of poisoning their pets, and were threatening them with violence just because my helmet camera was in use. One of my neighbour's cars was set on fire. And that neighbour didn't like my campaigning in the first place.

"It took a lot of effort to get the police to link all those incidents. Eventually, they did, but it never got anywhere. I'm pretty sure I know who it was, though. So, from day one, it has always been a battle with the police to get any positive work from them. Except for an odd police officer who was good."

David spent so much time and energy fighting for safer roads in his country that I wondered if he'd stop recording and reporting drivers if the government provided Scots with a proper, secure, segregated cycle infrastructure. "We won't get an environment that's completely safe for everyone for a long time," David said. "To some extent, third-party reporting is a bit of a sticking-plaster. It's covering a wound. If you have a society like in the Netherlands, then you probably don't need it. I've always said that the most important thing is infrastructure. The infrastructure guarantees some separation so it's then safe despite them [dangerous drivers]. Drivers will have to change. There has to be a change." After that outburst, he took another deep breath and turned on his cheerful face again. "When I was in Amsterdam, what amazed me was that when I went to a junction, they would stop. They would expect you to go past, even if you weren't quite there yet. It's important, especially for pedestrians. We're a long way from that. But if more of the infrastructure was there, the physical separation would encouraged it. Eventually, it would become second nature."

Even the Netherlands have problems, though. During the trip, David mentioned an event when an impatient driver tailgated him. During my roll through Scotland, the only motorists who passed me within inches were on Dutch plates. The situation changed only when I passed from the Lake District to Manchester – for worse. Everyone was passing me within inches.

Figure 1 Me and David in the summer of 2023

It was already late, and I still had ten miles before I could camp on the breathtaking Scottish hills. We said our goodbyes, took a selfie, and I was rolling. But the impression David left was still deep in my head. That level of persistence, goodwill and hope is difficult to match. And we had still only just scratched the surface. But we will meet David again quite soon.

Pioneers

Not the only one

It might have seemed that David, Andy, and Mike were the only ones wearing cameras to catch dangerous drivers back then. But of course, they weren't. YouTube was flooded with new profiles focused on documenting road conflicts from all perspectives – motorists, motorcyclists, and cyclists.

In early 2007, Paul Jones shared his scare of being cut up by a Stagecoach bus in Cambridge.[63] Not much later, TiNuts posted a video where a London bus driver invaded a cycle lane without checking.[64] AlexGreenBank showed how he was hooked by a Met patrol car that changed a lane in front of him on Westminster Bridge.[65] In July, Cab Davidson was passed within inches by an "Idiot Jeep Driver".[66] In November, TuneAfterTune luckily avoided a crash with a Mitsubishi Colt forcing its way head-on.[67]

More uploads appeared the following year, with less hope for safer encounters. Anthony Robson presented how it is to be an "Invisible cyclist" when an Edinburgh taxi driver cut him as he was approaching a junction.[68] The same happened to OnTheRoadUK2008 but with a London bus driver instead.[69] MrCellopane99 was closely passed two times in a row.[70]

The LeedsCyclist channel opens with him almost being taken off by a Leeds bus driver.[71] GadgetMind had to brake to avoid a classic SMIDSY[72] across the bus lane.[73] A similar situation happened to MyCycleClips, who had to avoid a white van driver jumping a red light across his path.[74] Cantankeroussquonk[75] and CommutingWithCamera[76] experienced the same thing.

TwoHat captured a SMIDSY caused by a motorcyclist.[77] RogerHotUK presented an argument for why painted cycle lanes don't work.[78] Bborp experienced a close shave with a Ford Focus,[79] and BristolTraffic enjoyed a naughty driver being towed.[80] All of that was just a fraction of the 2008 uploads. Every following year, more and more accounts and videos surfaced.

None of the above resulted in a driver being warned, fined, or prosecuted. But each documented the reality of British roads – vile, ignorant, with a profoundly rooted disregard for the safety of more vulnerable road users. The situation lasted until the end of the decade.

On rare occasions when a crash between a driver and a cyclist was recorded, the process was still long, stressful and slow. To this day, in Scotland and Northern Ireland, it has required burning out CD-ROMs with the video, visiting the police station and proving the cyclist's rights to officers who often weren't familiar with the Highway Code and were prejudiced against cyclists. It wasn't rare to be challenged for turning on no-turn-except-for-cyclists, like Shaun McDonald,[81] or cycling on a cycle lane, like Silvio Diego.[82]

The media should have paid more attention to the situation. The only cases where road crime was recorded were when some celebrities faced fines or bans for dangerous, drunk driving or speeding. Stories about using the phone while driving occurred a bit later. David Beckham's name pops up most often, among people such as Andy Cole, Dwight Yorke and Sir Alex Ferguson.[83] His ban in 1999 was lifted after appeal, and he avoided another one in 2001.[84] Finally, Beckham received a ban for phone use in 2019, just to be seen on the device later in the same year.[85] One would hope that such prominent figures being caught would discourage drivers from offending, but the trend continued in the following decades. Repeat offenders prove that the system is weak and, therefore, can be abused. Steve Coogan, Jim Davidson, Geri Halliwell, and Katie Price[86] filled the headlines in the following years.[87] The latter would go on to six bans by 2021, several crashes and risking jail for driving while being banned.[88] But worry not; the system was exceptionally soft on many more drives with *exceptional hardship*, which I mentioned earlier.

By the end of the 2010s, the UK had a perfect storm of widespread aggression, disrespect, and carelessness by motorists. Inadequate prosecution and policing led to a failure of prevention. And finally, we had technology to show the problem to the masses.

It was only a matter of time before headcam cyclists hit the national media. Amazingly, many will blame them for creating "the war between road users", forgetting that the war was started long before by the process of Traffication.[89]

In his brilliant book of that title, Paul F. Donald described how, after a short time of being used, primarily for pleasure, cars and therefore motorists "pushed pedestrians and other road users to the margins ... Before 1920, the press generally placed the blame for accidents on drivers ... but accounts of traffic accidents were increasingly fed to the newspapers, with appropriate spin and generous advertising revenue, by the motor industry itself; thus the finger of blame swung around". As the author pointed out, this gradual change, of one to two per cent annually, grew to have a profound effect within a lifetime. But hardly anyone noticed.

No. The pushback from the two-wheelers did not create the rift between road users. What surfacing videos caused, though, was an improvement in infrastructure, the law and public awareness. But for the message to stick, we needed one more element – a celebrity cyclist.

Pioneers

The mainstream

At the beginning of the 2010s, you could feel something was brewing, quite possibly because of ideas announced in 2008 by the then mayor of London, Ken Livingston. Not only did he design a bicycle hire scheme, but he also planned to upgrade the existing London Cycle Network with new Cycle Highways. Both projects came into existence a few years later under a new Mayor – Boris Johnson – who took all credit for both of them, hence the misnoma "Boris Bikes".

At this time, the media started to pick up the topic of cycling more frequently. The coverage wasn't negative at all. In an honest testimony in the *Guardian*, Erin Gill admitted receiving a £30 fine for pavement cycling to unveil the multitude of challenges and dangers city commuters face.[90] It wasn't the first time such a confession was made in the paper, as back in 1991 Robin P. Clarke, in his letter, said, "A child's bicycle, which can legally be pavement-ridden, can go just as fast downhill as an adult's, and is likely to be less competently controlled. Skateboards and roller skates have even more questionable breaking and steering. It hardly needs arguing that pavement motorists can be more dangerous than any pavement cyclist."[91] He struck a harrowing point. Five hundred and forty-eight pedestrians were killed by vehicles on pavements between 2005 and 2018, and only six by cyclists.[92],[93] The argument of pavement use has divided the public, and even today it is used as a low-blow response against any pro-cycling narrative. The issue was resolved back in 1999 by Home Office guidance that made fines for pavement cycling "not aimed at responsible cyclists who sometimes feel obligated to use the pavement out of fear of traffic and who show consideration to other pavement users when doing so". As the officials explained, "Chief police officers, who are responsible for enforcement, acknowledge that many cyclists, particularly children and young people, are afraid to cycle on the road; sensitivity and careful use of police discretion is required." Conservative minister Robert Goodwill confirmed the guidance in 2014.[94]

Cycling would finally get more investment. Promises of incoming cash flow appeared after a plea for increased funding from transport charities in early 2012.[95] Cycling was becoming cooler, with Boris Johnson promising £620m to improve the capital's network.[96] That, of course, caused ongoing opposition based on a naive assumption that cyclists were freeloaders and only drivers carry the cost of road uptake. In reality, the high cost of enabling motorists is being paid by non-drivers, and even the most enormous promised spending on cycle infrastructure was a drop in the ocean of general road expenses. How driving and the damage caused by car traffic is subsided was perfectly explained in Grant Ennis's *Dark PR*.

Cameras became both popular and effective, at least in the case of collisions. On August 23rd 2011, cyclist Iuckcan fell victim to two drivers in Greenford.[97] The first one, coming from the opposite direction, turned into the victim's path, causing him to fly over his bonnet and fall on the tarmac. The second one, after joining from a side street, drove over the fallen cyclist and his bike, trapping them under her car. Both drivers seemed to be oblivious to the commuter, who was covered in a bright hi-viz – and nearly killed him. Both were found guilty of driving without due care and attention in court and received ludicrously low sentences of six points and £230 for the first one and £130, plus £130 costs and £15 victim surcharge for the latter – in any case only possible thanks to the simple fact that Iuckan had a camera mounted on his helmet.

The community of headcam cyclists grew online, with more prominent figures known to insiders through their YouTube channel or Twitter. It wasn't just Magnatom and Cycling Mikey, but also such as:

- PompeyCycle
- Yangtse55 – who started to film dangerous drivers, to focus on unwise cyclists later.
- WestCountryTim
- Bazk666 – who founded his line of camera sign jerseys.
- MrGrumpyCyclist, a.k.a. MrHappyCyclist
- VeloEvol, known as EvoLucas

- Redvee
- SW19Cam
- CycleOptic
- 2rocship
- RadWagon1
- GrowingVegetable
- Bigsharnm
- BigBlokeOnABike
- TheFireUK
- CycleGaz
- Silvio Diego – with one of his most impactful videos showing how a driver pushes him onto the pavement.[98]
- 4ChordsNoNet
- and hundreds of others …

The mainstream

Neighbour

One new message on Twitter. Sender: 4ChordsNoNet. I opened it to see my post from the local volunteering group on Facebook. Wait – what? Does he know me? Have we met? I started to panic a little bit. There is a slight difference between your name being on one of the five-second fame headlines and getting recognised in your close community. But John had nothing malicious in mind. He wanted to help.

We shook hands at a charity event and scheduled a proper interview. For the place, I chose a small, cosy Italian cafe near my office.[99] The weather was great, and he found time while preparing for a significant family event. We both lived in southwest London, and that's how our roads crossed: helping out in the same organisation. John Richardson was one of the first headcamers I became acquainted with both online and in real life. He was also one of the first known.

Within his uniqueness, I felt a familiar vibe from John. Like David, he was prepared and eager to tell his part of the story. The difference was that John did not trigger the same controversy in the media. He kept his profile low. He had a massive impact on local third-party reporting but wouldn't grab too much time from the papers. Not because he wasn't interesting. He wasn't controversial. With John, we started with the background: What made you pick the camera? What do you try to achieve by that?

As it turned out, rather than one moment, it was a stream of events. Some left stronger memories than others. On the first occasion, a driver opened the door on him, resulting in a fall into the gutter and grazing himself. "You don't look out for cyclists, do you?" said the motorist, simply walking away as though nothing happened. The second time, a driver drove into the back of John's bike at the traffic lights but had enough integrity to take him home and pay for repairs. Strangely, I envied John, as after an elderly lady did the same to me, pushing me onto a busy roundabout, the Metropolitan Police collisions team just raised their hands and, after complaining, provided the driver's insurance details. The insurer never responded. Further faults, mostly to spokes and hub, appeared over time, but it was virtually impossible to prove they were results of the collision. Asked why the driver wasn't confronted with even a warning letter, the Met responded over a year later that "they hear our concerns".[100] The experience of most people I know is closer to mine than to John's, which made him a little bit luckier.

On the third occasion, a passenger opened their door on John. They got out, left their details, and drove away. As it turned out, none of the information was genuine. Fake numbers, fake names, fake addresses.

Once he had bought the camera, he had doubts about reporting. "I didn't want to come across as a 'grass', tell-tale or anything like that." His opinion quickly changed, though. The next time he was closely passed by a driver who got stuck immediately after in traffic, 4ChordsNoNet went alongside him and, in the heat of the moment, said, "I will upload that to YouTube." It wasn't a good idea, as the driver smashed the door against him, hit him and drove off. This resulted in the first report John made.

The traffic offences team responded that, as it was an assault, he had to report it to his local police station. "I'm not going down that road, and I'll leave it," he recalled. That process, while now improved, is still far more complicated and labour-intensive than reporting dangerous motorists. Usually, the MPS TORs team will proceed with a traffic offence and refer the assault to the victim's ward police team. They won't have easy access to original footage or reports, so the victim must meet face to face and go through a somewhat intimidating interview, during which the duty officer will "clean up" wording to "their standards". Of three accounts of assaults I had to report between 2019 and 2023, Wimbledon station acted on one with satisfying results. On the other, I was met with nonsense excuses like "number plates weren't readable on your footage, and face was too blurred to specify who was driving", even when they were good enough for the TORs team to send a warning letter and the face was as sharp as you can get.

After that last event, John reported close passes and mobile phone usage regularly. And he did not go out to find anyone. Everything happened simply on his daily commute to and from work. At that time, the Metropolitan Police did not prosecute either of the reported offences. Instead, they kept the reports in a database in case the driver got caught by the police for other crimes. Sometimes, the owners received warnings. "I had someone close pass me, and then about two weeks later they saw me again and they had a go at me [for being reported]," he laughed.

We spoke on many topics, from how the system improved over the years to mobile phone drivers and fatal collisions that motivated us to act. When asked if he thought reporting makes people hate cyclists, he took a deep breath, waited a moment, and replied, "I can see the argument, but I don't necessarily agree with it." He took another pause, looked around, then back at me, and continued: "Cyclists are always an easy target. You're not allowed to criticise someone's religion or nationality. You can get taken off social media or get prosecuted for it. Those people [who attack] will be homophobic, racist, Islamophobic or whatever it might be. They need a target to go for. And now cyclists are an easy target. Yes, it [third-party reporting] adds fuel to their fire. But those people need something to pick on." I couldn't argue with that take, as most of the abuse I tend to get or see usually comes from anonymous profiles full of examples of other hateful views.

Regarding roads, he wasn't worried as much about the aggressive motorists as the careless ones. This was especially true when we touched on the topic of close passes: "People pass you, you get out of their sight, you disappear. They don't care. Perhaps it's people's ignorance of their driving."

How can pushing those events on YouTube prevent such situations from happening? "I publish not to name and shame; it's for other people to see that a driver has been caught and that it could happen to them. They never know when someone's watching." In his mind, reporting is a collective thing. John admitted he is vulnerable but thinks he can look after himself. He hoped that his activity could prevent someone from being hurt to some degree. But after years of commuting, even with a defensive approach, he fell victim to – exactly – a careless driver.

On his way to work, he collided with a motorist who joined the road by turning right. The driver overtook him and turned left, immediately cutting into the path for the bike. It sent John flying. Despite wearing a helmet, he had to undergo life-saving surgery for multiple bleeds on the brain. "I've had no recollection of the crash at all. I don't remember it all at all. And it's only because I had the cameras on that I knew what happened. But even when watching it, nothing comes back. I watched it several times. No recollection at all."

This story sent chrills down my spine. Around the same time, not too far from where John was hit, another driver did precisely the same to me. I was rolling on a segregated cycle lane, CS7, along the main road, the A24. The driver pulled out from a side road on the right, turned right, passed me, and turned sharply left, cutting me off. I managed to jump aside and stop while shouting, "idiot!" It happened at apparently the most dangerous junction in London.[101] We met again in the court months later. The prosecutor brought three counts of driving without due care when, on each, the motorist failed to notice a large fat man in a hi-viz on a bike. Her defence was, "You called me an idiot." She was found guilty and received a reduced fine due to her private circumstances. I was lucky that nothing happened to me. John almost lost his life. You can find countless examples of similar scenarios.

While John became well known in the community, he did not grab the media's attention. His testimony shows the dark reality of the British roads, yet without undue drama. The rare exception was when he recorded a collision on the crowded CS3, reported in the *Evening Standard*,[102] and later in the *Telegraph*[103] and *MailOnline*.[104]

After meeting Richardson, I was wary. He's not searching for a limelight.[105] He's not putting himself in unnecessarily dangerous situations. He is careful and grounded, an asset to his local community. Yet, like others, he faces a disproportionately high threat and is met with hostility, arrogance and hate. Have we hit rock bottom as a society if we treat people this way?

He wasn't the only south London cyclist who pioneered third-party reporting. Along with names like sw19cam and thefireuk, one had an unprecedented impact: CycleGaz. It was he who first, in cooperation with the Metropolitan Police, saw that footage led to convictions.

His 51st report,[106] from December 2010, resulted in a £350 fine, six points, and £100 costs. The driver right-hooked him, causing a collision. That was at a time when the Met adequately addressed collisions.

Tailgating and an aggressive close pass in his 60th report from April 2011[107] cost the registered owner £400 and £85 fees, plus six points for not nominating the driver at the time of the incident. This outcome was ground-breaking for the prosecution of non-collision offences.

The one that made the most significant impact and is recollected as the first third-party report with a result was about an event from August 2012.[108] A lorry nearly took out a cyclist with a left hook in Oval. Gaz was behind them, recording. For the first time, he was asked to attend court. The driver was found guilty of careless driving and given three points, a £200 fine, £140 costs, and a £15 victim surcharge. VOSA inspected the company that owned the vehicle and improved their training. The video was used to push a redesign of the whole junction.

The mainstream

Broadcaster bullying of cyclists

Other personalities broke through in the media long before Mike van Erp and Jeremy Vine conquered the headlines. One that did it with unprecedented impact was Lewis, known as the Traffic Droid. In late 2011, the *Evening Standard* reported on his "Cyclist's crusade to film danger drivers".[109] In this brief piece, one could see already that his story was only about to get larger. "I don't go out looking for trouble. It just happens," he explained. "I see it every day, and I always stop to tell people off … Some people get upset. Some are puzzled … One chap got out and throttled me. But the camera is always rolling."

He had a bizarre yet ingenious idea for educating wrongdoers: "If they've been really bad, I hand them self-analysis cards so they can go on to YouTube and see for themselves." The famous red cards became his signature and were adopted by others.[110]

Lewis's actions, while well meaning, surfaced at a time when the media began a slow, hardly noticeable campaign of hate, misinformation, and prejudice. The BBC, which to this day does not follow established standards in road crash collision reporting,[111] began with a pseudo-scientific essay titled "The psychology of why cyclists enrage car drivers:.[112] The author started from a fair observation that the language used against cyclists online "would get people locked up if directed against an ethnic minority or religion, but it seems to be fair game, in many people's minds, when directed against cyclists". Then, the article shifted into a series of false statements. It accused cyclists of "doing the things that drivers aren't allowed to: overtaking queues of cars, moving at well below the speed limit or undertaking on the inside", but failed to mention that each of these actions is legal. But in this way, the author justified the projection of drivers' restrictions on other road users. Then it got even more twisted, with multiple paragraphs ranting about the "freeloader problem" normalising "an anger at people who break the rules, who take the benefits without contributing to the cost". The idea that only drivers fund road building and uptake through the legendary "road tax", or that cyclists are breaking more road rules, is typical ungrounded rubbish.

After such a welcome from the BBC, it was strange that Lewis agreed to join the production of the documentary "War on Britain's Roads".[113] The feature presented the severe issue of aggression, inadequate training, lack of prevention, and footballisation. The story of Alex Jane McVitty, tragically killed by a driver of a concrete-mixer lorry, and her mother, Cynthia Barlow's, fight to prevent further deaths, sent a strong message about vulnerability and improvements needed. As the film went on, each person involved came increasingly to agreement that some things had to change. But for some strange reason, the same picture reached over-simplistic and skewed conclusions, portraying the cyclists as – to say the least – a bit bonkers.

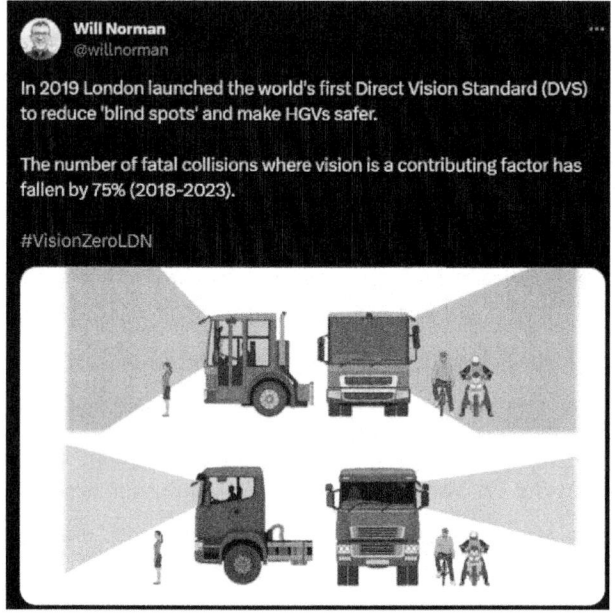

Figure 2 Will Norman's tweet showing the benefits of one of the changes originating from Cynthia Barlow's campaigns. 114

Another cyclist, a 24-year-old engineer, was portrayed as a head-strong, over-confident young lad. "I ride fast, and I enjoy riding fast. You can look at the speedometer, and you're doing 30mph. You're keeping up with the other traffic ... And it feels great when you're cycling and passing the traffic. Just seeing everyone stuck in their metal box." Many people believe that most cyclists move at that pace,[115] but the average speed for a commuter cyclist is 12mph. My personal is 13mph, with up to 20mph on the flat.

"Kind of feels like I deserve to be here," he continued. "I can go as fast as everyone else." While his argument made sense, the feature portrays him as arrogant. He was filmed from below, and the editor seemed fixated on his mouth. While describing a situation when a cab driver closely passed him, cut to the curb and assaulted him, the footage was mixed with the culprit parroting the cyclist's words. It seemed like the whole montage was intentionally obscene and degrading. This continued throughout the documentary.

Other guests were shown in a better light, including an older taxi driver, a cycling Police Constable, and a group of middle-aged professionals on bikes. The last group were assaulted by a driver who clipped them while passing. The incident initially resulted in an NFA[116] from the police. Still, after going viral on social media, it forced the attacker to turn himself in and be fined for common assault.

The same feature hosted David Brennan. The video of a lorry driver forcing his way onto the roundabout shocked everyone. Magnatom braked at the last second, narrowly avoiding landing under the vehicle. Everyone, even the taxi, agreed it was the motorist's fault.

"As I said from the start," David explained, "I wanted to post it online and get people talking about them. What was a complete revelation to me was how people reacted. There were people who would have loved to see me being squashed under that lorry, or if they ever find me, they will run me over".

As the viewer gets the feeling that the story may get a little bit more balanced, the narrator returns with yet another prejudice-loaded sentence: "Some decide to take control of the road, even if that will make them annoying to the other users." The young cyclist explained, "You need to take a very central position ... Some people see that as you antagonising other road users. You make them drive dangerously ... But I'm keeping myself safe. There isn't a space you can overtake. I'm not going to give you the space to overtake ... I suppose the person that gets antagonised by that is someone who hates other people being in their way, full stop."

He was right. Highway Code updates, finally enforced in 2022, advised cyclists to take a central, primary position wherever there is no space for a safe pass.

In a wrap-up about posting his footage online, the cyclist said it may have varying effects: "People can get a little annoyed. You need to block people's comments. What you need to try is to keep it so that they can look on their mistake and try to change, so next time they do better."

The youth's naivety and what seemed to be ill will from the producers resulted in a backlash. As the *Daily Mail* reported, many viewers described him as arrogant and antagonising.[117] Some directed actual threats like "I want to smack this guy" – Shelby Sadler – "I'd happily run him over" – Jerry – "This cyclist with glasses on actually deserves to be knocked off his bike and die!!!" – Kate Bailey. But the commuter shook off those threats, saying they came as no surprise: "I put stuff on YouTube and I get a lot worse than that."[118]

After the airing, he did not hide his disappointment about the documentary. "They kind of represented me as Jack-the-lad and cocky, an arrogant young guy ... I comment on bad cyclists as well." This fact was presented in his more likeable profile in the *Independent*.[119]

The *Daily Mail* reported that the documentary was condemned by the joint chairman of the Parliamentary Cycling Group, Labour MP Ian Austin, who described it as "stupid, sensationalist, simplistic, irresponsible nonsense".

Traffic Droid

The Traffic Droid also appeared on the infamous BBC documentary. But unlike with the young cyclist, producers did not use camera and montage tricks to skew viewers against him. In its proper context, his colourful persona was enough to achieve a screen-worthy drama.

"I see myself as a guardian angel," he said. "Other people see me as a vigilante. I find that strange because I don't go out at night looking for everyone committing traffic crimes." He explained that he uses the camera to trap bad drivers. He names and shames them. Then he puts them online to act as a deterrent. He also gives them calling cards so they can look up themselves online and "correct their ways".

In a tearful recollection, he admitted that he still felt hounded after a driver crashed into him years ago. Entering from a side road, the motorist sent him flying. "I could have died that night … That's why I decided I have to do something about it, to use the media, YouTube, to get the message across. Because it has to stop, or other people will get hurt or killed. It has to stop. That's why I created the Traffic Droid. The Traffic Droid came when I recovered."

This decisive moment was flushed away by the next clip, in which he's almost taken out by a trailer pulled by a close passing van driver. As Lewis approached him, the motorist walked out and assaulted him. But the feature's criticism was targeted at the cyclist: "What did you think would happen if you kept banging on the driver's window?"

"I see how it's starting in my head – don't hit that guy. And luckily, I had that restraint. It could have been very ugly. I could have taken this guy out, but hey, it's not my style. I don't fight." The clip resulted in No Further Action by the Metropolitan Police but sparked heated debate online.

In a short time, Traffic Droid became a public icon, recognised by supporters and haters alike. Often, he was used as a synonym for the headcam cyclist. His distinct looks, with a dark, military-like suit, heavily tinted goggles, and a multitude of cameras on his bike, made him stand out. His avant-garde manner of speech and emotional and energised delivery drew loads of attention. But was it him or a media personality?

A few years later, he reappeared on the first episode of another sensation-seeking feature – *The Complainers*, from Channel 4.[120] He challenged TFL[121] about bus drivers cutting in front of him or close passing. After watching his videos, officials deflected the blame and pointed fingers at Lewis. In one piece of footage, Droid took the primary position in the main (right) lane, and a motorist pushed between him and the other cyclist travelling in the bus lane. TFL representatives quickly dismissed the driver's dangerous behaviour and scrutinised Droid for his habit of challenging motorists.

When I finally met Lewis, he had a very sour recollection of the show: "I'll not forgive them [Channel 4]. We spent eight to nine months filming it. All the incidents. They came to court but didn't even use the material. They didn't use any of those. So, they trivialised the whole thing. They made me look stupid. I give them nine months of my life. Coming to my house. They publish rubbish. Nothing about how the process is going, how the police work. And the guys in TFL don't like me. A lot of bus drivers were fired. It wasn't my intention. But because of the action, they were. Same with the taxi drivers."

Over the years, Lewis's fame faded away. Others took the limelight. But his fight did not end. His profile is swarming with footage of taxis pushing in front of him, passing him within inches, tailgating, and sometimes crashing into him. It seems like he was targeted. While each of those incidents sends goosebumps down the spine, the media seems not to be interested. His struggle became a routine. His loud persona and mixing the road safety message with personal views on various dividing matters earned him cancellations in parts of social media. As a result, he stopped looking for attention.

I wanted to meet Lewis and learn more about him and his personality. Others had strong opinions about him, mainly because of his views on anything other than reporting. It was easier said than done; in his own words, he's "always on the move". And on the move, I caught him. He wasn't on his bike, nor in the combat suit. Hidden under a simple football cap, he sat on the top level of a double-decker. Not so loud, not so expressive. It was immediately visible how age and experience had tempered him. We started with his origins.

It was November 2009. He moved from London to Dunstable, but his love remained for the capital. Driving or taking the train was costly, so Lewis thought he might cycle in. He is a large, fit guy and always up for a challenge. As a private pilot, he drafted the route and rode his bike towards the A5 and London. Immediately, he felt aggression from drivers. It was a shock. Long before buying the first cameras or even a sporty outfit, he was targeted, close passed and undercut. Despite that, he persisted, lost his way a few times, and after a few attempts, found the best route through Elstree and Edgware towards central London.

Not long after, he bought some wine and rolled to his girlfriend's for the evening. A driver turned head-on into a T-junction without signalling or noticing Lewis. He "went like a helicopter". The outcome was tragic. Broken bones and ribs, months of therapy and learning to walk again. As he discovered several years later, the driver, despite being found by the police, ended up just with a driving awareness course and not a single point on his licence. Luckily, Lewis was able to sue him privately and receive compensation. The money went first and foremost on the cameras.

"It was a strange experience because initially how they treated us was not the same as a car driver. I felt I had to explain a lot of things. I didn't know [back then] what the process was, but I was lucky somebody saw it. I knew the person who hit me, and it was a hit-and-run. That's when the police became involved; I went to fill out some reports, and then they took it from there. But I didn't know how to report it at that time."

He wore eight cameras at once, the amount needed to cover all angles: one on the each hand, two facing forward, one on the helmet, one on the back, one on the chest. The last was a selfie camera on a stick, which additionally (as he said in *The Complainers*) made the bike more stable.

Figure 3 Source Traffic Droid – Lewis D. set-up

The fully equipped Droid returned in May the following year as Lewis had to commute to work in London. That was where the next incident happened. He was nearly knocked out by a high-end BMW while riding through Highgate. Lewis started to think about how he could fight back. He uploaded his videos to YouTube. Then he bumped into a reporter from local *Ham and High* newspaper, Josh Pettitt, who offered to write a story about him.[122] The fame scared him; he couldn't get used to seeing his face everywhere. His family wasn't prepared for that. Lewis recollected that his mother reacted to the article with a loud, "What the hell!?

"At first, I threw a card into the drivers' cars so they could look up themselves on YouTube. I also tried to report some to the police, but the Met weren't interested. I dug deeper as I wanted to learn how to get them prosecuted, but I was shocked. I went to the police station. Over 20 pages of filled accident reports. Burned CDs with the footage. Each time, it took over an hour just to be seen. And the attitude was always like I was wasting their time – Get over it. Did you enjoy almost getting yourself killed? they asked – No! It was the way the driver was driving."

After many attempts, Lewis encountered an open-minded female officer who took him seriously. She came to his office when he worked in telecoms at

Regent Street, and helped him fill out the reports. That gave him hope and rebuilt his will to try harder. He became a regular, and police staff started to take him seriously. However, the daily volume of up to 10 reports wasn't something all officers liked.

I also wanted to drill into his evident struggle against the cab drivers. Over the years, I have noticed fewer and fewer aggressive, careless, or plain dangerous on my route. But on his videos, many seemed to attack him unprovoked. Suspicion of him must have been linked to his early reports to RoadSafe.[123] As he filled out his complaints, they were supposedly referred to TFL. But the operator then delivered them directly to the drivers. The taxi community is quite tight and connected; therefore, by word of mouth, Traffic Droid became a nuisance, and his atypical image made him an easy target. By then, Lewis had started to refer to them as "Bullycabs".

During this conversation, I had the profound impression that the Droid before me was much more mature and cautious than the one from years ago. More careful than the one online. I wanted to learn about his observations during almost 14 years of recording. Primarily, I wanted to learn his views on people who had followed in his steps. "I think you got two types of people who are reporting. You have those because they've had a direct experience where they were almost killed. Then you have those who are inspired by what I and some others are doing, and they go out to catch people. That's the wrong thing. I wouldn't be using a camera if nothing happened to me. It was the sense of helplessness after the accident. I could have been killed. So don't wake up in the morning thinking, 'So today I'm going to ride everywhere and catch everyone in the world.' Don't do that. The only time you can catch them is when you're commuting."

That reminded me of an infamous statement from Essex Police which dismissed reports from cyclists, assuming they were the result of "hunting". What was Lewis's take on it? One week, he deliberately did not carry cameras on his rides and was hit three times. "It's worse. They work as a deterrent." Moving away from criticising the Essex force, Lewis reminded me about the issues with collision reporting with the Metropolitan Police. It wasn't the first time I had heard about these, and they matched my experience. In Lewis's case, a camera recording did not help when a private hire driver bumped into his leg. Apparently, the video didn't show the hit, but only the outcome of it.

We spent a long time exchanging stories from our rides and the sheer variety of aggression and carelessness. I asked about the worst of the worst situations, especially threats and violence. "The funny thing is that because the idea of law and order is very strong in me, I can get really angry. But I will restrain myself from getting into physical contact. I've been pushed and blocked, but don't want to hurt anyone. I don't want to get a criminal record because of someone else's stupidity. But in terms of someone coming out wanting to kill me, there were three or four occasions. One happened last year. It's really funny. I was cycling back home, and I saw four builders who were drinking beer in their van. I said, 'Drinking, are we?' And they went absolutely berserk. They all came out and tried to steal my camera. I called the police. The patrol came and arrested them. But they were released shortly after. If it had been the other way around, if I had punched them, I would have ended up with a record." On another occasion, he cycled early in the morning and experienced a terrible close pass, almost knocking him down. He used the loud horn he had at that time. The driver stopped, got out, tried to punch him. Lewis called the police, but no one came.

He returned to his childhood when asked where he got the resilience for all this. When he lived as a child in Nigeria, his parents and two sisters were almost executed by armed robbers. He grew up in an environment of threats and violence. Now, he doesn't want anything bad to happen to anybody.

Sherry

A few years after everyone was talking about the Traffic Droid, a new name, Dave Sherry, entered the scene. The media decided to give him a super-aggressive spin: "Most hated cyclist in the UK".[124]

He was briefly mentioned in the *Sunday Times* alongside drivers using dashcams.[125] While it was naive to seek any criticism of the motorists, the bike component sprang a series of more and more sensation-thirsty pieces in the paper. Later that year, an article dedicated to Dave portrayed him as a vigilante going after drivers using mobile phones at the wheel.[126] As the story went, he began his mission after a bus driver on a mobile telephone swung past at speed as he pedalled his bicycle in the opposite direction with his two-year-old daughter on the back.

The picture of Dave started to gain more vibrant colours. In a *Daily Mail* feature, Kathryn Knight painted him as a "self-styled scourge of reckless drivers".[127] The story presented the dangers drivers pose on their mobile phones and Sherry's role in reducing that risk.[128] Peter Hitchens in the *Mail* cheered this respectful presentation of him; he praised Dave as a "brave private individual", wished him good luck, and called phone-using drivers "stupid", saying the act itself was a "crime". Ultimately, he had a proper go at the police who were "endlessly moaning about non-existent staff shortages while having time and manpower to monitor Twitter and Facebook".[129]

Dave was a TV guest on morning shows for a couple of years. He appeared on the BBC's *Inside Out East*[130] and ITV's *This Morning*.[131] His most recent appearances had included one on *TalkTV*, where he patiently listened to an inconsistent rant by Jeremy Kyle.[132] Richard Spillet spun the "most hated" title for the first time in confusing peace that said Sherry used "hidden cameras" while mentioning that he "lets motorists know his views on their driving". It also showed Dave with a large helmet-mounted GoPro and eye-burning hi-viz vest with a camera sign on the back.[133]

"It might be strange that I'm also a bus driver too. But I'm just trying to make a difference. I sit on the fence. I'm a cyclist. I'm a driver. I'm just trying to ensure there is a space on the road for all of us by bringing bad drivers to justice. If I catch you, you're going to be very, very sorry. I'd rather act as a deterrent than see someone on the floor – it is like a war zone out there," he testified. The most worrying part of the story is that as a result of an assault on him, aside from cameras and the hi-viz, he had to wear 80-pound body armour. He was punched in the stomach by a furious van driver. Police confirmed the culprit received a caution for ABH[134] in June 2013. "He just saw red and went in for the attack. He properly knocked me back with a punch, and I smashed the back of my head on rocks behind me ... I had to go for an MRI scan and I had a minor concussion, but luckily no bleeding on the brain ... I've been verbally assaulted plenty of times too. But I don't have time to mess around with them any longer."

A year later, Kathryn Knight in the *Daily Mail* returned to enforce Sherry's mission's positive and heroic aspects.[135] While describing the heart-breaking story of 20-year-old Laura Thomas, killed when Ian Glover's lorry ploughed into her broken-down car while looking at his phone, Knight leaves no doubt: "This is just the kind of tragedy 'mobile vigilante' Dave Sherry is attempting to avert." At that time, the penalty for phone use was £100 and three points on your licence. Dave agreed that it wasn't enough. "People aren't learning," he said, "and the situation on the roads is getting worse ... Far stiffer penalties are the only things that will get people to put their mobiles away when they're in the car." It might be that this article, including Dave's words, that contributed to changes in sentencing the following year[136] to £200 and six points.

In 2019, Dave appeared again on the screen in the highly criticised[137] Channel 5 documentary, "Cyclists: Scourge of our roads?" He proved the prevalence of mobile phone drivers, but the most terrifying thing was the news of his collision the year before. In January 2018, Dave was cycling home through Epping when an HGV driver started to overtake him with incoming traffic from the opposite direction.[138] The pass was too close, and the end of the lorry hit Sherry, sending him into the gutter. The driver reportedly, thanks to mishandling by the police, managed to flee the country shortly after.[139] Previous articles reported tears on Dave's arms due to the incident, but I was about to learn the real toll of that horror. The first hint came in his appearance on GB News[140] in 2021, where he confirmed having a permanent disability after that crash.

Like David Brennan, Dave did not ask me to wait long before he shared his story. I caught him on the phone when he was at the gym. He was painfully straight to the point, not apologetic one bit, open and, as he described himself, "subtle as a sledgehammer". He invited me to his court cases. Unfortunately, I couldn't attend. Despite that, he patiently waited until we finally managed to sit down for a proper chat. Dave was the same person I saw on the telly. No surprises. Honest to the limits.

We established the timeline: over a decade ago, "some idiot" hit him on the bike of his bike with his young child in the back seat. "The old Bill said 'It's your word against his.'" He then learned the ropes of third-party reporting and the system's sluggishness with Lewis. "We used video evidence and filled MG11s[141] and 996s."[142] During that time, alongside other influential headcam cyclists, Sherry managed to get acquainted and work closely with RoadSafe in the Metropolitan Police. He mentioned key figures that helped to build and improve reporting: Andy, Stephanie, and Liz. I was honoured to see each name in my correspondence with the TORS unit. Unfortunately, the Metropolitan Police media office did not give the green light to interview them. Dave insisted on giving them credit. I will do that properly a bit later.

Sherry has a clear policy not to get involved in conversations on social media. He hates going into any form of politics and makes it clear that the reporting for him is very personal. Road safety for him is personal. But he doesn't like to show too many personal details about the culprits. "That's not good in my book. If someone's getting found guilty, let him just get along. They've been punished. Don't fucking publicise them on Twitter or YouTube. It's disrespectful. I would only use my videos to highlight and explain the story.

The mainstream

The arseholes who like to get aggressive, threatening and abusive portray why cyclists were getting victimised and discriminated against. I highlighted the idiots, and I enjoyed it. And yes, that made me Britain's most hated cyclist."

Despite years of struggle, Dave remains hopeful: "Things are changing, big time. We got the support of the courts and the police. We have the tools of the trade. We just need to stand by our morals, and it will make the road safer. The latest Highway Code changes have improved things. Put the shoe on the other foot, and it's making car drivers more responsible."

He stresses that reporting is about saving lives and preventing injuries. "If I could save one life, it's well worth the effort," he exclaimed, took a longer pause, put on his cheeky smile, and continued, "And you know what? I think we *are* saving lives out there. It's not just me. Back then, it was a few of us, and now it is more of us. You've got the good ones, and you got the bad ones."

His YouTube channel was suspended, and he was banned from the platform, without any warning or explanation: "no copyright strike or other infringements". It happened after he uploaded a video he filmed in Epping. The video left the uncanny impression of a link between the event and the platform. Yet it made him stop using the site, but he "did not lose a night's sleep because of it".

"There are individuals out there who are on a crusade. They can get blacklisted by the police and lose the respect of their fellow camera cyclists." Dave doesn't hide his dislike of those who seem to upload videos "for likes and views". "What is a thing that most don't do but should do when it comes to the reporting, then?" I asked. His answer was clear: "The rules of engagement: observe, retract, retreat."

We returned to the crash; he went silent for a while, then continued: "People don't know it yet, but I drive a London bus with a steering wheel adaption." That uninsured driver who went abroad scot-free left Dave with a life-changing disability. "But you know what? It makes you a strong person. I don't wallow. I'm not claiming disability benefits or anything like that. You know, it's just like you soldier on, mate. It makes you tough. And that's what I love about life. It's just carries on."

The mainstream

Jeremy

I sent a lengthy message on X explaining the book's goal and asking for an interview. The response was short and to the point: "Yes, let's do it!" Not long after, I stood waiting outside my office on a chilly March afternoon. (It was freezing!)

Jeremy stands out. A tall, slim man, smoothly riding a bike that seemed a bit too small for him. Perhaps I was too used to seeing his image on a Penny Farthing. One could see a perfect mixture of grace and comedy in his moves. It seemed like he had just finished filming his latest TikTok. Jeremy greeted me with a broad smile, locked his bike and grabbed the bags, apologising for how much gear he had to carry in that weather.

We went to the Greyhound, a local pub, usually full of journalists after work hours. Now, it was nearly empty, but still very cosy. I did not stammer, but the initial pressure of meeting someone like him made me struggle with the language. He listened carefully, with eyes full of interest and focus. A hint of caution as well. Yet after a few moments, the ice broke, and from a silent observer he turned into a passionate storyteller. Open, honest, but still accepting of remarks and questions from my side. He was genuinely interested in conversation rather than in delivering a monologue.

My notes were full of snippets from over 100 relevant articles and quotes I found in the archives. Naively trying to copy Steven Bartlett's interviewing style, I began by asking, "What made the person that sat in front of me?" and quoted an interview Jeremy Vine's brother, Tim, gave to the *Sunday Times* about their childhood.[143] The comedian sibling confessed that one-year-old Jeremy crawled out of the house and crossed the road. He recalled: "I was brought up in Cheam. It was different back then. It was like a village. There were hardly any cars. When I was two, or might even have been one and a half, I was crawling, and my dad left the front door open. I crawled down the garden path and across the main road and the avenue. Thank God, there was only one car every three minutes. He was washing the dishes, and he looked out the window, and he saw me. He said: 'What's that on the main road?' It was his son, and he ran out the road and got me back."

Tim described his childhood as very happy, with skateboarding, bike rides and kids coming to play. "Things were quieter and calmer, but I do think as well we didn't have any sort of analysis of risks." Jeremy clarified: "So nowhere a helmet or anything like that. It's a cycle to school and back. It's three and a half miles on a really rubbish bike. The cars would pass you really close, and you'd be in the gutter cycling. Once I left my bike in the village unlocked. I've forgotten that I left it. Then it was two weeks later, and it was still there.

"I remember as a teenager, I took this thing called Cycling Proficiency, and it taught you to ride in the gutter and that cars are fast and dangerous and you must always let them go. Now, I'm cycling on my own initiative. The crucial thing is I don't want to hurt anybody. I don't want to be hurt. If I'm going to be hurt, I'm going to stop cycling. I'm thinking every day about how I ensure that I don't take any significant risk. And I think if I went back 40, 50 years to Cheam, I would probably have cycled differently. I might well have worn a helmet when I was a kid. But at the time we had no appreciation of the risks, and it was great," he grinned. "It was a great childhood, and a bicycle was part of it.

"Now it's very dangerous. I mean the suburbs, Cheam, Mitcham, Morden, Wallington, those places south of London are brutal for cycling. The centre of London is probably the safest place to cycle in the whole country except for this borough [Royal Borough of Kensington and Chelsea]."

I couldn't resist mentioning Jay Foreman's episode,[144] which pointed out that the same borough was the only one without trams because trams were *used by the poor*. The scrutiny of RBKC was of great importance to us both. We were heavily invested in the topic and affected by that council's blunt negligence towards non-motorist commuters.

Jeremy took to cycling around 2011. As his work in TV was becoming more sedentary and less out in the terrain, he tried to incorporate exercise into his commute. In a later feature for the *Mail on Sunday*, Vine explained: "At 6ft 3in,

I could eat as many jam doughnuts as I wanted. For years, I binged on croissants and crisps and just got thinner. Then, in my mid-40s, my metabolism slowed and I became large and miserable. I remember crawling after my young child while playing at home and feeling, for the first time, a thick fold of skin on the back of my neck. In protest, I left my utterly ineffective gym (I can't blame them – I never went) and decided to make my seven-mile commute my daily exercise."[145]

Jeremy stopped to contemplate the delicious hummus and continued: "I was very wary of doing it because I was in that zone of thinking cycling is dangerous in London. I don't think it is. As you gradually do your commute more and more, you work out where the bad roads are. Kensington High Street is, obviously, a good example. When I started, I was intensely careful, and I'm still careful. The one thing that's changed, I think, is the technology. The cameras I use are astonishing. The uploads to social media. The fact that if something happens on my ride back, I can put it online tonight and it might have half a million people see it." It was precisely December 2012 when he published the first tweet about cycling, and, not much later, the first of his videos appeared on YouTube[146] and then on the video platform called Vine.[147]

Figure 4 One of the first Vine tweets from near misses.

His friend at work lent him a camera and said, "Try it because you'll want to review your journeys when you get home."[148] Jeremy recollected that event in his response to Jeremy Clarkson, who tried to gaslight the broadcaster in his *Times* column a month earlier[149]. Vine voiced his concerns about cyclists' and pedestrians' safety, but Clarkson denied any accusations of dangerous driving. Then he claimed that "about everyone over the age of 17 is a motorist" and that young motorists don't *tear about at break-neck speed*. Both statements were factually wrong then and today.[150] Jeremy responded with first-hand experience familiar to most two-wheelers. His stand was supported by the *Evening Standard*'s Andrew Neater, who quoted the same feelings from Olympic cycling medallist Victoria Pendleton and reported on massive underspending by TFL on cycling infrastructure.[151]

To give Jeremy Clarkson some credit, he did say something amazing in that article (which he may regret today): "There are two types of off-road car. There's an off-road car that is designed to go off road. A Range Rover, for instance. And then you have off-road cars that are not designed to go off road. These are called SUVs, and they annoy me.

"I look at everyone in their Honda CR-Vs and their BMW X3s and their Audi Q3s and I think, 'Are you all mad?' An ordinary estate or hatchback costs less to buy and less to run and is nicer to drive, more comfortable and just as practical. And it doesn't take up so much bloody space."

The love-hate relationship between the two Jeremys would continue over the years and usually resulted in heated debate amongst the readers. Mrs Lee from Warminster called cyclists "arrogant, in the middle of the road, holding up the transporters for a mile and travelling 5mph"; D.J. Kendal of Prenton complained about "teenagers on mountain bikes" riding on pavement and "through red lights" at the same time; and for the balance, Trevor Boardman, 73, from Wigan debunked myths about road tax and not stopping on the zebra.[152] The infamous Rod Liddle tried to piggyback on Clarkson's position[153] but failed miserably in suggesting that drivers were on the roads before the cyclists. His readers trivialised Liddle in the letter, starting on precisely that point,[154] but the goal was achieved, and as the *Sunday Times* editor wrote, they "had our biggest mailbag to the date". He was soon forgotten, but the damage was done. The language Liddle used has been parroted until today by most anti-cycling moaners.

On many occasions, meanwhile, Peter Hitchens supported Vine, trashed silly and ungrounded claims by Clarkson, and confirmed ever-lasting respect and bike/professional bromance with the former.

From that moment, the Radio 2 broadcaster snowball grew, with more cases he was involved in asked about for comment or debated about. When an Audi A7 driver assaulted a cyclist who called him out for encroaching the cycle box, Jeremy said, "Everyone is talking about this. Clearly, the cyclist was foolish to pick a fight, but the Audi man is violent and should be caught."[155] He understood that the platform gave him a unique opportunity to reach the masses. His profile allowed him to criticise all parties without being cancelled or accused of anti-bike sentiment. He made mistakes and owned up to them.

When he received a ticket for speeding at 16mph on a five mph stretch in Hyde Park,[156] he admitted, "I feel embarrassed, and I apologise."[157] In response to the event, Sam Creighton in the *Mail* asked, "Were police radar gunning joggers too?"[158] Danny Boyle called Vine a *Speeding Demon*[159] in the *Telegraph*. Donnchadh McCarthy used the story to criticise the Metropolitan Police for refusing to lend support for a blanket 20mph limit, in the wake of yet another London cyclist's death caused by a speeding driver.[160]

2014 was already tragic for cyclists in the capital. By June, there were eight deaths, seven of which were caused by HGV drivers, six of which victims were women. The most recent was a 26-year-old PwC consultant, Ms Ying Tao.

Jeremy became a victim of a dangerous driver himself. Eighteen months earlier, Ross Lydall reported[161] that Vine was knocked off his bike. The driver was sentenced and fined £3,200, unheard of at that time. Jeremy confessed to getting two more drivers sentenced: a black taxi driver was fined £200 and sent on a driving improvement course, and another bully driver was *busted* by the police.[162] He was obviously lucky, as his misfortune happened when a young, brave officer changed the Met policy regarding road crime. "I can report it to the police. That was all done by Andy Cox. That brilliant police officer who gave us a portal where we can report." I was pleased to hear that name, as I was waiting to meet Andy just after he settled back in London after almost three years serving in Lincolnshire.

In 2015, three more cyclists were killed by HGV drivers in the Square Mile: Victor Manuel Ben-Rodriguez, 32, and Janina Gehlau, 26. Despite that, the City of London Corporation considered abandoning its plans to address safety concerns. Ross Lydall yet again reached out for Jeremy's help. In response, Vine called out the *farcical lack of safety* at Bank.[163]

I was interested in his reporting. "When I come down this road,[164] I always film people on their mobiles. I think it's important that drivers on this road be excessively careful. And I'm seeing fewer of them. I think people are beginning to realise that cyclists are filming them and are starting to be more careful. I see driver after driver sitting there at traffic lights and they have their hands literally folded in their lap like they're not going to touch their phone. I'll sometimes go a whole day and won't see a phone driver. I reported loads of phone drivers.

"I probably report one person every fortnight. That's not many. And it has to do with social media. For example, I was cycling the other morning and a milkman came past me. And again, the same situation: you're in front of the lights, in the cycle box. The van behind you wants to pass, and you can't move left quickly enough. Why should you? And as he moves past, he goes: 'You're a fucking piece of shit.' Then he drives off, and of course, I will catch him. Two minutes later, I was ahead of him, and I said: 'Why did you call me a piece of shit?' And he said: 'You didn't move out the way. You got to stay on the left.' So, I say, 'Okay, well, fair enough, but I think you've got to be more polite.' So, I uploaded it, and it's a brilliant little film. People, of course, could identify his company, and I felt a bit bad about that. But a couple of weeks ago, 'Hi! Jeremy! How are you doing?' and it was the same guy. I said, 'I felt so bad about that film I took it down. I didn't want to get you in trouble.' He said, 'Don't worry, I learned from it.' And that's what should happen, you know, he understands me, and I understand him."

It reminded me of a video with a postman who almost knocked Jeremy down. "That guy was interesting because he was clearly a very good person. As soon as he saw me, he started talking to me. But he had done a ridiculous turn. And one of the things I can see is that, because we're getting cycle lanes now, drivers have really got to understand that they cannot turn left across a cycle lane until it's clear. And I think maybe the Mayor of London needs to do an advertising campaign because it's a matter of fact they don't get it."

In one response to Jeremy Clarkson, Vine wrote: "If nothing else, cycling in a major British city reminds you to make a will and tell your mum you love her." And in several interviews and columns, Jeremy mentioned the fear that his family felt each time he went out cycling. "I always say goodbye to my wife in the morning in the manner of a Japanese fighter pilot in 1943. She's never sure if I'm going to come back," he told the *Radio Times*.[165]

Jeremy

Like many other cyclists, I have experienced something similar and received a fair share of fear from my family. I wondered what they felt about Jeremy's commute and mission:

"I think they know I love it. There's something about being in this quite competitive zone and trying to get home alive that's quite energising. I remember talking to a cyclist down here, and I said, 'God, it's terrible tonight.' And he just said, 'Yeah, but we love it, don't we?' It's like a video game where you've only got one life. My wife obviously does worry a bit. I often show her my videos; I show what's happened. Every day, I have something about the way drivers behave, and I think she knows I'm very cautious. What's interesting about social media is that you get a lot of feedback on your films. And people always blame the cyclist, whatever happens. It's incredible. I was told I wasn't wearing bright enough clothes. I've got one of the brightest lights in the market, Exposure Joystick. I've got to buy an illuminated jacket – you saw it, this reflective jacket. Then I'm told I'm too bright, you know? You just can't win."

Attack

As a massive celebrity, Jeremy quickly became a regular headline cyclist. In February 2015, *Metro*,[166] the *Mail*,[167] and the *Times*[168] reminded everyone about Dave Sherry, his body armour, the drivers convicted for ABH[169] and the price of his cameras. A day earlier, *MailOnline* dug out the Traffic Droid.[170] But from August 2016, the limelight was solely on Vine. And no, not because he became a new face of *Crimewatch*,[171] but for an entirely different, and unpleasant, reason.

While cycling next to the council building down Hornton Street in RBKC, Jeremy was abused and threatened by a female driver. The street was relatively steep and narrow, with parked cars. Vine carefully rolled down the hill. An impatient motorist sat on his back and started to smash the horn.[172] When the journalist stopped to check what was wrong, to his surprise, 22-year-old Shanique Syrena Pearson jumped out of the car and threw a meaty rant.

The *Mail* quoted the motorist as shouting, "Why did you do that? You don't respect your fu***** life. I could have hit you, and been done for murder. Get off the f***** road. You lot p*** me off."[173] According to the *Telegraph*, when Jeremy pulled next to the driver a moment later, she shouted, "If you take a picture of my car again, I'm going to knock you out because that's my personal belongings."[174] The *Metro* reported that she mimicked firing a gun at him.[175] The story made headlines across all the media, including the *Times*,[176] the *Sun*,[177] the *Daily Mirror*[178] and the *Guardian*.[179]

Everyone seemed to agree that Jeremy was a victim and Ms Pearson an aggressive perpetrator. Therefore, it was even more horrifying when Sarah Vine (not related) tried to rationalise the motorist's behaviour: "I'd be lying if I said I had never expressed similar sentiments internally when trapped behind a painfully slow, wobbly, middle-aged cyclist who refused to pull over and then stops abruptly to deliver a sanctimonious road safety lecture."[180] It was another example that an insane hatred of cyclists predated mainstream third-party reporting. Like the previous Liddle nonsense rant, this one resulted in more trash publications. In the *Sun*, an unnamed journalist sympathised with the driver, saying that "cyclists are getting very arsy and self-righteous."[181] Jeremy didn't take it too personally. Years later, Vine, Sarah, reported on a cycling stroll with Jeremy and described herself as a cyclist.[182] What a twist!

Jeremy Clarkson wouldn't be himself if he didn't turn the story on its head to remind us about his existence: "There was a time when you could take these morons [cyclists] to task. You could shake your fist and shout and point out that it's absurd for a fully grown adult to be playing in public on what is a kids' toy. But no more ... Today they all wear helmet cameras to record your rage."[183] In other words, he blames the victim for finally being able to catch the offender red-handed. Yet again, Clarkson proves to be a bully.

There were voices of sanity as well. In the *Evening Standard*, Rosamund Urwin recollected when she was tailgated and tooted by an impatient driver because she tried to avoid being doored. "I'm going to run you off the road, you fat b****," shouted a female motorist while doing a punishment pass. Another lady she interviewed ended up with fractured thyroid cartilage and severely damaged vocal cords when a door struck her neck.[184] In letters to the *Metro*, Lyndon Jonen from Monmouth stood up for Jeremy: "If Jeremy Vine had slipped, she could have run him over. My daughter is a keen cyclist and has encountered this kind of attitude from motorists. As an ex-professional driver, this behaviour makes my blood boil." Toby Wilsdon from Sussex suggested that the answer to cyclists being hit by car doors is to educate the drivers. Nick B. from London, a driver with over 30 years' experience, was amazed how "belligerent drivers can be" as they "fail to appreciate how damaging a car door being opened can be". Matt from Essex explained that "cyclists wear cameras for this very reason – someone being impatient and endangering their life."[185]

A few days later, Ms Pearson told the *Sun* that she had been slated online, with elements of racism. She insisted the police hadn't contacted her.[186] She must have jinxed it, as the *Evening Standard* reported that the following day she was arrested[187] and later charged with multiple offences: driving without reasonable consideration to other road users, failing to licence a vehicle and using threatening, abusive or insulting words or behaviour.[188] Two days after the charges, Clarkson did what he does best: blamed the cyclist again: "The man (or woman) did absolutely nothing wrong at all." Either Clarkson did not see the event video (posted by each newspaper, including one he worked for) or had a total disregard for the motorist to the level that he didn't bother to recognise their gender. "The. Roads. Are. For. Cars."[189] Desperately trying to sound a fanfare for rationalism, it sounded like the cry of a cat dying under the wheels of his beloved four-wheeler.

During the first hearing in front of Hammersmith Magistrates' Court, Ms Pearson's lawyer accused Vine: "I suggest that you have racially stereotyped her as a black person and that [gun] gesture is associated with black people." She denied all the charges[190] but was found guilty a month later. "I have no doubt you intended Mr Vine should believe immediate unlawful violence would be used against him, given you made threats against him," District Judge Timothy King said. "You swore, shouted, and refused to allow Mr Vine to respond to points you made, and you placed your hands on his bike."[191] The judge had no objections about Jeremy's trustworthiness and behaviour: "His manner of cycling was perfectly appropriate," he said.[192] Soon after, the *Mail* reported that the defendant already had 15 previous convictions for offences, including one for causing harm, and that she tweeted during the court case to brag that she would be "straight back behind the wheel".[193]

"HURRAH," Peter Hitchens exclaimed in the *Mail on Sunday*, "for the broadcaster Jeremy Vine, like me a cyclist, for standing up to a bullying driver who treated him like a second-class citizen." The columnists did not spare Clarkson, who thought that cyclists "shouldn't be on the road as they don't pay road tax", calling out his "nonsense" and reminding him where the road funding comes from.[194]

The *Sun* changed its tone about Ms Pearson after she lost her challenge at Isleworth Crown Court. The paper called her a "yob". They wrote that at the time of the incident, she had a suspended sentence for theft, assault and resisting arrest, which now she had to serve, making it nine months in total.[195]

Jeremy

The victory was sour for Jeremy Vine. During an event publicising his memoir,[196] he said, "That particular incident ... was an eye-opener for me. The lady was jailed because she was already on a suspended sentence ... But I regret that I was a part of it. My friends said, 'Oh, but you were a victim of a crime,' but I ended up feeling I wanted to apologise to her. On the day in court, she came in with a suitcase because she expected to be sent to prison. I would have been happy with just an apology."[197]

I asked him about the event, and he said: "You can see if the person in the car is violent or if the car has made them violent. I was coming down [Hornton Street,] a steep hill, one way. She's behind me. God knows what she thinks. She can't overtake me, so she starts hooting. I then slow down and say, "What's wrong?" She goes completely mad and threatens to knock me out. It's all on camera, and she's then prosecuted. But what was interesting was she had 16 previous offences, she was on a suspended sentence for a crime and violence, and she was driving a car around London. She has no control over herself. There are a million uninsured drivers. There are some very, very angry people behind the wheel of cars. And they blame people, young kids on the pavement."

It rang a terrifying truth. Over ten times more people are killed by motorists on the pavements than by cyclists.[198] Yes. I've mentioned this before.

In a previously referred to response to Clarkson, Jeremy recollected the story of a driver who jumped a red light, passing inches from him. Vine gently knocked on the man's passenger-side window and said, "Sir, just to let you know, you nearly killed me back there," to hear in response, "I. WANT. TO. KILL. YOU."[199] That sounded familiar and sent cold sweat down my spine. Not only because just next to the place where we were sitting, a Mini (don't ask me why Mini) driver tried to ram me from my bike on purpose three times. (Each time he was prosecuted.)

Jeremy became the listener when I told him about that and other recent events. Not long before our meeting, I had been to court in a case of assault. On my way to work, I noticed a motorist who drove erratically for half a mile while shouting through his handheld phone without seeing me and my camera.

I cycled on a secured lane and caught up with him at each successive junction. When his passenger realised that they were being observed, the driver turned from the right-hand turning lane (one of three) across the intersection, blocking the A24 in Colliers Wood. It was a peak hour. He got out and threatened me with, "You started with the wrong geezer." I stood calmly, telling him to get back into his van and not make things worse for himself. Ultimately, he pushed me, causing my bike to fall. He wasn't so tough in the magistrates court. Following advice from his solicitor, he pleaded guilty. I didn't even have to enter the courtroom. I simply showed up.

I asked Jeremy if he had expected Mrs Pearson to get out of the car and assault him. "I wouldn't be able to defend myself. Normally, these people don't get out of their cars because they don't want to leave their precious car. I remember somebody telling me they went to Fulham Football Club in the company of a guy called Jimmy Hill. Jimmy Hill was a former Fulham player who became a very famous TV presenter. He's dead now. But this player went with Jimmy Hill and the Fulham fans all saw Hill and they all started shouting, "Jimmy Hill's a wanker," and Jimmy said, "You see, they still sing for me." I was on Kensington High Street and a taxi driver shouted out "Wanker!" And I was thinking, yeah, they're still singing for me. Normally, I'm very polite. And they always say, "You've got to move over." So, I say, "Well, you're slower than me, so why didn't you move over for me?" They can't deal with that logic. Why didn't you move over for the cyclist!

Jeremy

A voice of concern

Jeremy Vine became a spokesperson for everything cycling-related. He kept posting his journeys on social media with clips that grabbed the attention of the masses. Footage showing a motorist driving on the cycle lane the wrong way against the heavy traffic would get over 40K views.[200] When I wrote this, his Twitter/X had almost 800K followers, and his latest video had over 160K impressions.[201] While he kept reporting, it did not catch much media attention, but the footage that landed on his profile enabled a debate and helped push many improvements.

He continued to use his platform to highlight the lack of care and ignorance of all road users, without any exceptions. When a cyclist escaped death by inches after sliding through gates at a level crossing, Jeremy wrote, "The barrier is there for a reason. And when this jerk has to be scraped off the front of a train, the poor driver needs counselling for years."[202] On another occasion, he criticised Wheelie Kay, who posted a video of himself careering into a moving car while riding along a dual carriageway on his back wheel. "Amazing video. The lesson here is that there are clowns who cycle and clowns who drive. The clown on the bike doesn't hurt anyone. Put him in a car, different story."[203]

While already suffering from a disability, 2_Wheeled_Wolf has been intentionally closely passed twice by the same driver, knocked off his bike and assaulted; Jeremy asked what Essex Police would do.[204] As in cases reported by other cyclists, the police sided with the motorist. Wolf described it all to me: "I used to report drivers to Essex Police but not anymore as they are useless, biased and liars. Not one driver I reported was actioned on in over ten years." I will come back to them later in the book.

After posting some of his videos, Vine was accused of provoking the events or not being defensive enough. I had mixed feelings. From my sofa position, I imagined a few situations where he could do better, but I wasn't sure if I would make the same judgement in the heat of the moment. Most recently, his Brompton bike ended under a lorry that reversed on him after turning into a cycle lane from another cycle lane.[205] It was widely discussed, with professionals not being able to find common ground on whose fault the event was. His use of 360 cameras and clever editing with dramatic zoom-ins and zoom-outs often made it difficult to assess the moment. I've seen many of his and similar videos, and my impression was that he kept on the defensive, preventive side of things. But being slightly worried that he may end up hurt, I asked where he stood in terms of avoiding such situations in the first place:

"I think I'm probably quite a risk-averse. I'm somebody who for years didn't get on bikes, as I thought it was dangerous. It's a desire not to be hurt. I do have a fear of being hurt. I must be quite rules-based. So, when I get up in the morning, I go on to the CS9 Cycle Lane; it's 5:45 and I hit this light straightaway that shouldn't be there, and it's a 90-second light, and I'm there in the middle of January, and it's freezing, and I'm staying. I'm so rules-based. And I realise that I get offended when other people break the rules. That's the problem. There's a story about a woman in Australia who stopped at some traffic lights in the middle of nowhere and they never changed because they were broken. She just stayed there and had to be dragged from her car, suffering from dehydration, in the end. So, I think I'm secretly a traffic policeman. I just think, let's make it orderly. But the trouble with what's happening in London is you've got people who are prosperous, they buy two cars. They see the advert saying it goes 110mph and they can't get it above eight mph, and they are furious. They get stuck in their metal box. This whole psychology is fascinating to me.

"I hate that one has to be so careful. It's the same when I drive. I do have a car, and I drive probably 200 to 300 miles a year. And my wife doesn't like me driving because she says I go so slow. I'm amazed that the little street that we live on is 20 miles an hour; people go down at 35, and it's only 200 yards long. They roll down it in delivery vans. I don't get it."

Jeremy used his position to drive change in the capital. He presented his incident with Ms Pearson to the London Assembly Transport Committee, asking for infrastructure to separate cyclists from dangerous drivers: "Sadly, I have come to the conclusion we'll never eliminate the number of really angry, dangerous drivers and therefore, sadly, the answer is [road] layout."[206] As to the counter-argument suggesting the removal of such features: "People say these cycle lanes should be removed because they are empty. The driver's mindset is that a road isn't working unless it's got a traffic jam on it. It is a bit like taking a picture of the M1 at 2 a.m. and saying it should be shut down."[207]

He did not stop there, and joined the London Cycling Campaign initiative "Stay Wider of the Rider", which eventually led to clarification of the passing distances in the Highway Code.[208] Together with Chris Boardman, he criticised the idea of Tory cycling minister Jesse Norman, who wanted to impose stricter laws to protect vulnerable road users from cyclists. "When I'm on a bike, I'm a vulnerable road user. In 2016, there were 1,700 road deaths; three were caused by cyclists," said Vine.[209]

Gemma Dobson was clipped by a driver and had a liquid thrown over her.[210] When she called the police, PC Ian Heathy from Surrey Police did not hang up properly and she heard a three-minute "taking a piss" out of her incident. Jeremy used his platform to call him out.

Vine was consistent and unapologetic with his message. When interviewed by Peter Levy for BBC *Look North*,[211] he quickly dismissed every cliché the host threw at him. When Levy said drivers were becoming second-class citizens, Vine responded, "Cyclists were here first. In a lot of cities, the roads aren't really designed for cars. In fact, designing cities around cars has been one of the most historic mistakes of our society. That's why you feel so oppressed as a pedestrian or cyclist. You feel endangered. And it shouldn't be the case." Then Levy quoted Nick Freeman and suggested insurance and penalty points for cyclists. Jeremy came back with, "No, because you want to encourage people to cycle … which will make you fitter, less of a burden on the NHS, make you happier and safer to everyone else around you. What's not to like?"

In the end, with a forced smile, the host tried to bite his guest with "but they are not contributing anything to the roads, which is the –" Jeremy stopped him there: "Rubbish. Rubbish. Drivers are subsidised by the general taxpayer. Drivers do not pay the cost of the roads; they pay a bit of it. All of us are paying for the roads, cyclists included. By the way, there was a road rage incident where someone attacked me and went to jail, and it turned out that only one of us was paying tax on the car, and it wasn't the driver. So, as they say – go figure."[212]

When fashion icon Susannah Constantine said, "Drive into cyclists wearing Lycra, kill the lot of them and go and die in jail," Jeremy did not hold back. "The last minority you can legally wish death on are cyclists," and he offered her a ride together.[213]

Each year, different topics required his support. After some were won, new ones emerged. The cycle highway network grew around London (while still a drop in the sea of London roads), parts of the City became closed to motor traffic, and work on pedestrianising the Strand began. The light even shone on Kensington and Chelsea for a moment (I will return to that).

With the 2020 pandemic, the Boris Johnson-led government and councils (regardless of the party in control) started fast-rolling massive active travel improvement projects, including new pop-up cycle lanes and low traffic neighbourhoods. The latter's success is still debated today, and the speed at which they were applied caused a massive rift in society. Jeremy tried to help explain the topic to the masses: "In a city as compact as London, you can't justify people driving around in two-tonne metal boxes with an empty armchair beside them and an empty sofa behind them. It's just nuts. But once you start to say, 'Right, if you want to drive in a big metal box, that's fine, but you can't go down here, here and here,' people go completely mad about it. To the point where somebody says, 'Your neighbourhood is going to be an LTN,' and everyone goes, 'You're fucking joking! I don't want that.'"[214]

He must have had an impact, as shrinking hard-line motoring groups started to file complaints about his alleged bias against drivers. Loved by the tabloid press and shouty talk shows, FairFuelUk chief Howard Cox told the *Sun* that the BBC (including Vine) was "biased in favour of well financed green environmental positions".[215] This gaslighting is nothing new, as described in Paul F. Donald's previously quoted book *Traffication* and Grant Ennis's *Dark PR*. It is the car and the petrol industry that has money behind it. It's the one that controls the headlines. Cox and his friends have run multiple surveys on their social profiles. They were quoted around the press with ignorance of a microscopic respondent number, and no verification. It's a common tactic. RBKC backed the removal of the cycling infrastructure by a poll that openly logged votes from around the world.[216] A petition opposing Wales's default 20mph speed limit was widely criticised for the same reason. While the Senedd denied signs of tampering and duplication, saying that voters must confirm their email,[217] Google Trends has shown increased Welsh postcode look-ups simultaneously. I doubt an email address is a valid proof of address.

While running his Channel 5 show, Vine pitted guests of opposing views against each other to engage them in an argument. He took massive pride in staying unbiased and giving a platform to everyone. When commenting on the impartiality row in the BBC, he said, "The conclusion I came to was that you can have values, but you can't have views, and that's fundamentally how I operate."[218] For two years, he was silenced by the BBC for breaching impartiality rules when he criticised individuals who objected to introducing the traffic-calming scheme near his house in Chiswick.[219] The most vocal of them, Cllr Joanna Biddolph, was later suspended from the Conservatives for "disclosing confidential information" and "misusing her position as a councillor".[220]

Jeremy

Q and A

As time passed, I nervously scanned my notes. So many questions still had to be asked. Discussions with Vine could open me to other important figures in this book. Being a professional journalist with decades of experience made him a perfect person for a debate, so just for a moment I wanted to turn devil's advocate. "It's often brought up that when cyclists are being called out, we turn fast to whataboutery on motorists. Are we unable to take criticism?" I asked.

"I think the answer is that cyclists don't pose any real danger to people. And therefore, the idea is that any safety advice has to go to drivers. It can't go anywhere else. The traffic lights I mentioned, where I sit for 90 seconds: I have done a little film saying, can anyone tell me why I'm waiting at this light? Because I don't know. And the answer will be because it's the rules. When we had just bicycles and not cars, we didn't have traffic lights. So, traffic lights are for cars, but cyclists have to obey them. And I do, but there is a part of me that thinks we only have them because they're there for cars. I do think e-scooters are a problem on the pavements. People who cycle on the payments obviously cause a lot of upset and anger, but not very much danger."

That's where I decided to throw a curve ball. The oldest article I found in the archives contained "Cycle" and "Jeremy Vine". "It's very difficult to overstate the inconvenience I feel about living in London, the rudeness and anger everywhere. Like the fact that seemingly every smoker throws their cigarette butts into the street, and cyclists think they can cycle on the pavement. It's very irritating …"[221] He looked up at me up from his plate – still enjoying the hummus – smiled, and laughed. "That's pretty good research. Good journalism." I blushed.

"When I see kids or teenagers cycling on the pavement, I think – good, when they get a bit older, they'll be ready for the road. Previously, I found teenagers cycling on the payment really annoying. Not anymore. In our area, we have these young lads who used to cycle really slowly and block cars, and the drivers got so upset. Actually, I think that's great. That's what they should be doing. As long as the car is doing 15 miles an hour no one's going to die. But yes, I think I wouldn't like to be caught knocking someone over on the pavement. That's for sure. That would not go well for me."

I mentioned the recent case of Auriol Grey, a pedestrian who was jailed for manslaughter for pushing a cyclist, Celia Ward, under traffic.[222] The sentence and the media coverage were heavier than for the drivers who kill cyclists and often walk scot-free.

"I'm very conscious that pedestrians are the most vulnerable, and there are certain areas where you have to be very careful as a cyclist because of conflict. Hammersmith in front of King Street is one where people come across the lane. Another one, of course, is Oxford Street. An incredible amount of encroachment onto the road. I'm not complaining about them doing this because I understand pedestrians walk across the road with headphones on and their backs to me. I have to be ready for that. And it's good training. I just thought to myself, of course, they take the risk, as the driver wouldn't be able to react in time. I have be ready for anything they do."

Again, this sounded very familiar. Just a few hundred yards from where we sat, I had to test my brakes as a former editor of one of our papers stepped in front of my bike without checking. There is a video, but it stays private.

"The area where we met, Kensington, the same as Bank in the 2010s, looks like a never-ending building site, with an absolute lack of segregated infrastructure. This creates a massive conflict with HGV and van drivers," Jeremy pointed out. In response, I said: "On my way to work in RBKC, but also earlier on the A24, I noticed a humongous amount of tradesmen tapping on their phones while driving. As a white-collar worker, when reporting them, on many occasions, I met the argument that by doing so I was discriminating against the working class.

"Firstly, 1700 people die every year because of road violence," Jeremy continued, "and some of those will be guys in vans. So, I think the fact that we're all concerned about safety is not a bad thing. We all know mobile phone use the wheel is an absolute hazard. I do think that there has to be a trade-off between delivery and working vehicles and black cabs, as well as the safety of vulnerable commuters. Now, I was staying in Edinburgh a few years ago, in what was called a pedestrianised street. We rented a flat to go to the Fringe. And what amazed me was that the pedestrian street, Guy Street, was full of lorries all day long because there was some sort of loading exemption. It just shows that you have to properly enforce pedestrianisation. You have to make sure that people don't abuse it, and people who drive for a living will complain, but in the end they will work around new rules, and we've got problems in the city with pollution. We have problems with road danger. You know, I spent the first ten years of my daughter's life tending to be careful of, you know, cars flying down our street. It's ridiculous. So, I think in the end we have to have a cultural change, and I'm sure that in the end it'll be better for those van drivers, cos their kids will be safer."

Should more people report? We're often called snitches and weasels. During Ms Pearson's case, Jeremy told the *Guardian*, "I hate to overload our hard-working London police with footage from my commute, but I feel the person you see on the video will at some point hurt someone very badly."[223]

Many critics, especially on social media, accused Jeremy and others of tarnishing the cyclist's reputation and creating broader division by reporting. "It's difficult. The main issue is how cyclists are seen. If we look as if we're SAS or are tooled with cameras and all sorts of kit, we can put people off cycling. On the weekend, when I'm cycling up and down my high street in Chiswick, I don't usually wear a camera because I think you need to have a different image. I don't usually wear a helmet either, but for commuting, I do. I think the main way to get greater safety is through enforcement, but I'm not worried about the police workload because I think we're saving them work, actually. We're saving them work when we prevent a person from killing somebody further down the line. In the end, enforcement is the way and so we try to ensure that we keep reporting. Yes, I do think people should wear cameras. But to be honest, the main thing is just to get them cycling and have them be safe. But I think, you know, it is a faff having cameras because of mounting them and charging the batteries the whole time. Then I found this thing: until I had a camera on showing a picture of myself, I didn't get as many views. Then, instead of getting half a million, you get a million.

"My stat is always that there's 15,000 km of road in London and 173 km of segregated lanes for the cyclist. It's really not enough.

"At the weekend, just for a mile, I joined a women's cycle group. There's a group of Cycle Sisters, Muslim women, an amazing bunch of people. They've never cycled before, most of them. They don't go fast. They just do it for the company. It's very nice, so moving to see it. But you need segregated cycle lanes for that."

The Battle of Kensington

After our chat, Jeremy took a smiley selfie with me, donned his wet kit, jumped on a simple, worn-down bike, and pedalled back home. I returned to work thinking of the best route to avoid the High Street.

The relatively short stretch of road between Kensington Olympia and the Royal Albert Hall became a bane for both of us and thousands of commuters travelling between west and central London. Close calls, intimidation, bullying, and drivers on their phones. All are sandwiched on a road with no cycle lane and virtually no parking enforcement. I actively discouraged using Putney and Hammersmith bridges. But the alternatives were equally bad: New Kings Road and Battersea Bridge – a literal death trap for cyclists. This forced me to take long detours to reach Wimbledon. For many, the Royal Borough of Kensington and Chelsea is synonymous with petrol addiction. It's often called the Royal Borough of Killing Children. Supercars, SUVs, swarms of PHVs and construction traffic, all sprinkled with taxi drivers. Despite a long campaign by Better Streets for Kensington and Chelsea, the Tory-led council continuously ignored the issue.[224] Improvements had broad support from nineteen local schools, five universities, five local hospitals and another four healthcare providers, the Royal College of Music London, Royal Geography Society, Royal Albert Hall, seven local community organisations, including the RBKC Youth Council, and many local businesses. According to estimates, up to 4,000 cyclists use this route daily. All that fell on the deaf ears of the council.

In 2020, ongoing work on the street increased tension. In June, Jeremy recorded a long stretch of the road blocked by construction. "Tell me you're installing a pop-up cycle lane," he joked on his video.[225]

The idea wasn't new. Recognising the value of such infrastructure, the *Daily Mail* and General Trust plc submitted testimony to the Parliamentary Transport Select Committee, which was evidence for the Active Travel inquiry. The document supported the implementation of active travel choices. "In order to encourage active travel, local authorities are placing particular emphasis on new cycle paths and cycle highways. This is to be welcomed. We believe it presents an ideal opportunity, not only for cycling but for using other modes, including shared mobility solutions like e-scooters."[226]

After the country-wide standstill caused by the pandemic, many people were eager to escape "home arrest" and return to their workplaces. By October 2020, the cycle lane had been completed and an initial six-month trial had begun. Yet, as the traffic slowly grew, Thames Water works near Holland Park caused a bottleneck and congestion. In December, the *Mail on Sunday* released a feature by Nigel Havers, moaning about how the cycle lane had destroyed the High Street. Havers was a formerly famous actor who received a driving ban for drunk driving. After being caught, he claimed that he "had no regrets".[227] [228] "It never used to be like this. We used to relish our brisk morning walks down Kensington High Street, where we have lived on and off for the past 40 years. It was one of life's simple pleasures. But that all changed almost overnight after my local council – without notice – installed these dreaded new cycle lanes which have caused havoc across the country."[229]

Figure 5 Typical situation while crossing High Street Kensington

The piece puzzled many, including myself. Maybe four decades ago it was different, but at least for the past several years this street had been nothing like Nigel described. No brisk cycling or walking to the shops on the lunch break. Only fumes and the perfume or sweat of pedestrians cramped together on narrow pavements, topped with a headache from the constant honking and exploding exhausts of sports cars. When I tried to walk on the green man towards Church Street, I usually had to walk around a van and a cab that had stopped in the middle of the crossing.

On a bike, I felt fear when drivers passed me by inches to test my brakes, as the congestion did not allow them to go wider. I felt despair when many vehicles, including the Tunisian Ambassador and the Met, were parked on a double yellow. Many cars were left idling, and wardens were too scared to address it. I asked one to speak to the Diplomatic Police unit that clogged the junction's left turn lane, creating a blind spot just in front of the pedestrian crossing. He said that he wouldn't do anything in fear for his job. That is the High Street Kensington I know from then and the one I see today. The cycle lane was a godsend. And it was murdered in its infancy.

A week later, the *Mail on Sunday* continued to beat the drum, praising Worthing council for removing the bollards and suggesting Kensington would be next. They quoted a petition:[230] "More than 3,000 residents and businesses signed ... calling on the Royal Borough of Kensington and Chelsea to remove bollards."[231] Even if the actual residents backed it, the number would represent less than two per cent of the borough's population, where more than half of households don't have access to a car or van. Publicly available data has shown the form was full of entries from the rest of the country and abroad. The claim was made-up rubbish. Later, the article quoted Nick Freeman calling for number plates for cyclists, but did not mention other reasons why the traffic was worsening.

To keep a balanced view, the paper invited Jeremy to present his opinion, which he did in a beautifully spicy way. "Scrap cycle lanes, Nigel, and I'll swap my bike for a Chelsea tractor.[232] Let's see if that stops jams!" the headline said.[233] Vine did not use any sugar-coating in his response: "In central London, the average daytime speed of a car, pre-Covid, was 7.8mph. On two wheels, I average 9.8mph. So, my modest little bicycle, costing less than £200, is faster than a £200,000 Maserati. But as I cycled, I got angry every time I saw that a fellow cyclist had been killed – the victims often young, smart, professional women, their lives suddenly ended by a truck turning left. I got angry as I began to grasp the unacceptable level of physical danger I was exposed to as impatient drivers pushed past me or turned across me at lights and junctions. I got angry as I watched car adverts that made breaking speed limits look sexy and boasted of safety features which protected only the driver, not the person they hit … One of the most astonishing statistics tells us that motorists in London drove a total 22.6billion miles in 2019, across only 9,000 miles of road! So, we know that if we pave over the whole of Britain, it will just create one monstrous traffic jam, and the inescapable conclusion is that road space needs to be taken from motor vehicles and given to more active forms of travel – yep, cycling foremost … Make no mistake, cycle lanes will save lives. But it will take a while before they start to be used by the number of people the critics demand they see. We didn't wait till planes were in the air to start building airports."

His words led the minds and hearts of many, including myself. Clouded by fever from another infection, I lay down at home and felt hurt by the council trying to destroy the glimpse of hope the lane gave. Jeremy's words were like a spell of hope and sanity on the pages of the paper that had started all that mess. Loads of outstanding journalists from other Kensington-based titles like *Metro* and the *Evening Standard* stood united to defend the bollards. Many of them I knew personally. Boris Johnson, then Prime Minister, went "ballistic" and defended the lane.[234] I took my laptop and wrote to the council:

"I've been assaulted many times on Kensington and Chelsea roads and a few times almost lost my life thanks to dangerous drivers (once on purpose). In our team, we have people permanently disabled after being hit by cars while cycling. We all used that lane, and it made our journey safer. I'm incredibly disappointed to hear that you are planning to remove the cycle lane on Kensington High Street. It has proved incredibly popular with key workers like teachers and hospital staff, many of whom felt unable to cycle on this dangerous road without the lanes, and it is also increasingly used by families."

Then I did something stupid, yet some, including Jeremy, called it courageous. I posted my letter on Twitter. And even though it starts with "This is my PRIVATE stand on it. I'm not imposing or suggesting the official position of any institution. Anyhow, in the current situation, as my personal safety is at stake, I voice my concerns,"[235] I should have expected it might go the wrong way. Well. I'm Polish, and we have something called ułańska fantazja, which is essentially courage combined with stupidity.

Road.cc picked up the tweet and made a massive article headlining my employer's name.[236] My fever skyrocketed. Dumb as I might have been, one person I could always count on was my boss, who shielded me from further ramifications after giving me a fatherly telling off. Then he enforced on me the rules of further engagement. These rules allowed me to write this book while being transparent and avoiding conflicts. As I learned years later, Jeremy also defended me and many other media professionals who spoke up. He saved us from harmful side effects of this – what seemed to many – generation clash in the professional fabric of the borough.

The same article that had put me on the roast revealed further inconsistencies around the lane's removal. Kensington Business Forum rejected claims that it opposed cycle lanes. In their press release, they wrote, "We support any project which helps our business community and commend the council's efforts to design and implement the temporary cycle lanes so quickly under a government directive." Later, they wrote, "We recently passed on the business views, both of those in favour and against cycle lanes, as a representative body of Kensington W8 Business. The views shared with Kensington and Chelsea are of local businesses and not those of our Executive Committee. Regrettably, this has been represented, in certain public forums, as our opposition to cycle lanes. This is not the case."

Nevertheless, the bollards were gone, and everyone was forced to risk their life when crossing that section of London. The whole borough is a blank spot on the map of cycling infrastructure in the capital, with a large proportion of road traffic collisions involving cyclists. Better Streets challenged the council in the high court about the removal of the provision just seven weeks into the trial. Still, they lost in 2023,[237] and in August the council announced work on reintroducing the lane in the form of an "advisory cycle lane" (paint)[238] after a consultation that was criticised as gaslighting and giving no option for authentic, safe infrastructure. Together with many others, Jeremy kept pushing for more, proving to this day how hollow and misleading the "fake lane" has been.

Lauren O'Brien is one of the better known cycling social media activists trying to improve that stretch. In her tweets, she shows the reality every two-wheeler must face there. "This is the reality of cycling in a city like London. My partner and I don't go anywhere without out GoPros; we realised pretty quickly after moving to the city that they are out best protection when dealing with the state of some drivers on the roads."[239] On another occasion, she shared a video of her filtering heavy traffic on Kensington High Street with a big black Range Rover parked on double yellows and holding everyone back. "What is holding up all this traffic, I hear you ask? Take a wild guess. Clue: it isn't a cycle lane …"[240] Day later, she shared a clip of a gold Smart (no MOT) that continuously invaded the advisory cycle lane, preventing her from using it. "Ever wonder why cyclists ask for segregated cycle lanes or, at the very least, wands on the road? This is why. It's just a painted line to drivers unless you properly segregate it. Until that happens, it isn't safe to use."

The force

Camera footage won't do much good if it can't be used to improve safety. Social media was the only platform that achieved that for a long time. It proved the problem exists. It put pressure on the legislators and educated viewers. Drivers quickly learned about their friends' or relatives' riding experience. Many stated that they had never imagined how scary it could be for a cyclist on the road, and promised to change their behaviour. Others always blamed the cyclists for anything, regardless of the facts. To this day, some deny any reason why a driver could be prosecuted. Oh, how wrong they are.

Police had to work out how to process, assess and use the new form of evidence. There wasn't enough legislation to help them. Even the Highway Code is mainly guidance: only some bits are covered by the law. While it can still be used against offenders, it leaves a lot of leeway. It would be a problem in countries using civil law, but not in the UK with its common law. Case law and precedents enforce assumptions and allow policies to materialise. They help find loopholes and enable daring legal professionals to punish criminals. Even when they lose, like in the infamous Barreto case,[241] there's a chance to fix the bills[242]. But it happens only because the police are allowed to act on their interpretation of the law in the first place. It all depends on the will of the officers.

I have had quite a mixed experience with the police in the past. Within the Metropolitan Police, I experienced uneven support, care, and professionalism. While the unit responsible for traffic offence reporting was great, collisions or assaults weren't always taken seriously. I'm not alone in this. Yet, compared to London, many parts of the country seem far behind. Sometimes the poor performance is due to different legislation, like in Scotland and Northern Ireland. In other situations, it appears to originate from a very public conflict between officials and the people – like in Essex. I wanted to be fair and represent the topic correctly. To do that, I reached out to every police force in the United Kingdom with the following questions:

- When did you start to accept video evidence from members of the public to prosecute road traffic offences?
- When did you provide an online service allowing members of the public to upload evidence?
- For the last four years, what was the number of reports per road user type (e.g. pedestrian, cyclist, motorcyclist, driver)?
- For the last four years, what was the number of reports per gender (or title if gender was not recorded)?
- For the last four years, how many reports resulted in warnings, conditional offers, or prosecution?

Answers were likely to vary, and they did. Police are regionalised, usually around county borders, with their own hierarchy and supervision by local commissioners. Whereas in some parts, organisations will be resistant to change and improvement, in others, ambitious and eager officers can drive innovation and, after achieving success, spread it to the other parts of the country (and beyond).

There must have been a source of third-party reporting in the police. When I asked the community, all pointed to two ambitious officers: Andy Cox and Mark Hodson. But what could the organisation say about them? Would it recognise them or claim the achievement for itself?

It wasn't much of a surprise that the first question about accepting footage got mixed up with the second about providing an online tool to upload it. For example, the Metropolitan Police said they had taken evidence recordings from the public since 2016, while CycleGaz confirmed that his videos were accepted before 2010. Police Scotland did not answer the question and went on about lack of funds, when we know that David Brennan's videos had been accepted since 2010, even if their process still seems medieval in 2023.

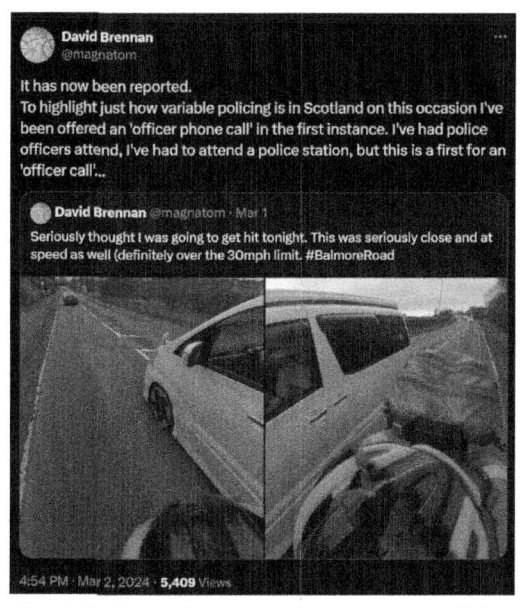

Figure 6 David Brennan's tweet about a close pass report in 2023. 243

As corporate memory struggles, it's safe to assume the dates usually represent when the force made a conscious decision to work with the public against road crime. The Hampshire and Isle of Wight Constabulary claimed to have started accepting third-party evidence around 2010. Kent Police stated they always accepted such footage, with the full digitalisation of the process in 2022. The same answer came from Leicestershire (portal created in 2020), Merseyside (portal since 2018), West Mercia (joined OpSnap in 2018), and Wiltshire. Others were more specific:

- 2016: Cumbria, Essex, Metropolitan Police, City of London, Norfolk, North Yorkshire, Suffolk.
- 2017: Avon and Somerset, Dyfed-Powys Police, Gwent, South Wales.
- 2018: Cambridgeshire, Staffordshire, Thames Valley, Warwickshire.
- 2019: Derbyshire, Devon and Cornwall, Dorset, Greater Manchester, Hertfordshire , Lancashire (they accepted it for

several years before but had trouble locating records), Northumbria, Nottinghamshire.
- 2020: Gloucestershire.
- 2021: Lincolnshire.
- 2023: Durham.

Northamptonshire and West Yorkshire did not respond to this question in the FOI request. Cheshire, Humberside, and South Yorkshire did not respond to my Freedom of Information Requests in good time. Cleveland and Surrey refused to provide information on all questions, taking issue with some. North Wales and Sussex are still processing the FOI request at the time of writing.

The Police Service for Northern Ireland couldn't answer the question, but they stated they had accepted some evidence via various services since 2019.

West Midlands responded that they enabled the upload portal in 2020 but forgot to respond to the first question. Luckily, we already knew the answer.

Disruptors

One thing you can't say about Mark Hodson is that he's quiet. No. Once you ask him your first question, he becomes a gift that keeps giving, even when you're already satisfied with the answer. Direct, opinionated, energetic, and unapologetic – this is the impression you get wherever you meet him on social media, in one of his talks or in a face-to-face conversation. Unsurprisingly, he claims – and has every right to do so – to be one of the spices that brewed third-party reporting as we know it today.

If Mark were a jalapeno, his work partner, Stephen Hudson, would be a vanilla pod – in a good sense. Mark was a fire that melted the ideas, and Steve was the mould that let them settle, cool and come out as hoped. "He was really sort of the one who made sure that everything got done properly. He was very much the one that kept everything in check and stopped me going off on to the next thing before we finished something." Both are seasoned traffic officers from West Midlands Police who changed how the police work.

Mark worked in the force for seven years before he was moved to traffic. Before that, he did loads of response work and student officer training. In his own words, the job was *extremely physical* and required him to be in exceptional shape. "You get in your traffic car and you chase a stolen car. The stolen car eventually gets stopped by tactical crashes. You get out of your car. You run after the bad guys who've been driving it. You got a fight with them, and then you lock them off." That requires a lot of exercise, and the bike was the perfect solution. A mountain bike, in his case.

His brother-in-law was a professional motorcycle racer and used MTBs for fitness. Mark tried it, and the adrenaline side quickly dragged him in. As a self-declared petrolhead with a love for cars and motorbikes, especially 1960-70 motor racing, he loved the feeling of downhill.

Steve, on the contrary, was a racer commuting to work on a slick roadie. When they worked together, he convinced Mark and a few other colleagues to do the same. "It was from about 2012 when I really became a dedicated community utility cyclist," Mark recollected. "It became my main form of transport. It just killed two birds with one stone. I got to work, got my miles, and got the fitness done. If I was on an afternoon shift, working late, I'd leave a couple of hours early and do a 60-mile circuit into work."

One of the hardest things he had to do once he joined the traffic was take care of victims' families. For a long time, Mark was one of the very few trained liaison officers in the unit – the person who was between the investigation into an RTC and the relatives.

"I saw the impact. Unless you deal with the families and RTCs, you don't see the overall impact. Going through the interviews with the offenders, it intrigued me how people who were normally law-abiding in every other way broke so many laws in a car and posed so much danger to other people. It struck me that the people you see in the interview were just like anybody else. If you went on the street and asked if that chap looked like a criminal, no, he did not. But that chap over there *is* a criminal doing 20mph over the speed limit every day, and unfortunately, one day, those circumstances meant he killed somebody, and now he's a criminal. But prior to that, he's always been a criminal."

The duo started to wonder how to make people realise they were the real problem and what they were doing was wrong. In this, Mark discovered what was to be his life's work. In the past, he worked for a top-tier accountant company. A career that could make him a wealthy person. But he joined the force to get something personally – the ability to improve the world around him. "There are two things you can do as a police officer: you can go to work every day, put the uniform on, do the job and have a significant impact on people's lives; or you can go to work, do the job, have significant impact and try to change something, so you don't have to do the same work day in, day out."

It became evident to him that people wouldn't walk or cycle places or make hybrid journeys using public transport because they were generally fearful of the way others drove. Having children growing up, it frustrated him that he couldn't let them cycle to the school two miles away because of his fears.

They couldn't avoid mistakes along the way. One of the first campaigns they ran in 2014 was about HGV blind spots. It did not bring the expected results but allowed them to gather feedback and re-evaluate their strategy. The problem was that rather than addressing the root problem like Cynthia Barlow did, they focused on educating the victims. As a result, instead of targeting the vulnerable road users, the duo decided to pay more attention to the cause: dangerous driving. The public and media still had a very motoring-centric mindset. Invited to their event, the ITV crew left disappointed that they could not film a scene of "a cyclist being mowed down by a truck driver". They wanted drama but received information instead.

Their brainstorming led to a new addition to the daily commute – a helmet camera. While cycling in a small town in Warwickshire, Mark was narrowly overtaken by a white van driver, squeezing between him and two parked cars. As it turned out, the driver was on his phone as well. It must have been a surprise when it turned out that the person he had victimised was a police officer. He may have been the first driver outside of London to be prosecuted based on the footage from a third-party report. His denial was firm, as he argued in court that the footage was doctored, confusing the Garmin headset beep sound with some editing artefact.

The force

Figure 7 Source Mark Hodson

Mark did not hesitate to name names where credit was due. Many forces struggled to facilitate the growing importance of social media and limited their communications to fire-fighting and damage control. But inspector Kerry Blakeman, "a pioneer of police social media", helped WMP to break down the wall between the officers and the public. "I could get my message directly across to the people," Mark recollected. "And there was a genuine hunger from the public to interact in the way they could never do before. They are interested in the nuts and bolts of what we're doing and why." Cutting out the middleman and putting a face to the profile perfectly fitted Mark's personality. "My style of doing it was that I would talk to somebody on Twitter like I talk to them on the street. If somebody's been an idiot, I'd say: you're an idiot. It's not the corporate face of West Midlands Police; you're talking to a police officer. If you try to cause trouble, you'll get the same response. If you want to get results to protect some people, you have to be prepared to upset others. You've got to identify your problem group and not be hesitant or afraid of upsetting them. You'd notice very quickly that except for some who would never change, the majority of people don't like to be associated with the problem group. Nobody does."

He threw me a series of off-the-cuff examples: "We stop a person who drove too close to a cyclist during our close pass operation. They go to court.

They hear they are a problem. They're scaring people every day. Others see it and say they won't do that again, as I don't want to be identified as a problem. If you have a group of parents who see the problem of parking outside schools and start taking photos and bringing it to the school's Facebook page, no parent wants their car to be there. They will quickly change their behaviour."

With the initial success on Twitter, the team recognised that they needed a longer format to tell the story entirely. They decided to start a blog. In Mark's words, using the social platform was like shouting at a bloke across the road, while writing posts was like having a cup of coffee and a cake and having a half-hour conversation. And the new medium went huge. Especially the entry that initialised Operation Close Pass. The problem was that the demand grew and the pair struggled to keep up. Luckily, it all happened *in the right place, at the right time, with the right people around*.

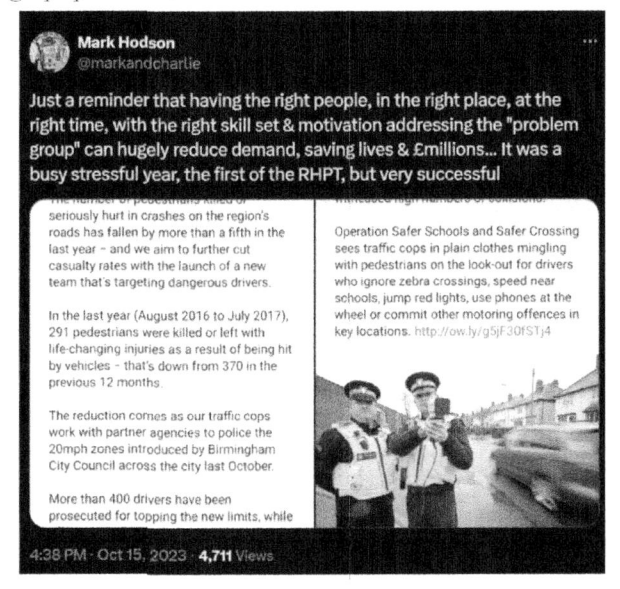

Figure 8 Source Mark Hodson on Twitter 244

The initiative had growing support from the Chief Constable and the Police and Crime Commissioner, David Jamieson, an ex-Labour MP and under-secretary in the Department of Transport responsible for changes to section 165 of the Road Traffic Act.[245] After scrambling qualified people, the WMP

The force

created the first evidence-led Road Harm Reduction Team. With adequate commissioner funding, the team then attends conferences and spreads the ideas nationwide. They were also invited to Australia and Canada, but due to lack of time and workload, they could never go.

Mark attributed a large part of Operation Close Pass's success to Brig Ford, an ex-journalist turned WMP spokesperson. He brought along Chris Boardman, a national treasure whose mother died while cycling not long before.[246] His professional touch turned this to the most successful campaign the West Midlands ever had. Millions were reached in the first week before the topic went worldwide. "It didn't matter if people agreed or not. All of a sudden, everyone was aware of what you could and couldn't do. I thought this was just the easiest police work. I can change behaviour sitting on my phone and putting out a few simple messages in the right place." It went so well that when walking to court, officers would hear the magistrates say, "That's the bloke from the TV," and were fully aware of the legislation and what the summoned driver did wrong. "If they knew, the drivers must have known as well."

More people saw prosecutions happening and started to contribute. The demand for officers serving in the RTC fell, which was great, since the 2012 cuts hit traffic hardest, as it was one of the most expensive departments in training and equipment; but it increased demand for public report-processing. That's when another success-hungry officer stepped in, Stuart Baker. Before he took over the traffic investigation unit and unloaded Steve and Mark, they processed 300 prosecutions annually. Most ended with fixed penalties, as the evidence was unquestionably good. A small portion of those ended in court, usually for not naming the driver. Their problem was a lack of not-guilty pleas to verify the law and the system in the court. With his team, Stu bumped up the number of prosecutions to one thousand and kept growing it.

They also observed that courts tend to take evidence from members of the public differently from that supplied by the police. In the opinion of many people, courts and the police are given some target for the number of prosecutions. "It's an urban myth." Mark exhaled. Yet, when a video from an individual backs the case, the courts seem to give it more weight, inspect it with less scrutiny, and declare harsher sentences for the offending motorists. Often, the officials see the witness as a victim and a good citizen.

The success attracted talent: a marketing professor, academics and law practitioners. All wanted to be close and to contribute. Officers knew the police didn't have all the answers and needed to speak to people and create partnerships. They paired with traffic defence barristers as well, who "at the end of the day don't want to see people killed and injured". They started to exchange information and ideas, run imaginary trials and switch roles to understand all points of view.

The worst battles weren't on the streets, though. It was within the four walls of police stations where the most enormous pushback occurred. "Police forces are very conservative in the way they work. They don't like change. They don't like creativity. They don't like taking risks. But we got to the stage when other forces started copying us, being up front on social media. People think that we say things to curry favour from our supporting groups. Whether that's, you know, vulnerable road users or law-abiding drivers who are sick of the way others are driving, we are doing that from a very selfish point of view. *I want you to go to work and do less work every day.* I didn't want to go and give those death messages. I didn't want to deal with the grieving family for 12 months. I didn't want to investigate another fatal RTC. I wanted to go to work and have a day where I didn't have to deal with the carnage that offending drivers distribute on our road network every day."

After the first year of the Operation Close Pass and 20mph enforcement, the cycling-related cases fell by 20% and pedestrian-related by 21%. "If you cut burglary by 20% in a year, you'd get a knighthood," Mark laughed. "The cost of every fatality is £2.2 million. If you reduce your fatalities by a factor of 10, it's £20 million. That's a lot of money." And it wasn't what they expected to see in the first place. Just before starting the campaign in 2016, Stephen asked Mark what he considered a successful outcome. "I'd be happy if it just grows, some other forces copy it, and I get a bottle of Scotch out of it." It went nationwide, yet the bottle never arrived.

Mark directly links third-party reporting, active travel, and general safety. "You create a better society where people are able to go out and do things. And if you focus on vulnerable road users, you're going to get more eyes and ears. You have more witnesses, so you can reduce crime because the criminals don't like being seen. The more people who get out of their metal boxes, where they're isolated, and onto the streets, reduces more crime. These people breathe fresh air, walk, and exercise. You reduce demand for the NHS, mental health support, and obesity problems. Whenever I'm not after dangerous drivers, I'm really into active travel. It's really a silver bullet to everything that we're currently struggling with."

Successful trial

In October 2016, South Wales Police, GoSafe and the Road Casualty Reduction Partnership started a pilot called Operation Snap. It encouraged drivers to upload the evidence from their dashcams. By August 2017, as the *Sunday Times* reported, 129 cases had been dealt with and had ended with fines, driver awareness training, or in court.[247]

The pilot by South Wales Police in conjunction with GoSafe was officially launched on December 19, 2017. In their memo, the force quoted South Wales Assistant Chief Constable Jeremy Vaughan, who admitted that "This [OpSnap] provides us with the ability [to] target those who drive dangerously and reduce the number of fatal or serious road-related accidents that occur on our roads. Operation Snap is for all road users, from pedestrians to cyclists, motorcyclists, horse riders and drivers of all vehicles." Teresa Healy, Partnership Manager at GoSafe, added: "Operation Snap is the culmination of partners working together to respond to community needs; to deliver a solution which allows road users and the wider community to actively contribute to road safety. This operation also allows us to protect vulnerable road users who would not otherwise have the means to submit their footage easily to the police.

"… This operation acts as a deterrent to those who choose to drive dangerously. By enabling the public to submit footage, we will reduce the number of serious or fatal collisions that occur on our roads."

Inspector Steve Davies, who delivered Operation Snap on behalf of South Wales Police, stated: "Police officers cannot be everywhere, as much as they try, but with Operation Snap the police could be anywhere.

"The aim of this initiative is to change driver behaviour and their mindset behind the wheel. We want drivers to ask themselves two questions: firstly, am I being recorded? And secondly, do I really want to take that chance?"

Of all the forces in the UK, North Wales was the fastest and most eager to help me with my research. Shortly after my first emails, Sgt Ian Price offered his help. I was so excited that I accidentally invited my whole department while setting up the Microsoft Teams meeting.[248] It caused a few of my colleagues to freak out and my bosses to make a series of friendly jokes by the water cooler.

At first, I was primarily interested in how the unified system's introduction changed how officers worked. Did it simplify the process or become a burden? "It created an additional demand," he replied, "owing to the fact that it's been widely publicised as a means of reporting. Previously, when people used to report incidents on the road without any corroboration,[249] it would be finalised with no investigation into it. Whereas, when you have corroboration, then you've got some legitimacy around the complaint. The corroboration, in this instance, would be done through a dashcam or headcam. The initiative improved the efficiency of dealing with such complaints. Previous to all those things, if you phoned the police and stated you were a witness of dangerous driving, 'I've got it on my dashcam', you'd have to make an appointment with a police officer. The officer may not get there, and you would have to reschedule it. Once you meet, they need to view the footage, take the witness's written statement, and take the evidence. So, for example, take the SD card. That's an element of seizure, which is a nuisance to the members of the public because they'd have to buy a new card. Then it would have to be uploaded to the police system. There may be some IT compatibility issues. By the time everything was carried out, on average, 23 hours of officer time was taken up in processing. Today, we're probably looking more in line of about four hours. That's a huge improvement."

Those figures have an actual translation to prosecution as well. In the UK, the force currently has 14 days to deliver the Notice of Intended Prosecution to the vehicle's registered keeper. The time counts from the time of the offence. "Once you press the submit button, we'll get a notification within minutes. The officer would then view the footage and statement and decide whether it matches the criteria and take some form of action if necessary." What happens after 14 days? Usually, the driver goes scot-free, but as Stg Price mentioned, some exemptions could be applied to the most serious offences and crimes.

The system had many iterations and some hiccups along the way. Officers must transfer footage from the dashcam system to evidence.com, a software widely used by UK police forces and made by American Axon. They can share the link with the Crown Prosecution Service to proceed when it's done. Back in 2018, only a few prosecutors were using the system, so they had to burn DVDs and hand them to the CPS lawyer on the day of the trial, and while it was inconvenient, it was also very prone to errors. "We've moved on in the technology world since then, albeit only five years ago. It's quite remarkable," cheered Ian.

He also saw how keeping a good relationship with the public can benefit everyone in the long run. "We get a lot of people who repeatedly provide us with footage, probably because they've had a good experience. They know the outcome and see it's worth reporting incidents to us. They tend to be from the cyclist commute community, but a growing number of submissions are coming from people who ride horses. Certain areas in our force have a lot of interest in equine activities. We've had interactions with them over the years; they have told friends and their friends. We work with the British Horse Society and try to identify those areas. They have their system to report dangerous places or situations, which they can use if there is not enough evidence to go to the police or they don't have confidence in reporting to us. This was unfortunate, but we got in touch with the local representative, and as a result it generated more submissions to us."

Sergeant Price admitted that it creates more work for the force, but on the other hand it allows them to act where it wasn't previously possible. It has also helped improve the signage, making drivers more aware of horse riders and how motorists should pass them. It works both ways, as well. Some vulnerable road users could quickly get agitated. The whole system allows for correcting the behaviour of both groups.

Similarly to Mark, Ian recognised the value of using social media to raise awareness in the public and build prosperous relations. "We had a guy live-streaming himself driving in the local town and later on a section of the bypass with a national speed limit. He was doing 120mph whilst filming himself on his phone. Later, he would drive through other towns, sometimes doing 80mph, overtaking cars, being near pedestrians, etc. The subsequent inquiry resulted in 23 months in prison for dangerous driving. When that was publicised, we received loads of positive feedback." He admits there is a criticism along the lines of "Big Brother is watching you" but dismisses it, stating that the incidents were always happening. The only thing that has changed is that the force can do something about it, thanks to the usage of cameras and social media.

From 0 to 15 thousand

The success of West Midlands and North Wales gained a lot of interest from safety campaigners, officials and active travel activists around the country. Still, without changing the way of thinking in the capital, their message could get lost between polarised opinions across local forces. Someone had to break the ice in London. Greater London, as the City of London, despite having one of the most enormous amounts of commuter cyclists in the country, seems to have kept quite a cold relationship with non-motorised road users to the present day. One could be blocked and stopped for legally cycling on the road there.[250]

For the Metropolitan area, the solution was obvious. Jeremy Vine mentioned Andy Cox in a split second; others did as well. While the duo of Mark and Stephen is mainly known to people who are actively interested in the topic, almost everyone has heard about Andy Cox. There is a good reason for it: He was surrounded by a fantastic team and supportive supervisors.

Andy joined the force in 1999 and rose through the ranks in Northamptonshire. While focused on crime-based policing, he received a call from his Chief Constable saying: "'Congratulations, Andy, you're promoted. We want to put you on road policing. You'd love it. You will change it. It will be different, and you'll enjoy it' – and he was absolutely right." Soon after, he achieved his first success in the area, and word spread around the country. Despite being quickly moved to another field to make a similar impact, he wanted to continue improving road safety. When he joined the Metropolitan Police in 2016, Andy asked to be allocated to that department. He was refused, yet he worked his way back in 2017. He went ahead and became the lead of the VisionZero campaign in 2019.

The force

> **Squarehighways** ✓
> @Squarehighways
>
> @nikir79 you can find information on how to report a road traffic incident in the Square Mile to @CityPolice on: cityoflondon.police.uk/contact-city-p...
>
> 4:11 PM · Jun 15, 2015

Figure 9 One of the first tweets with a link to the online upload portal from the City of London Police

During one of the first meetings of the campaign, Andy met with all of London's main partners: TFL and senior Metropolitan Police officers. He asked: "And how does the public report?" One of the leads responded that the force has a link on the website to contact them. "Great, let's check it!" Andy exclaimed, to learn a few moments later that the feature was difficult to find, almost hidden on purpose. "It's ludicrous, nobody's going to be able to find it!". The lead responded: "That's the point." Andy tweeted the link, and the rest is in history. Over the first two years, the Met went from four to 30,000 reports.

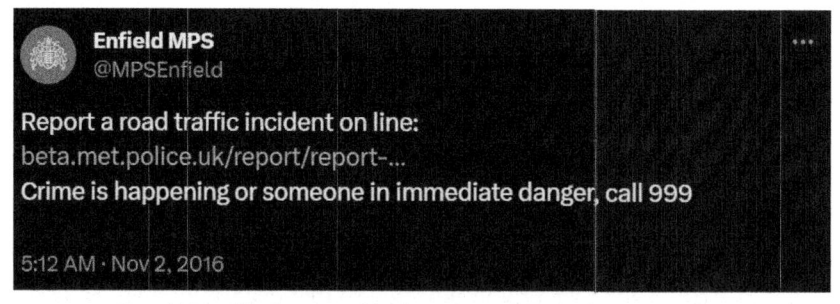

> **Enfield MPS**
> @MPSEnfield
>
> Report a road traffic incident on line: beta.met.police.uk/report/report-...
> Crime is happening or someone in immediate danger, call 999
>
> 5:12 AM · Nov 2, 2016

Figure 10 One of the first tweets with link to online upload portal from Enfield MPS

As Mark Hodson mentioned, the police don't like extra demands. The profoundly ingrained idea was (and often still is) that reducing barriers to reporting crime gives officers more work. Like Mark, Andy disagreed. "If you look at the police resource perspective for every fatal crash we go to, that has a huge impact on our resources and finances. First responders, road police, investigators, forensics, court cases, support to the family, witnesses, CCTV, phones to download, road marking examination and loads more. That's a huge amount of money. If you prevent a fatality, you don't have to do that. It's about £2.3 million to the economy for every fatal crash. And if you look at the workload. We have four to five people dying and about 60 people seriously injured on UK roads each day."

Andy also mentioned that the effort to improve force efficiency is far from finished. They still work on streamlining and making the whole process more professional to facilitate better third-party reporting for enforcement and protection and as a deterrent.

As Andy's team marketed the initiative, more people reported. The online portal succeeded, with over 10,000 reports in 2022[251] and closer to 15 in 2023. Jeremy Vine offered his platforms and used the features as well. The media got interested in the topic through the *Sunday Times*, *Time*, the *Mail*, radio, and television. Some have supportive or alarming spins, but they raise awareness that drivers must always expect to be observed. "What did I want to happen? First, police can't sort road dangers on their own. Second, the public must be frustrated when they see dangerous and reckless drives; they want to be part of the solution. Three: More people die on UK roads than by murder and terrorism combined. It's an absolute priority as part of our police purpose to save lives, detect crime, and solve crime. And it's part of our police purpose to win public confidence and support victims.

"In any other crime, sexual assault, burglary, violence, we ask the public to come forward with information. The fact we weren't doing that for road crime was wrong."

The force

Fix the justice system

We need to stop momentarily and see the situation's gravity. This will require me to repeat some facts and numbers. But it's essential. Take a moment to contemplate the figures. According to the Department of Transport, in 2016, 1,792 people died, 24,101 were seriously injured, and 155,491 were slightly injured in road collisions. Twenty-six per cent of pedestrian casualties were children, from newborns to 15 years old.[252] In 2020, 28,742 people were killed or seriously injured.[253] One every 18 minutes.

As if that wasn't enough, many drivers involved in incidents aren't even insured. There are over 100,000 uninsured drivers in the UK. Every 20 minutes, someone is hit by an uninsured hit-and-run driver. Every four minutes, an uninsured vehicle is seized. Those collisions cost the economy nearly £500 million annually.[254]

Every fatality is a tragedy. Every single one should be prevented. At least, their number should be reduced. Sentencing and strict fines are proven ways to achieve that. But the deterrent doesn't seem to be applied to everyone equally. It's often believed that cyclists aren't accountable. How could they be, without number plates,[255] insurance, and the legendary road tax? Each year, the media comes up with stories like the tragic death of Kim Briggs and demands harsher sentencing for causing collisions by cycling. It rattles many people who see the cognitive dissonance of the outlets. The level of threat from the motorists is incomparably greater. Yet the prosecution seems more lenient on them. Collisions with bikes are a perfect topic for the papers. They are rare enough not to bore the audience and prey on pre-existing societal divisions. Change cyclists to pedestrians (who don't wear number plates either), and you have a winning headline. When Auriol Grey pushed 77-year-old commuter cyclist Celia Ward into the road under oncoming traffic, the whole nation lived the trial. When drug-fuelled thugs drive into a bus stop full of people, it's just another day in London. Even when a Range Rover driver rams into a primary school in Wimbledon, killing two children, most papers write the story like the vehicle was self-driving and the motorist was possibly a victim, only to lose interest week later. That driver hasn't been publicly named yet.

Every single cyclist who has caused death in the recent history of the UK was sentenced and jailed. Many drivers go away with nothing or a suspended sentence. It is a fact that in today's Britain, if one wants to kill someone and go scot-free, the weapon of choice is a motor vehicle.

At this point, I have to acknowledge an exception. A tragic event that shook the nation just before I was ready to begin this book. Hilda Griffiths died two months after the collision with a cyclist in June 2022.[256] Reports said that Brian Fitzgerald was cycling at between 25 and 29mph when the pedestrian walked in front of his bike. According to him and several victims, he had no time to react. The story was covered by all media, leading to a motion by Sir Ian Duncan Smith to introduce new legislation to prosecute "killing by dangerous cycling".[257] Even in the active travel community, opinions were divided. Mark Hodson called out poor prosecution,[258] but Daniel ShenSmith described in detail why the police had no realistic prospect of prosecution.[259]

I want to be clear: I don't condone riding fast in places like Regents Park and I believe that cyclists have a responsibility for pedestrians' safety regardless of whether their actions are sensible. But I agree with Chris Boardman[260] that the law is based on "fear, not the data". James May rightly points out that most cyclists aren't even capable of breaching 20mph limits.[261] And it's not only because Duncan Smith comes across as a hypocrite after defending vandals destroying ULEZ cameras;[262] it's because it deflects from the real issue – dangerous driving. I will come back to this story in a later chapter, "

The language".

> **James May** ✓
> @MrJamesMay
>
> When has a cyclist killed someone but not been identified?
>
> 8:00 PM · May 13, 2024 · **9,320** Views
>
> 💬 4   🔁 3   ♥ 132   🔖 1   ↑

Figure 11 James May on X263

I may enrage some. But if setting much more rigorous sentencing guidelines for anyone who causes death or injury on our roads, including cyclists, pedestrians, and horse-riders, everyone would win. Not only will it shut up Littlejohns and Liddles alike, but it will also address the existing issue – deaths caused by dangerous driving. I have no sympathy for those who risk others' lives, regardless of their mode of transport. When a bicycle is a crowbar, and an SUV is an M16,[264] if you run blindfolded into the crowd and smash someone's brain you should still taste the consequences. And yes, it will be one to three people annually. But then we can demand that 1,700 victims of motorists are given the same justice. I'm all for it.

Subsequent governments failed to address the issue. As Adam Tranter rightly listed: "Things that the government could do (and have said they would do), but haven't, instead prioritising the creation of dangerous cycling laws:

- New laws for hit-and-run offenders, campaigned for by @RoadPeace
- Publishing of England road safety strategy
- Undertake full review of motoring offences and penalties, first promised in 2014
- Transport's Roads policing review: calls for evidence began on 13 July 2020 with recommendations due in Spring 2021; to date, no update has been published

- Pavement parking consultation review – closed November 2020. No update has been published
- Allowing death by careless driving sentences to be appealed by families under the unduly lenient sentences scheme
- Establishing the Road Crash Investigation Bureau: promised, then quietly shelved
- Clarify the difference between careless and dangerous driving."[265]

We must remember that a sentence's role is to punish the culprit and enforce behaviours in the broader public. If the criminals can expect no consequences for their actions, even more eyes on the streets from the public or "bobbies on the beat" won't discourage them. If there is a crime, there must be a punishment.

What consequences can meet the dangerous drivers who haven't killed anyone yet? Close passing, speeding, or using a mobile device while controlling a vehicle – the Crown Prosecution Service views all of those as dangerous driving.[266] When caught by officers, traffic cameras, or reported by a member of the public, police are given five choices: no further action, a warning letter, a fixed penalty, retraining, or referral to the court. Any of them can happen after the initial triage. Except when caught red-handed, the vehicle's registered keeper will receive a NIP: Notice of Intended Prosecution. It requires them to name the person controlling the vehicle at the given time. That includes a passenger supervising a learner driver, so if you use a phone as a driving instructor or while teaching your children to drive, you commit an offence. Failure to name the driver will result in the court case with a default outcome of six points and £200 – it's the easiest outcome for CPS to win and can be done in the defendant's absence. Sometimes, the NIP will be followed with a conditional offer of a fixed penalty or driver/speed awareness course. A considerable number of drivers will choose the former and pay. If that's a one-off, it may be the best option, with usually no more than six points and £200.[267] If the driver already has points on their licence or has passed their licence exam less than two years before the event, it will lead to a court case for disqualification.[268] New drivers are more likely to have to retake the test, while more experienced ones can get away with a massive fine and months of ban. That refers to low-tonnage private vehicles. Drivers of HGVs can expect multiple thousand-pound penalties for offences like phone use. TFL-controlled motorists like private hire and taxi drivers will lose their badges after just a single offence of this kind.

Retraining is an interesting form of repentance offered to those without previous convictions and allows them to avoid penalty points. They usually cost less than FPNs but are as good, as the offender is willing to learn from them. A decade ago, I attended one organised by the Thames Valley Police for doing 33mph in a 30mph zone. It shocked me to the bones and made me a better and more careful driver, cyclist, and pedestrian. It should be part of regular driver training. But some people attend just to tick the box, and re-offend shortly after.

One outcome that causes most of the controversy is the warning letter. It's meant to be used at officers' discretion towards motorists most likely to accept the reprimand. It's different from a verbal warning, as the record is kept within the force and can be brought up in case of future offences. This form was a default way to react to most offences back in the day. For instance, it was a standard procedure in London during the era of the Road Safe workgroup. Nowadays, it's proven to be ineffective at large and has adverse side-effects. It doesn't prevent reoffending and destroys public confidence in the force. Across the country, most forces stopped using this method, but some, most famously Essex Police, stubbornly facilitated it despite wide criticism from the public, academics and colleagues. Essex Police used to go easy on motorists, but there may be changes for the better, as the number of fines for phone use doubled between 2021 and 2022 in their area.[269] At the same time, this force is widely criticised for its pick-and-choose attitude to submitted evidence, based on which road users group submitted it. "We accept these if they are reported by cyclists who record it in passing while on their commute but not from those who proactively seek examples of poor driving."[270] This did not play well with the community, and many people complained about their reports being dropped, with commentary that (quoting one of the locals) "the recording was made by a cyclist with a headcam; therefore, he was looking for dangerous drivers". The criticism also came from legal professionals such as Daniel ShenSmitch, known as Black Belt Barrister[271] and specialist cycling senior solicitor Rory McCarron.[272] Together with many members of the public, their reports were dismissed at the officers' whim. The data seems to confirm there's a problem.[273] In March 2022, existing loopholes blocking mobile phone prosecution were fixed, yet only 33 reports were processed during that year, 50 ended with warnings, and 125 were not actioned due to *insufficient evidence*. Only three of the actioned reports were from pedal cyclists. The majority were from motorists.

After speaking to members of the public who used third-party reporting, I failed to find one who was satisfied with the handling, outcome, or attitude.

To be fair to Essex Police, they weren't the only ones criticised, but no others received unanimously negative feedback. It's difficult to provide reliable statistics, as volumes of affected reports and people's willingness to complain in public differ hugely. North Yorkshire Police had several big gaffes, like giving road safety advice instead of prosecuting a driver who, after close passing a cyclist, reversed to altercate and ran over a dog.[274] Staffordshire Police rattled many people by bluntly down-playing a phone-using lorry driver by going at first for the lesser offence of not being in proper control to ending with caution. The driver had already nine points. Oddly, that event was broadcast nationwide on the *Blue Light – Emergency Response* TV show.[275] Home Counties forces like Thames Valley Police, Hertfordshire Police, Hampshire, and Surrey Police received a fair number of complaints, especially about the lack of feedback. In the latter's case, it is strange. Surrey VanGuard and Road Safe teams are known for their proactive and unapologetic approach to road crime, which can be matched only by Mark Hodson's iron-hand tactics. At some point, TVP focused on scaring rather than protecting, and stopped Cllr Katherine Miles in Oxford to tell her she shouldn't cycle with her children as it wasn't safe.[276] The

City of London Police has a long-term dispute with the commuters, showing a lack of proper training and Highway Code knowledge, but have improved since. Even the Metropolitan Police with the high standards of TORS teams fall short when actual collisions occur. Once, an elderly motorist drove into my bike and pushed me onto a roundabout while I was waiting for it to clear before entering. In the eyes of the Met collision team, there was "no public interest in prosecution", and the driver did not receive even a warning letter. It's beyond comprehension. How does checking if a potentially dangerous motorist is fit for driving not in the public interest? My complaint took over a year to be processed and brought no results. This experience is shared. CBikeLondon complained, "Just had a final update from police about a driver who ran into me (and my then one-year-old onboard) during an inpatient undertake attempt on a narrow residential road, and then proceeded to assault me. 'Words of advice' is all I'm getting."[277] ShamRockSoup reported their collision with Wandsworth Council contracted minibus, scraping his elbow, and despite "crystal clear 360 footage", the department decided to take No Further Action.[278] "I can get a close pass; they will be prosecuted, but collisions won't," Axolotol explained. "I have two instances; one was a Range Rover on Queenway, the other was an elderly driver. I stopped in the cycle box towards the right side as I had to go ahead. The driver entered the cycle box and tapped my bike. So, that is actually a collision. Another one close passed me. I passed him later and gave a thumbs-down, and he tapped my bike while passing me again. I reported that to TORS. TORS escalated that to collisions. Collisions don't do anything because there is a massive queue. Because there was no injury or damage, collisions can't do anything. I spoke to a collision person, and she said there are too many collisions and they can't handle it. If there is damage, they refer you to the insurance company." I hear that argument over and over – *no damage*. I don't accept it. The occurrence I had left me with trauma and fear. After some events, I couldn't use my bike for weeks. The fact the flesh is not hurt doesn't mean there is no damage.

When Andy Cox tweeted about the importance of police feedback to the reports, many replied with criticism of the Met not doing that anymore. Some addressed the same issue elsewhere. "I gave up submitting as you have zero feedback," Ralpha Phil said about Hampshire Police.[279] Many forces incorrectly use GDPR as an excuse for not providing details to the witness.[280]

The forces that got stellar reviews from the interviewees were Welsh constabularies and Avon and Somerset Police.[281] Wales, as a country, has pioneered many improvements outside the already mentioned operation OpSnap. The 20mph speed limit drove the petrol lobby up the wall and led to cringeworthy campaigns by local Conservatives.

Regarding the warning letters, Mark Hodson's message is clear. There must be visible punishment. It must discourage others from doing the same. Word of advice: it does not work; but conditioning does, for the vast majority – 95% in his opinion. And the remaining 5%? "Some of them are mentally ill, and there are mentally ill people driving cars. They won't receive the message and need specialist treatment; and people who are just criminals and are not interested in other people's safety."

Andy Cox took a more balanced approach: "It's all about proportionality. What is the risk of harm? What's the driving history? I don't think we should enforce the most harmful, most risky behaviours as a part of our strategy to save lives. There has to be some discretion and some independent assessment of that but in a broadly safe and constant remit. If we think driving is risky, then warnings will be few in between, but it's a lesser form. If there is an obvious opportunity to learn from one mistake, then there's a benefit to warnings. Anyone who follows me knows how much I dislike speeding. For example, community speed watch, which is, in essence, the community stepping up and trying to enhance people's awareness and the risks posed, shows some benefit in terms of reducing repeat offending. There is a way to use rehabilitation prevention and warnings. Everyone knows the traffic laws, and everybody, therefore, should appreciate the risk they pose."

In the greater picture, he sees that the reporting itself has a more significant benefit to the public regardless of whether it ends up with a warning or prosecution. "We see evidence of drivers who changed in consequence. There are cases of people who reported some drivers, and they then say they saw that driver behaving so much better now. There is no end of benefit in my mind around it. But it's a massive culture shift about the very dangerous aspects for people to understand."

"The attitude towards driving in this country is amazing," Mark continued with evident sarcasm. "You can get somebody in an interview room, and if they've stolen off their grandmother, given the evidence, they'll say: 'Oh, yeah, I'm a really bad person. Yeah, I shouldn't have done that, broken the law. I'm really embarrassed. You know what a bad person I am.' But show them evidence of dangerous driving, and they will think that the reaction you get is like you'd slit their family pet's throat or something. People take driving so seriously that everybody thinks they're the best driver in the world. There's no such thing as a driver who doesn't make a mistake. Even highly trained drivers like myself never have a 100% drive. There are too many variables involved. I always say you have to drive in a manner that, when you make a mistake, it's easy to negate it. You have a protective bubble around you. You look for the right people. You look for the vulnerable road users. You recognise vulnerable situations. The thing that always goes back to the camera is people asking how you judge who you can report and who you let go. Where is your line in the sand? I don't have a line in the sand. The line in the sand is the minimum standard for me. It's the test standard. If somebody can't drive at that standard, they shouldn't be on the road. The reason is, it's not like you're looking to get this person or another because every time you sit there and interview a driver who's killed someone on the road, they aren't the person you think they'd be. It's someone like me, someone like you. It's somebody who hasn't been fulfilling their responsibility to everybody else on the road at the time. That's why you're interviewing them about it. They commit an offence that results in somebody's death, so don't ever think that you're doing the wrong thing because this person seems like a nice person, because they're a nurse going to work, because they're a teacher, because it's a driver who needs their license. They are quite possibly going to be the person who kills, the next person who takes a life. As much as you can say that people learn lessons from being told, they don't do that. I can tell you they don't. Never! I stopped the same driver three times in one week for the same behaviour. In my early days, I was in traffic and learned the hard way. I've been to community speed watch operations where the same person is at three warning letters for speeding past the same school. Warnings don't change people. It's only fear of prosecution. Something's going to change their life and impact them in some negative way that changes that. It's basic psychology. Warnings letters are like the traffic light symbols on junk food. People look at it and go – yeah, it's bad for me, whatever that is. But then, if you opened up your pack of junk food and it was covered in anthrax, you wouldn't like to have it. If someone opens that letter and there is a Notice of Intended Prosecution, you think, I'm never gonna do that again. People shouldn't worry about who the reports are about or the reasons why. Because, unfortunately, normal people inflict damage on society."

Even with the best police efforts, those who cause the most extensive damage are often let go by an inadequate justice system. From prosecutors down-playing the events, prejudiced judges and magistrates, to silly sentencing. The current guidelines allow 18 years of custody, with a life sentence for the worst, for causing death by dangerous driving, after June 28th 2022. Otherwise, the top limit is 14 years. The minimum disqualification is expected to be at least five years.[282] According to a YouGov poll, over half of respondents supported life bans for such offenders.[283] It would be anyhow naïve to expect courts to apply those eagerly.

Two weeks after passing his driving test, Harry Bennett killed 77-year-old cyclist Geoffrey Dean. Traces of ketamine, cocaine and alcohol were found in his system, and he drove up to 51mph in a 30mph zone when the event took place. He avoided jail and received a three-year ban after the PROSECUTOR told the judge that the incident was "just below" the dangerous driving threshold.[284]

Banned, uninsured driver John Brazil was speeding when he hit a 60-year-old woman on a pedestrian crossing. He received an unusually high sentence of nine years and nine months, plus a 10-year driving ban. It's still not close to the guidelines.

Melissa McKelligot ignored a give way sign and smashed into several cyclists, leaving them with life-changing injuries: hip replacement, partially collapsed lung, fractures to spine, etc. Court result: 225 hours of unpaid community work and driving ban for 93 weeks.[285]

RoadPeace is a charity that supports victims of road crimes and death prevention. One of their campaigns is Fix Our Broken Justice System, which tries to challenge such silly sentencing. On their blog, Rebecca Morris, head of communications, compared the tragic loss of two young women, Ellie Edwards and Frankie Hough.[286] Ellie was shot by Connor Chapman, who rightfully received a life sentence with a minimum of 48 years behind bars. Frankie, who was 17 weeks pregnant at the time, had a puncture while driving with her two sons and nephew on M66 and pulled over on the hard shoulder to make a call. Her car was hit by a BMW being driven erratically by Adil Iqbal, who was seen weaving in between vehicles, dangerously undertaking and reaching speeds of up to 123mph. Frankie died. Her children were seriously injured. Iqbal was jailed for 12 years and banned from driving for 13 years.[287]

The difference? The weapon of choice.

"If you want to kill somebody, use a car." George Monbiot [288]

David Danglish, Elaine Sullivan and Paul Mullen were killed on the A1(M) in County Durham in 2021 after Ion Onut crashed his lorry into their vehicles while browsing dating sites. The sentence: eight years and 10 months. He will be allowed to drive again after 14 years and five months.[289] In 2016, a Tesco lorry driver, Florin Oprea, hit cyclist Julie Dinsdale. As a result, she lost her leg, but Blackfriars Crown Court decided that a fine of £625 would be adequate.[290]

The force

After "quite sharply pulling onto the kerb, rolling back slightly, and accelerating", Peter Williams ran over a four-year-old girl riding her scooter on the pavement. Liverpool Crown Court found him not guilty of the offence of causing death by careless driving.[291] Lance Flavell was seen driving his van five days after being disqualified, but Norwich Magistrates Court decided not to extend his ban and hand him a fine and points. They explained, "We have given you the opportunity to get back to work as soon as possible," despite the fact he wasn't currently employed.[292]

Sania Shabbir, aged 27, used her phone while driving. As a result, she crashed into and killed Martyn Gall, aged 41, and seriously injured James Middleton, 33. Birmingham Crown Court sentenced her to four and a half years for killing by dangerous driving and two and a half for causing injury, to be served concurrently. She can drive if she passes an extended course in four years and nine months.[293]

If I wanted to list just a fraction of cases where people who chose to drive in a dangerous matter ended someone's life, this book would be many times thicker. And that would probably account for just one year. With the support of RoadPeace, Calvin Buckley, Frankie Hough's partner, has made fighting for harsher sentences his life mission. He shares their story and works hard to ensure no other family must endure what they did. Same as Kim Briggs's partner does. The same as some who want to go hard on dangerous cyclists who kill an average of two people annually in the UK, we need to stop protecting criminals behind the wheel who – again – kill 1,700 in the same period.

"I went to court; the judge was mostly on her phone while the driver harangued me about bad cyclists. Case was dismissed. I tried to file a complaint but was told you can't really do that." Travis, owner of the famous cycling cat Sigrid, recollected his experience of the court's attitude.[294] That was in response to another thread presenting a similar story: "Absolutely horrible day in (remote) court regarding Theo getting pushed off his bike three years ago. A driver went out of their way to antagonise us, changed direction to follow us, threw stuff at us and eventually came alongside to have his passenger push Theo off his bike while we genuinely just did our best to ignore them (I was at my most unwell at the time and this 30-minute spin was part of my attempted rehabilitation). Despite being the victims, we were dealt with rudely by the judge; I was called disingenuous because apparently there was no way I could have heard a driver shout 'Push him' and seen Theo's crash while riding in front of them. She believed that the driver had no responsibility because 'we all have to pass cyclists within 1.5m sometimes' and all context leading up to the incident was shrugged off. Care less about losing the case – we knew that was a risk. But I'm so angry at how we were treated; I don't for a second believe the judge was impartial and nor did she behave professionally. She made faces and interrupted every time our solicitor spoke. Honestly, I got the impression she sympathised with the defendant driving the car (who didn't even show up, by the way) more than she did us, as victims of an unprovoked violent assault. I don't know how to go forward. Apparently, there are no grounds for appeal; we will formally complain, but I'm just at a loss."[295]

The force

An envious cop

As officers around the country work hard to save people's lives, some put their egos above the public interest. Some would go after a person who proves there are areas where the force under-performs. As is often the case with Eastern European dictators, such individuals' tactics fall apart due to the incompetence of the only people willing to follow their lead.

I don't mean here situations where officers are mistaken. It happened in the case of a cyclist accused of allegedly dangerous cycling based on his report of a phone-using motorist. Media outlets were hated to celebrate their victory, only to retract a few days later when the Met admitted their error and apologised.

The following story is based on several accounts from the same period and place. In all cases, the interviewees felt confident enough to share their experience, were ready to defend their stand in court if challenged, but were required to keep names and locations edited. It isn't my aim to set a fire but to raise awareness and initiate debate – some of which can and should be behind the closed doors of constabularies.

In the period when police asked people to come forward with footage of dangerous driving, including the force in question, some submissions were actioned in a way that did not match the seriousness of the situation nor public expectation. Or rather, there was inaction in cases that resulted in life-long consequences for the victims. Individuals publicly raised their complaints in one way or another, only to receive bullying correspondence forcing them to retract their criticism. It worked for the majority, but in one case it backfired.

The officials picked footage that wasn't used in any report but was posted on social media. It showed dangerous driving by a motorist and a brief exchange between the driver and a cyclist. The traffic section of the nearby force contacted the author, asking them to come to their station under caution for several things, including "officer impersonation". But in none of the videos was a person seen to behave or dress like an officer. It did not fit the definition of a public order offence either.

The force

The first strange thing about the situation was which section made the demand. Events of this kind are dealt with by the criminal unit, usually from the local station. In that case, it was traffic. After getting solicitors' advice, the cyclist decided not to fall for the bullying tactics and didn't attend.

The court date and files arrived several months later, including a witness statement. The latter seemed inconsistent, including the event being described as happening months before it took place.

The victim attended the first proceeding and pleaded not guilty. After a few weeks' wait, they received a letter confirming that the case had been dropped due to a lack of evidence – as their lawyer had predicted.

Harassed members of the public contacted the department lead to demand an apology and reprimand the official whose name was on the whole paper trail. It was denied. Words of penance came from above, though. A superintendent sent a lengthy letter trying to damage-control the situation. In response, he learned that the day before the hearing, the officers involved sent out the charge papers, and the Crown Prosecution Service confirmed that the person had committed no offence, yet they pursued it. That amounted to a malicious prosecution. The reporter learned later they had likely been investigated for policing standards gross misconduct.

Thanks to their perseverance and professional legal support, the source had the upper hand. But by other accounts, the relationship ended in burned bridges, lack of trust in the police unit, and victims left alone without any justice given, bullied and scared of having any meaningful contact with the police.

Luckily, it seems that it was a rare exception to the overwhelming good, but not perfect, dynamic around third-party reporting.

Record, retreat, report

The main benefit of seeing the whole phenomenon of third-party reporting from the officer's point of view is the ability to take a critical glance at ourselves – members of the public – who, in the Peelian way, want to be part of the policing.

Except for the already mentioned Speed Awareness Course, I received a Notice of Intended Prosecution for inconsiderate cycling. It's a valuable memory. A TORS officer accused me of cycling between lanes while I was on the left side of the right-turning lane on the South Circular in Clapham. He accepted my explanation, and all concluded with a warning. However, the primary outcome was an improved standard of my commute and a years-long relationship with the force. When you take that responsibility into your own hands and provide the force with your evidence, you start recognising the names under each email. They become familiar and close. Andy, Lisa, Stephanie, Ross, Jennifer, Graham, Jodi, and Claire: they not only took seriously my statements and fears, but they did that for thousands of others in London alone. They provided feedback when they could and criticism when they felt they should. They are barely known to anyone but are essential to the overall success of the movement. Thanks to them, we have fewer dangerous drivers on our roads, some have improved their standards, and many of us stopped doing wrong things.

One of the most controversial and debated topics around third-party reporting is confrontation. Should the witness avoid getting involved, or should they voice their concern to the offender – who, in many cases, may not be aware of the risk they're posing or the law they break? What if they continue ahead and hit someone while staring at their phone? "As long people are not confrontational, they don't commit any criminal offences themselves, as long they record in a public space by whatever electronic means, whether it's a head camera, dashcam, a mobile phone. All they can do is send it for us to review, and we will review it following the law," Andy Cox explained. "If there is an offence in the evidence, we will follow the law. People who have reported footage before have also been prosecuted themselves on very rare occasions." So, should we interact? "My advice is that it's a personal choice. For me, the important thing is if, as a reporting person, are you safe and legal. If you record the footage and send it to us, we will review it and take action when appropriate. So, it's an individual choice. I don't advocate knocking on windows and stuff like that. My advice is, if you record, send it to us, no more than that, and we will take action. Your job is not to intervene."

Mark Hodson is far more direct: "I have a thing about people who want to do a police officer's job and berate a driver. The only reason I have a thing about it is because people don't realise how volatile drivers can be. And you'll never know who you're dealing with. In my early days with traffic, I was very much into giving people a telling-off when giving them a ticket. But not so much now. It's a business transaction. You get a ticket. I don't care what you think, on your way. I'll see you in court if you want to argue purely because people get so rammed up. We've had some really nasty incidents with road rage in this country, and people need to remember that. Record, retreat and report. Just do that. Leave the talking to drivers to the police officers. That's it. All right: give them a shake of the head or a wag of the finger" – he laughed. "What people don't realise, especially when I'm working on the motorway, if we're happy with the car being insured and taxed, we won't stop that car for committing an offence. We'll just record the footage and send an NIP by post. It's a much more efficient transaction, and you'll get the desired result without somebody trying to justify what they did. They would come with all sorts of rubbish, and in the time you stop and talk to one driver, you can deal with three others … I get blamed for being the most argumentative person in the uniform. So, it's really the case of do as I say, not what I do. I know people will be saying: You're the worst sometimes. If my wife could hear this. 'Amount of the times I've been with you in the car, and you lean through your window and tell people to put their phones down.'

"For example, Jeremy Vine: he puts some really good stuff out, and some people hate Jeremy Vine. He's got a different perspective from me because he's a journalist, and he needs the audience figures. He needs controversy. Some people sort of really get wound up with Cycling Mikey. I love Cycling Mikey. He did so much for awareness, but again, I do worry sometimes. He doesn't have that protection I've got from the uniform and the badge. So, it's always the case of record, retreat and report. Don't get involved. Sometimes you can't help it, though. Coming out with that expletive sentence where you question somebody's parentage, and you're shaking your head furiously.

"When you watch the original WMP clips for Operation Close Pass. There is a red Fiesta coming out of the T junction and straight on to me. It's me on the bike. Steve says there, during the presentation: Mark is sending a cheery a hello to the person who just pulled out. And it's me making the wanker sign. You can't help it sometimes, but keep it to the minimum. Leave the whole face-to-face behaviour change to the professionals.

"It's not vigilantism; it's being a witness. It's passing the evidence to the police. I think people need to look into the dictionary to see what a vigilante is. If you got concerned about stuff you see it's good in terms of Peelian principles. It's people taking care of themselves; it's the camera giving them a bit of empowerment. They are not just victims anymore; they can do something about it. They can give the evidence to the police, and it works pretty well. It really is important in changing behaviour."

The Channel 4 *Complainers* show I mentioned brought another powerful story: a bus driver must learn how to cope with complaints and unsatisfied customers. After repeated reprimands from management, he had to attend a customer relations course, on which the coaches taught the parent-adult-child model developed by Eric Berne in the 1950s. This component of transactional analysis in psychology helped me to manage such situations. Often, when we see someone behaving dangerously, we either come from the parents' position – telling them off; or we have a tantrum like a child. They respond like a child as well. It leads to no good. Being an adult, taking a step back, and limiting yourself to reporting may be the best course of action in most cases.

"I'm in a privileged position when I've interviewed so many offending drivers," Mark continued. "I must be the first officer who started doing post-offending intelligence interviews. We started doing interviews on the back of the third-party reporting back in 2014. And those were people who had already got their fines and points and didn't have to say nice things to be treated easier. And the things they said about their changing behaviour, and what the solicitors' defending motorists did through the third-party reporting, was amazing. I thought it was brilliant, like what we've always dreamt of. You can have that 'police officer' on the street at any given time, but it's not the real officer, it's someone who will give the police the evidence. But now it's clamped down on with all the rubbish about vigilantes, and police forces don't invest enough time and money in it."

Figure 12 Surrey RoadSafe X account about their usage of helmet mounted cameras 296.

The masses

By this point, you must be really looking forward to reading about Cycling Mikey. We all knew him back then. He was one of many prominent third-party reporters on Twitter and YouTube. But he wasn't the only one.

On December 30th 2019, I uploaded my last – 301st – report that year. Volkswagen Golf, a driver on the phone, attended a driving awareness course. It was the 23,682nd submission to the Metropolitan Police alone. You couldn't say it was a tiny fraction of "lycra-clad lunatics" anymore. Third-party reporting became a substantial communal movement fighting road crime. To make it even more shocking, most of the uploads were done by motorists.[297] The whole phenomenon only grew more prominent in the following years.

It's virtually impossible to grasp how large it all became. While campaigning against phones behind the wheel and conducting research for this book, I met many like-minded people. Most I will fail to mention.

Some have come forward to share their experiences, often unaware they were the local heroes making the change – the David Brennan's, Droids and CycleGazs, among others.

The masses

When the feedback works

"At the start, it wasn't about reporting, but just in case I was knocked off. I got my first action camera in 2016. I tend to commute along country lanes. I thought that if I got hit by one of those people who close passed me, I would have evidence to show that it wasn't my fault. So, if I got hit – and I thought I would at some point – my family would know what happened and have a successful claim on the insurance." James stopped to think. "I had a really horrible close, squeaky pass. There was a car coming the other way and the driver of a Volvo overtook me by inches. I just saw her yakking away, looking at her passengers. The motorist coming from the opposite direction had to break sharply to avoid the collision as well. She was going fast. I was amazed at how easily I could have been smashed up there. So, I contacted the local police. They didn't have the upload portal at that time, but they came back to me. A couple of officers rang me and gave me a visit. I burned them a copy of the footage on a CD-ROM. That tells you how long ago it was," he chuckled. "And they went around to see her home, showed her the footage, and explained the law. She was very upset about the distress she had caused me. Her husband was a 'keen cyclist', apparently. They did not prosecute her but passed on to me her sincere apologies and her assurance that she would take greater care in future. I was happy to accept that because I have achieved my objective. I think she passed me a few more times on that road, giving me plenty of room."

Meeting James was a refresher. He commuted in the Avon and Somerset area, where most opinions about the police were surprisingly positive. What matters is that it was often followed by reports of drivers improving after an officer's intervention. "I had another case on a notorious local blind bend. I made an online report, and initially not much has happened with it. It's a local accident black spot with countless crashes. The driver was going around the bend at full speed, on the wrong side of the road. If someone had been coming around that bend just a split second earlier, there would have been a head-on crash. I contacted my local beat officer, who was very familiar with that spot.

He said, 'Just leave that with me, James. Thank you for bringing that to my attention.' And he went to speak to her. I remember her passing me time and time again. Each time safely. Very careful."

One might imagine that James lives in an idyllic world where people are open to criticism and own their mistakes. But he had to own one of his own as well. "I had a warning once for inconsiderate cycling. I stopped to speak to a driver who passed me too close. I didn't realise I had blocked a lane. A driver came up behind me and patiently waited whilst I finished my chat. I then sort of waved my apologies to him and he drove off quite happily. I was told not to confront drivers because you don't know who you're dealing with. There are people in the area that police know are armed and could pull a gun on you, or are likely to have a very short temper, have a knife, or stick a screwdriver into you."

I asked James why he decided to post his events on YouTube. "I know the police send only a couple of still images to the drivers; in the majority of cases, that's enough. I wasn't summoned too often as a witness, except in cases where the driver was indeed very stupid. Uploading the footage with a registration place allows them to find it and see what they did wrong. To see what exactly happened. So, it's an opportunity to educate themselves to a fuller extent and understand why they are being prosecuted. Some of my friends found those videos and said they didn't realise how much space they really need to leave around cyclists. And they started to be more careful. Even my dad – an ex-police officer who used to cycle to work – said that to me. But when he commuted, he had a uniform on and the roads used to be much quieter; it was back in the 70s and 80s. It's important to spread the word about how to drive safely and that there are people carrying cameras, and your actions can have consequences. It may be a cyclist, horse rider, motorcyclist, or another driver."

I felt a similar vibe from Axolotol, a commuter cyclist from London, when I asked why he uploaded his videos. "Education. It doesn't make any difference to me if somebody gets prosecuted. What makes a difference is if they stop doing the shit they are doing. Just don't be dangerous. And everyone's happy, right? I don't want people to lose their licence. I don't want people to have to pay fines. Just be a decent human being, drive with respect and treat other people well. You're not getting held up by anything. It's the city. I understand the difference in the country. I'm gonna overtake at the next set of traffic lights and get three or four cars in front. What's the point?

"There was a recent case of a taxi van driver near Lancaster Gate who right-hooked me. That got over 500K views on Twitter. I did not report him. He seemed like a decent guy, just ignorant of the law. I was in the cycle lane, at the bottom of the hill, about a car length behind him when he started turning. I immediately changed gear and put on the brakes; I thought for a moment he still might let me go as he had to give way in this situation, but he just cut across. So, I tapped him on the back of his van to give him a warning, like, Hey man, I'm here; not like, You're in trouble. And he started yelling at me. I was about just to carry on, but as he started shouting and I came back. Let's talk about this. He said: 'What are you doing? I had my left indicator on.' I responded: 'I have a priority in this situation; you have to give way.' We both calmed down. He said to me to be more careful; I asked him to check the Highway Code. I did not report him because I don't think he did that maliciously. I feel he probably will check the Highway Code. But this is a big education piece, as there are more than half a million people who saw this and have been arguing about it on Twitter. If that teaches people, it's like what the Highway Code says: be careful because otherwise you'd endanger people. To me, it's more important than some guy getting a fine. A fine teaches one person, but putting that on social media teaches the masses. There are always a lot of arguments on such a thread, and some people write ridiculous things. But you see it when they give up, as they see they have lost.

"I don't want to go home and waste my life filling reports. It takes me about an hour because I take the raw video and overlay it with the GPS information so it has the time, location, date and speed I was travelling. So, when the CPS gets it, there is no dispute. But it takes half an hour doing that, half an hour filling out a report. If it's a long video, it takes ages to upload. It's just a waste of my life, and I don't want to do it."

Granny

A brutal history can cast strong people. Strong people can be a massive support to others. One strong woman who stands against danger in a challenging environment and sends waves of hope and support around has become a mother figure to many involved in commuter cycling and third-party reporting. Even though the latter is almost non-existent where she lives. As the Police Service for Northern Ireland described in response to an FOI request, "Work is ongoing to develop a Road Traffic-only-related digital upload service. This is still in the early stages of planning and subject to budgetary constraints."

Anne, known to all as Cycle Granny,[298] has cycled her whole life. She grew up in the suburbs, where going about on a bike was common. She never wore a helmet and never had any issues. Neither was she into cars, but she began to drive larger vehicles for a living at some point. Afterwards, she picked motorbikes as a passion. Anne went from job to job, facing difficulties in the Northern Irish job market while studying to become a medical photographer. She went for it once she got a chance to become a bus driver. That was her first proper, relatively secure work, even though she had to operate through the worst period of the Troubles.[299] "Once, a London bus driver decided to move to Ireland. Thought it would be fine. We told him it's really hard, but he bought a big place in Belfast. Three months later, he got hijacked and beaten up. He was back to London very fast," she recollected. "I need to tag that story because it's really a basis for everything that goes on here. Basically, there are police no-go areas in Belfast."

After the buses, Anne continued to chase her dream career, but the recession hit the country. She had to sell the house and motorbike and returned to commuting by cycle. Drivers in East Belfast were relatively okay around the bikes. But as she moved to the West, "It was a different ball game. The drivers are terrible. There's no law there. There are an awful lot of illegal vehicles. No one respects cycle and bus lanes." She recollected a crash from that period: "I was cycling there for three years. I was cycling on the left side of the road, going ahead, and a taxi driver turned left into me and knocked me off my bike. I got up. My bike was damaged. I was shocked. I tried to get the registration, but he just drove away." When she contacted the police, they just shrugged their shoulders and said they wouldn't 'drop everything' as she couldn't remember the plates and had no footage. Anne decided to buy her first camera, which was the cheapest thing she could get from eBay for around £24.

It didn't take long before a similar situation happened again. A taxi driver left-hooked her and drove away. She reported that to the police, as the footage was clear. Initially, they didn't want to have anything to do with it. They weren't supportive at all, and the case did not go anywhere. Northern Ireland doesn't have anything like the workflows of England and Wales. The victim must complain, and the crash is referred to the court. The whole proceeding can take years.

"I report only situations where my life has been in danger. I have two upcoming court cases soon. First, a young buck in a car nearly hit me while speeding in a bus lane; second, a woman hit me on a roundabout. The date is still not set and it happened almost a year ago."

West Belfast, the Catholic side of the city, has a historical distrust of the police. Traffic offences aren't high on the force's agenda. "When they go, they need a whole team of cops. You can't go as one or two. I remember once I cycled and a SWAT team arrived. No talking to anybody, just heads up against the wall and checking our names. They never know if a sniper could hit them. We have peace now, but they shot a policeman just a few months ago when he was on a football pitch." And that translates to road safety enforcement: "We get the bus lane camera only one day a month because it has to be protected by the police. Otherwise, it will be stolen or destroyed. That makes the commute hard and not safe at all. Police officers often don't know the Highway Code themselves. I have shown them a video of an HGV pulling in front of me into the cycle/bus lane and they said the driver had the right of way. I tried to explain that HGVs can't use the bus lane, but no luck. They have no idea what an Advanced Stop Line[300] is or what the cycle box is for. When I took a primary position to protect myself, they told me I was at fault for the close pass because I wasn't far left enough."

All Anne could do was file complaints. "There's nothing I can do legally, but I can encourage and educate. I know some of my videos are used in the police training. I was contacted by the ombudsman and he put me in touch with a person responsible for education around traffic law for the regular officers."

There are no alternative routes for her commute either. Each is equally dangerous. Even the public transport – tram-like Glider buses – is operated with disregard to the vulnerable road users. Bog Meadows and other parks which could be used as cycle bypasses are often closed or unlit, making it especially dangerous for women at night. Even on the road, Anne is often subject to bullying that seems unmatched by her male peers. Most of that comes from private hire drivers, who seem to be triggered by a lady "in their way" while in the bus/cycle lane – which they are not allowed to use.

Figure 13 Anne with number plates on her bike

The masses

The fear of losing one's life while commuting is nothing alien to Anne. Her nephew Michael was killed by a driver with impaired vision. That wasn't the only tragedy she experienced first hand. As a bus driver, she saw with her own eyes how fragile life is. "It's always the speed. People argue about 20mph down the back of the city hall. They say it's too slow. It's not. The boy I saw killed would be alive if the driver went slower. Drivers don't slow down when they see pedestrians on the road. The lorry driver was in front of me going towards the pedestrian crossing, where the boy was passing on green. A taxi driver goes in the right lane, it's a four-lane road. He doesn't see the boy and doesn't expect him to be there as the truck is not slowing down. When the boy passes the lorry, he's hit by the car, falls under the truck, and the vehicle runs him over. Brains all over the street. The HGV driver jumps out in shock and tries to put his head together. I've seen it many times. I've seen a whole family get knocked down at once. I've seen a woman get knocked down at the lights, and the driver blamed me for stopping on red. I take risks by cycling, but equally, I can get killed on the pavement. When I get on my bike, it's like I'm going to the war. I feel like in the rain in Vietnam. It's wrecking me psychologically. I tried to take the bus. It takes 45 minutes, and 17 by bike. If I drove the car, it would take me half an hour plus 20 to find a parking spot."

Michael's tragedy deeply affected her and their whole family to the extent that her relatives asked her to live-track each ride. "I was going home one night and didn't get back from work until nearly half ten. All the roads were closed. My phone died. My family couldn't reach me, and they heard someone had died on the road. In the meantime, they have rung the police and all hospitals. As a result, they bought me a new phone and installed a tracker app."

Anne is a highly respected figure in the cycling community. When she visited London for one of the medical conferences, Mike van Erp, Lewis the Traffic Droid, and TV producer and eco-campaigner Carla Francome took her for a ride around the capital. She has always been a beacon of resistance and hope, especially supporting many female cyclists. But even while exposed to so many challenges from motorists, she never tried to make people hate them.

"I'm a professional driver. I know there can be good drivers. I know what it feels like when a driver kills someone. My friend has killed a person while driving a bus. There are genuine accidents, like when a driver reverses and a person steps behind his bus. Back in our day, we didn't have rear cameras. The person saw the bus reversing but still stepped out. And the driver still blamed himself. There are people who are sincere about the death they have caused. We need to get away from hating one group or another. People depend on their mode of transport. We need to be stricter on the bad ones. There are too many young drivers who have an 'I don't care' attitude. They will drive in their school uniform in the bus lane, but if you tell them that, they will just say, 'Fuck off, what's the business?'"

On January 3rd 2024, Anne was cycling back from her work in ophthalmology at the Belfast Health and Social Care Trust when two young men injured her with a golf ball. This time, the police promised to review the CCTV but later dropped the case as the footage did not identify the culprits.[301]

The masses

Adolescent boys hate women on bikes

In a 2018 article for the BBC, Anna Allatt asked: "The bicycle was once a symbol of women's emancipation, with suffragettes taking to two wheels to spread their message of equal rights. However, the last figures show a big gender divide in cycling. Why?"[302] Sexist attitudes among male road users may be the main reason. But general road safety is not far behind.

Female and minority cyclists are more likely to experience road aggression, sexism, and prejudice. It would be a big mistake not to mention it, but I knew that I needed help understanding it from people experiencing it first hand. Asking was the right thing to do as I wasn't immune from ungrounded biases. Unconsciously, I expected my guests to be fragile victims without any strength.

One could argue that Anne the Cycle Granny's horrid experiences were primarily due to the Troubles in Northern Ireland and aren't relevant to the rest of the Union. But they are. Unlit paths, overgrown parks, and cycle routes away from the main arteries efficiently prevent women and other more vulnerable groups from cycling. Please forgive me for that classification. By no means do I try to paint any part of society as weak, but we can't turn a blind eye to the fact that women, children, LGBTQ+, disabled, and ethnic minorities fall victim to far more violence, including road crime, than blokes like me.

Despite this situation, women lead the change for safer roads. Not without reason. Each year, Cycling UK publish their "100 Women in Cycling" list.[303] It's an inventory of individuals who significantly impact how we commute. I must admit that before doing research for this book, I was ignorant of that fact and unaware of the depth of their involvement. But even with limited knowledge, I was familiar with Kamar Omar and her Cycling Sisters movement promoting active travel amongst Muslim women; Carla Francome, Jo Rigby, Sarah Berry and Ruth Mayorcas promoting cycling and fighting for safer infrastructure in London; and Harrie Larrington-Spencer proving disability is no barrier for cycling. It was Nazan Fennel who sparked long-term resistance from pedestrians against murderous driving in Birmingham.

One place that gave me the impression of having a humongous number of such icons was Sheffield. I couldn't get hold of Cycling In A Skirt, an NHS professional and absolute legend of the local movement, as she was in the middle of cancer treatment while continuing her campaigning (and she won!).

Luckily, I met Rebecca, a cycling instructor from the same city, and a pharmacist. She had started to commute on her bike recently, and she was soon forced to use the camera and third-party reporting. As a medical professional working in various GP practices around the town, she found that mode of transport worked the best for her. First, one day a week, two, three and then the whole week. "I did it for about a year, and odd things happened. That kind of got me a bit cross. Made me feel a bit frightened. Someone drove past me too close, too fast, and shouted something like 'Fucker' out of the window at me. It might have just been lads being stupid. But it felt quite intimidating, and there was absolutely nothing I could do about it. I didn't even manage to catch the regs. You're kind of like, What the hell was that? There was another cyclist ahead of me on an e-bike. She got the same shouty experience. I think that was the final catalyst. I joined Twitter and sort of talked about it. I'd seen people reporting. That was the point at which I bought the cameras. And since then, just knowing I've got them on makes me feel much calmer if something happens. I don't feel like there's this need to try and catch up with the driver and remonstrate. If I get angry, I can just shout and swear and then go home and report it to the police and be reasonably confident that they'll deal with it. I think it feels like a security to me now. I hate saying that I feel a bit naked without the camera on."

This was an interesting point. I noticed that once you start using cameras, you see more questionable behaviour from drivers. I wondered how that change affected Rebecca's peace of mind. "I don't think having a camera is making me more anxious. I think it makes me less anxious. Because if something happens, I have evidence. I just feel like it is a bit inevitable. Someday something is gonna happen." Tina, an experienced CTC National Standard Cycle Training instructor from Stevenage, Herefordshire, responded alongside the same lines, with an extra kick: "Cameras don't make me feel safer or more anxious. They make me feel a little bit more confident when I'm in a confrontation 'cause I can go: Well, there's a camera here, mate. You're on camera. Whatever you say, it's on camera. But I had a couple of those where I've had to point out that there's been a camera. But I don't feel that the camera makes a difference to me in a security sense. It's reassuring you know that if you're dead, there's some evidence as to why it happened, and that's really why I carry it, and I do it on pretty much most of my rides."

Rebecca reduced her hours as a pharmacist and trained as a cycling instructor. "I was instructing and riding back from the school with my male colleague. In single file because of the nature of the road. A van driver was very aggressive with overtaking despite both of us having Pass-Pixies[304] on our backs. He overtook, hooted, and then pulled up immediately. We had to go around him. He wound his window down, ready to have a go at us, and then he saw a camera on my head and thought better of it. So, he wasn't triggered by the camera. I think many drivers are triggered by the fact that cyclists exist on the road."

"The scariest thing is that the most dangerous driving I see happens when I'm working,"[305] Tina confessed. "But because we're with children, we can't use cameras. If I could have my cameras on, I reckon I would be reporting three or four a day. But our governing body says we're not allowed to use cameras at the moment." That came as a shock, as no specific legislation prevents such use, especially since buses serving schools use dashcams and have interior cameras.

The first time I heard about Tina's town, Stevenage, was in one of Jay Foreman's videos discussing cycling infrastructure.[306] It is a perfect example of what happens when you build great cycle routes and make them very easy and comfortable to drive. Outside the town, Hertfordshire is essentially a network of main roads between settlements. As a seasoned cyclist, Tina got used to being closely overtaken regularly. Aggressive motorists pushed her too hard and she decided to equip herself with cameras. She used to report the first ones

151

through the council, which ensured the culprits were prosecuted, but since she moved to a publicly available reporting system, she has had no feedback from the police. While frustrating, she did not stop, but she was selective. "I've put in not very many. I am selective. They've got to be pretty bad before I put them in. If I did them all, I would never do anything apart from put them in. So, I don't bother." Despite her best efforts and strong character, she didn't convince others to follow her lead and buy a camera. "We are a female-led organisation in terms of instructors. I'm the only one that runs a camera out of the entire team. I don't know how many people would consider it. But a lot of them cycle, and we have had some injured instructors in the team through drivers.

"With close passes," Rebecca continued, "I don't always see the driver, yet I have been surprised that on the occasions when I have a good look at the driver, I have been surprised by how many of them are women. Because I sort of assume that women would be somehow nicer. Yeah, I'm gender stereotyping here. There are particular spots on my commute at the top of a hill, and there's a road coming from the right on the summit. Down that road is a school. There's a lot of school traffic at the time I'm cycling past. I'm going up the hill and people overtake me approaching the summit. People that live in and know the area. They know there is a summit, a junction, and they don't see anything. And there's often someone waiting to turn out of the side road. That's one of my biggies for reporting. There was a woman overtaking me, and she could tell that I'm shouting. She gives me a finger. I'm like – Sorry, what? I'd usually indicate to them to stay back. She gives me a finger – a woman with a secondary school-aged daughter in the passenger seat. And the child is showing me a finger as well. I had an odd person pull out on me from that junction. They look down the road and not towards me."

Rebecca's situation is well researched. During a speech by Brian Deegan while on the panel,[307] Mark Hodson referred to Dr Graham Hole's research, which tried to explain crashes between motorcyclists and drivers joining the road. As it turns out, drivers in such situations are actively looking for a gap, so their brain ignores a smaller road user in the gap – a bicyclist or a motorcyclist.

While cycling, Rebecca did not feel worse treated due to her gender, but more because of the apparel. "There's a difference between when I'm on my hybrid bike versus an e-bike. On a normal bike, I'm leaning forward and got hi-viz jacked on. I look like a sporty cyclist. On an e-bike, I'm very upright, more likely wearing normal clothes: a skirt and long boots. I still have a helmet on, and my hair is very long. The perception is that their assessment of me before they actually get to me makes a difference."

She wasn't alone in that feeling. Tina said: "It's interesting 'cause I generally ride a drop-handlebar bike. So, I look like a cyclist. But a few weeks ago, I rode that bike wearing a dress. The behaviour was definitely different. They gave me more room. People gave way and allowed me out of junctions. They were just nice to me and I'm riding along. What's happened? Literally. It was a girly dress, and it was summer."

Even a confident and experienced instructor like Tina wouldn't dare to cycle away from public spaces at night. "I'm now in a cycle hub that I manage. This is a place in the middle of the park. The only reason I'm happy to be here tonight on my own is because my husband is outside with the cycle club. So, I'm comfortable in here on my own, but normally I would not do it because it's in a park. I mean, the place is beautiful, it's just gorgeous, but after about 5 – no."

This echoes what Anne told me before, and Rebecca had the same feelings: "There is a risk of unpleasant encounters with drivers because the alternative is a lonely backwater router that doesn't feel safe. During the day I'd cycle through Encliff Park, which is tricky. Full of people walking. It's pleasant enough to pedal through, and it keeps you off the busy road for a bit. I won't do that at night on my own because it's all woodland. So, I end up riding the busier roads. There are many other routes which are shut after 5 p.m."

A Canadian lady in the UK loved cycling until a truck driver carrying a skip decided she shouldn't be on "his turf". As she rode on a rural road, she was tailgated. Both the passenger and the driver shouted through their windows. They started to throw things at her, then slowly drove into her back, then pulled back. They continued to follow, driving wider and closer many times and shouting that the "fat cunt shouldn't be on the road". Frightened, she tried to ignore them, and when they drove off she felt relief that it was over. But it wasn't. Without any warning, the driver reversed into her, giving her zero space. When their back light caught her bike, she sailed into the hedge and the gutter.

When she stood up, the bike was flattened. The helmet was on the ground. She noticed blood dripping onto her shirt. She has a dent in her head to this day. Back then, bruises, scrapes, a bloody mess. They laughed when they left.

When she gave her statement to the police, the officers were fixated on her helmet. Nothing came of it, as there was no footage. Since then, she has hardly ever had the courage to ride her bike.

"Makes me anxious out and about. Some of the cycle paths are isolated and the fear comes if you see a male. Then you go on the road and get it from drivers."[308] To those words, Elisabeth, a disabled cyclist, reacted to the video made for the Women's Freedom Ride in 2024. As I came to learn, her feelings weren't unique.

On March 3rd 2024, the London Cycling Campaign organised the Women's Freedom Ride. It was promoted with a video containing blood-boiling accounts of female cyclists:[309]

"A complete stranger walked up behind me and slapped me on the arse. It was so hard it bruised through my clothing … I was riding to work."

"He blocked our path; my kids and I couldn't pass. His face was contorted and furious. He screamed at me that I was disgusting for putting my children at risk … I was cycling my kids to school."

"'Go back to where you came from.' There was so much anger in his voice … I was cycling to the office."

"He stopped in front of me, and he said, 'Get of my way you fucking old cow … I was cycling to meet my friend."

"'You can fuck off and suck your mother.' It was the way he said it. It made me sick to my stomach ... I was cycling to work."

"He came at me really fast. I thought he was going to hit me. At the last moment, he slowed down and shouted, 'Bitch,' right in my face ... I was riding to the park."

According to the campaigners, nine out of 10 women cycling in London have received aggression or abuse from other road users.

The masses

Prove you're not a camel

In some respects, the United Kingdom is exceptional. Some argue that third-party reporting conflicts with the presumption of innocence. It doesn't. Everyone is not guilty until they plead guilty or are proven guilty in court. Workflows like NIP and FPN simply offload the juridical system and let offenders own their faults and carry on.

One thing our system doesn't do is force the victim to prove they aren't the criminal – at least in the majority of cases, except for a few oddities mentioned before. This wasn't the case – and as I hear it still isn't – in Poland, where I experienced third-party reporting for the first time.

It isn't the fact that most of Europe employs civil law instead of common law. In the layperson's terms, the former is more loose and shaped by case law, while the latter is strict and literal and, for this reason, sometimes heartless.

Eastern Europe loves bureaucracy, and judges are predominantly prejudiced against vulnerable road users. In the end, Poland has draconian jay-walking laws. It must be a vestige of the communist past or Prussian influence, deeply embedded in Polish policing. The sheer obsession with going after vulnerable road users and the expectation that you must prove you're not a wrongdoer. Complaints about some UK forces bullying cyclists for showing their failures seem trivial in comparison.

And so we have it: my first experience with a bike, camera, and authority. (A young lad naïvely thinks that the juridical system may be on his side in such a setting.) We cycled in a single file close to the side of the road. There was no cycle lane, and in Poland they are obligatory. As the most brightly dressed person, I wanted to move from the head to the column's tail. There was no traffic behind me, so I pulled inwards and let the column pass, then joined back at the end. When I finished the move, a red Volkswagen Golf zoomed past us inches away, far above the speed limit, forcing the driver coming from the opposite direction onto the grass, and zig-zagged ahead. It was all captured by a camera on my helmet. It wasn't GoPro, but some cheap early edition 1080p no-name device connected by a thick cable to a power bank in the backpack. The Traffic Droid would be proud.

Figure 14 Me with my first headcam setup.

Back home, I wrote my report and sent it to the police, hoping the culprit would be found and fined. We were summoned to the police station. My friend heading the column was accused of "filtering on the wrong side". That's where the civil law beauty kicked in. Instead of allowing everything not forbidden by default, it forbids everything not verbosely allowed. And in the case of filtering on the right side (left in the UK), a cyclist could pass any other vehicle but another bicycle.

We were gobsmacked. My friend did not accept the fine, and we ended up in court, where the judge had enough sense to drop the case but at the same time accused us of "cycling on the road". But there were no cycle lanes anywhere. We were in the middle of the forest. When we asked where we should be, the judge said she did not care as long as it was not on the road.

That experience deterred me from further reporting for years. Cameras stayed as a deterrent and an insurance policy, but my trust in the authorities returned only when I moved to London. Before that, I wasn't reporting anything while living in the Chilterns, as Thames Valley Police presented quite appalling sentiments to cyclists. Seeing how the Metropolitan Police reacted in defence of commuters shocked me. And it was lucky when Andy Cox orchestrated an evolutionary leap in road policing.

A new "headcam community" seemed to form on Twitter and YouTube. Why not join? I had a headcam and plenty of events to discuss. I wasn't welcomed, though. As you have learned, linking me to my employer wasn't too tricky, and I got quickly cancelled. To this day, I remember the meme sent to me by one of the bikers with a sketch from *That Mitchell and Webb Look*: "Are we the baddies?"

Yet again, I had to prove to others that I wasn't who they thought I was. Just as the court thought I was in the wrong by even being on my bike on the road, the community here thought that I must be some sort of infiltrating journo-rookie. As in an old Eastern proverb, I had to prove I was not a camel.

Today, it's just a funny story. Most of those who vowed to block me changed their mind, and we stayed in quite a positive relationship.

Over a decade ago, when I still lived in Poland, my work was sedentary, traffic in my area was insane, parking was even worse, and the distance wasn't too bad – about eight miles one way. It was a healthier, cheaper and faster option to jump on the bike than sit frustrated in traffic. It also helped my mental health. I'm not alone. The University of Edinburgh conducted research proving that cycling to the office makes commuters less likely to be prescribed antidepressants.[310]

I had a camera at the back in case someone drove into me, so my family could know how it happened. But I didn't have to use it often, only when going for a longer ride, as within the city; otherwise I was spoiled with segregated infrastructure. Cycle lanes varied in quality but were everywhere, wide, divided from the traffic, and often went straight to the destination (it was 2010 in "poor" Eastern Europe). I was always forced to share the road with other vehicles in the UK. No matter how defensive I tried to be, it seemed someone would kill me soon. That feeling stays with me to this day. On the evening I wrote this chapter, I was almost taken out three times by aggressive drivers pushing too close when they had no chance of a safe overtake.

A grocery delivery driver pushed me off the bus lane in Battersea and made me start reporting. But the one that made me decide to go full on happened a few months later. It was one of the worst encounters I've ever had.

It was a rainy evening, and I was cycling through the Clapham Common on the A205 South Circular Road. It was narrow, and the traffic from the opposite direction was massive. I was cycling relatively close to the curb when I heard a loud sound approaching. An enormous new shiny Mercedes-Benz SUV zoomed past inches from me. The only thing visible on the black-as-night car was the lit-up screen of the phone in the driver's hand. I panicked at first but then got a massive adrenaline spike and felt stirred with anger. Full steam on, I followed him and met him at the lights (which always happens there). I screamed at the driver. He first denied anything had happened, then played dumb. He did not notice the camera. I vented, had enough, and the lights changed to green, so I decided to move. But then he overtook me again, stopping in the middle of the junction and blocking it, obstructing me and everyone else. He cried through the window: "Please don't report me, I have children, I cannot lose that job." I nodded, just to be able to move on and avoid more congestion (horns beeping all around). But deep in my mind, I thought: "Where the f**k do you think I'm cycling back to? To my children. I want to arrive home alive." The driver received a £660 fine, plus fees and eight points on his driving licence.

That moment led me to make over a thousand reports, the majority of which were prosecuted in some form. I have attended multiple court cases. It wasn't the last time I felt endangered on the road, but it was one of the last moments when I felt powerless. The more I reported, the more feedback I got from the police, the stronger I felt. At some point, my anger grew into a sense of duty – or mission, if you prefer. But that did not last forever.

I had periods of guilt, tiredness, and mental lows. I was helpless when I got some unknown liquid thrown over me. The police failed to do anything about it. I've already mentioned the pensioner who drove into my bike.

During that journey, I experienced a spectrum of emotions, and one thing did not change. I always knew that the main reason for it all was to make the roads I shared with others safer. I wanted to try other approaches, and that is how the idea of this book came along.

If you read the stories about Mike van Erp or other cyclists with the cameras, or (worse) read social media commenting on their actions, you will find words, names, and descriptions in which "zealot" will be one of the mildest slurs. You will find the same foul language targeted towards any cyclist, no matter if they are MAMIL like me, children biking to school, or casually dressed commuters. Media of all sorts thrives on othering cyclists. It is a business, and emotions are the currency. We all remember from history how othering ends.

The people, emotions, worries, fears, and motives are not shown to the masses. It seems that anyone who jumps on the bike does it to steal your roads, and anyone with a camera is a stalker who wants to destroy your life and career. Never is the same amount of effort used to remind people that to be caught red-handed, one must do something wrong in the first place. How often are you told that those people aren't zealots but someone's partners, children, or parents? Nurses, doctors, teachers, handypersons? Does anyone tell you their taxes pay for the same roads and amenities? That some of them have had friends or family members killed by distracted drivers?

I want to remind you of that. I want to show you the people behind the bike and the camera. Hopefully, you won't ever again allow anyone to divide you from others on the road. I want to prove that none of those people is a camel.

The masses

Too many to mention

"Set up and ready to go. Thanks to the driver who close passed us then ran over and damaged my wheel," James 2.0. a.k.a. KiwiCycling wrote on his Twitter – "You have motivated me to start reporting dangerous drivers and your insurance has funded the cam. If it saves one life, it will be worth it."[311]

Testimonies like that can be found almost every day on social media. "Since I tweeted about the new team dealing with #3rdPartyReports at WMP, I've been getting feedback from a surprising number of people who were reporting, gave up, but have started reporting again and are getting feedback. It's early days, but it's looking positive right now," Jaj991 from Coventry posted the other day. He planned to meet me when I did my charity cycle, but my bike broke down. It's a shame, as his input was essential in the early stages of writing. "Reported two incidents 08/09/2023 and have had a response today: 'I have reviewed your submissions and both drivers have been reported for prosecution.' Both were running red lights. Updates on 10/09/2023, one FPN and one being offered a driver improvement course. FPN was for a driver who drove off while still using his phone. The course was for a driver who used his phone while stationary." [312]

Chris purchased his camera as a safeguard for his commute to work. His first ride resulted in a 12-month ban and £700 costs for the close passing driver.[313] It was a shocking outcome, as West Midlands Police, which took the driver to court, experienced structural changes and was criticised by many complaining about reduced support for third-party reports. "I've commuted by bike for a number of years now and have witnessed some horrendous driving," Chris told Road.cc. "The week before the close pass, I had a driver pull out on me on a roundabout, who then proceeded to try and blame the incident on me as a cyclist for 'not giving way to a car'. When I arrived at work that morning, I ordered myself a 360 camera for the handlebars."

The volume of reports grows massively each year to the degree that local forces struggle to process them. The traffic departments are usually small and underfunded – Mark has explained that already. Even the Met has reached maximum capacity. Charlotte Baker asked for an update, as she did not receive NIP confirmation after she reported a video of a PHV driver running a red light on Kensington High Street. In response, the Met officer confirmed that due to the large volume of reports, they did not manage to send out the NIP in time. The driver received a warning letter instead.[314]

The unspeakable

It's always exciting when digging deeper into the archives to find some bits that have missed, forgotten, or abandoned. Just as David Brennan showed up in the papers as a young genius scientist fighting misogynistic prejudice, my next guest appeared in the media in a different context from how we know him today.

A 2007 feature in the *Guardian* trumpets the excitement: "From time to time, if they were lucky, our audience also enjoyed an amazing display of flicks, jumps and death-defying swerves from the teacher ... a champion speed-skater, who wore an arresting, body-hugging, blue and black lycra outfit and helmet, and swooped around us like a more can-do version of Spider-Man, bouncing off the kerbs and shouting encouragement as we learned, bent almost double, to push ourselves along on first one leg, then the other."[315]

Two years later, the *Times* played the same tune: "I contacted ... one of London's leading skating tutors, and arranged to meet him at his regular haunt next to the Albert Memorial in Kensington Gardens. Surrounded by skaters scissoring their feet around rows of tiny traffic cones ... he wasted no time getting me strapped into my blades and up on my feet ... The lesson was a revelation."[316]

More recently, a quite unusual story popped up in the *Forces Magazine*: "A quick-thinking young soldier conducting King's Life Guard duties at Horse Guards has been praised online and by a senior officer for how he handled an encounter with a young man with Down's syndrome ... The young man with Down's syndrome, Ibrahim, 17, and his friend ... wanted their photo taken with the Trooper of the Blues and Royals but were keen to ensure they were respectful around the soldier.

"Some rubbed their eyes in disbelief when watching the video. 'Is it him?' they asked:

"'[Ibrahim] was nervous around the guard, probably because I was being careful to give the soldier space and because the guard has such emphatic body language ... The Dutch-Zimbabwean man seen with Ibrahim has worked with the 17-year-old and his family for a decade, often cycling, skating, swimming, and kayaking with him, saying: 'He's pretty important to me, as much as my own two sons are. Funnily enough, he and my 14-year-old are quite good friends and enjoy doing things together. Yesterday, we were kayaking along the Grand Union Canal and a man we chatted to recognised Ibrahim ... One of Ibrahim's relatives was a senior Army officer in another country, and one of my ancestors was Admiral Michiel de Ruyter, one of the most skilled admirals in history."[317]

A father, trainer, skater, carer. Those aren't the words often used to present Mike van Erp. More people know him as a Cycling Mikey or Gandalf. His name became a symbol on the level only Jeremy Vine and Traffic Droid achieved. If you cycled with a camera in the 2010s, someone could ask you, "Are you the Traffic Droid?" Nowadays, it's common to ask, "Are you Cycling Mikey?" I always respond, "Mike is the slim one; I'm fat."

It is somewhat surprising how the symbol surpassed the person. Mike was in the headlines across the industry, a guest on many TV shows, torn apart by blood-thirsty online motorist groups and forums. His name even popped up on American CBS News.[318] His face was everywhere, but many people who knew his name had no idea what he looked like, what he did for a living, or what kind of life he had. In tones of abuse on social media, foam-mouthed critics accuse him of being twisted and wicked, a failure, abuser, criminalist, snitch, or weasel.

"That comes mostly from your men who are probably not very good drivers," he explained. "They feel I should be part of their group, and you shouldn't report members of your own group, which is basically a criminal group of road pirates. I feel that's where the most water comes from: younger, very car-centric people who are obviously doing stuff like speeding or using their phones. Football is a very common thing, probably because it attracts those who tend to be more tribal. It's a bit like psychopaths like to buy SUVs.

That doesn't make all people who buy SUVs psychopaths." We will come back to that …

On many occasions, anonymous opponents on social media would go after Mike, portraying him as waging war on cars, not being able to afford one or having a licence in the first place. "I learned how to drive in an old school Land Rover which was left over from the war. It was just a chassis, two seats and the dashboard, in a gliding club on a grass runway. That was a proper SUV. I still remember my first drive. I put it into reverse because the Land Rover's reverse was very close to first. You couldn't really tell the difference until you had a bit of experience. I let the clutch out with a bang, and Brian, a gliding instructor who was teaching me, nearly went over the dashboard because there were no seatbelts or windscreen. This way, I learned how to handle a car in a slippery situation and skidding."

The unspeakable

The Bush and the Corner

Almost every morning, I ride through what some call the Mikey Turf or Mikey Bush. This relatively short street between Hyde and Kensington Parks is always full of drivers who are too busy with their phones to notice that someone is watching. Yet on this occasion my camera wasn't focused on them. As I passed the bridge over the Serpentine, I saw in the distance a smooth Gazelle e-bike and a smiling Mike waving. It was a meeting I had waited long for. After years of messages, tips, experience exchanges and mutual support online, I finally met a rich character who should think about writing down his story on paper one day.

Most of us knew Mike, who had been hugely active since 2006. But it was 2020 when he became the new face of third-party reporting. In his statement about an event from November 3rd 2019, he wrote: "I spotted this driver texting on his phone. I stopped and, whilst waiting for traffic to clear, could see the driver typing on his phone. I then crossed to the driver's side, where I saw his iPhone lit up with the classic blue and grey message bubbles of Apple iMessage, with text and a message in the process of being typed but not sent." He had no idea the driver was *Sherlock Holmes, Snatch, Lock, Stock and Two Smoking Barrels director Guy Ritchie*.[319] As the *Evening Standard* reported, the motorist pleaded guilty in writing. Because he already had nine points from three speeding offences, he didn't contest the imminent six-month ban, along with a £666 fine and £166 costs and court fees. He did not attend court, which was scaled down to a single justice procedure.

As the paper continued, Ritchie was caught out similarly to his friend David Beckham, who had also got a six-month driving ban a year before for the same offence. He was reported by a member of the public and sentenced by the same court in Bromley. The *Mirror* clarified that Richie had nine points from three speeding offences before this.[320]

But, as I mentioned, this was far from Mike's beginnings. The *Metro* reported that by then he had caught 358 drivers in a year, leading to 574 penalty points and £35,400 in fines.[321] In a piece for the *Mail,* Mike draws attention to how easy it was to report the footage to the Metropolitan Police. "London is possibly the camera cyclist capital of the world. It only takes a few minutes to submit a video. You just fill out a form online and send it. You do occasionally have to go to court, I have had to do it maybe five to ten times."[322]

In the following interview on the *Jeremy Vine Show,*[323] Mike defended Richie, saying he was very polite compared to many other drivers. Challenged by a co-host, Dr Tessa Dunlop, he explained that while his channel was motorised, it wasn't creating any serious income. He has made a point that he isn't the only one, and for thousands of other camera cyclists, the primary motivation is how badly drivers behave towards cyclists. To her next question about influencing the relationship between drivers and cyclists, he pointed out that he's Dutch. In his words, the Netherlands is famous for how easy and comfortable it is to drive and cycle there. Finally, the poor relationship is manufactured by the motoring industry. That point is well argued in the previously mentioned book Trafficaiton.

In a letter to the *Times* a few days later, reader Hohn Slinger Rugby suggested: "Sir, You report that a cyclist used a helmet camera to report enough driving offences to result in £35,000 of fines and 574 licence points ('Cycling vigilante snatches Guy Ritchie', News, Jul 24). If one person, untrained in surveillance, can enforce the law so effectively, it is likely that road safety could be improved if the police used plain-clothes cyclists in towns and cities. A new category of officer could be created, akin to PCSOs. They could be funded by the fines, allowing as many as were needed to reduce criminal behaviour, to be hired on short-term contracts. Helmets off to Mike van Erp for showing how easily technology can be used to enforce the law."[324] The idea wasn't ever picked; still, third-party reporting only grew in popularity over the following years. In the Sunday edition of the paper, columnist Camilla Long recollected how her instructor "barked" at her during the driving lesson when she reached for her phone to check it: "Turn off the engine. Never, ever touch your phone if it is on." "For this reason, I have no sympathy for the annoying film director," she wrote.[325] Their readers did not share the sentiment, rolling with the cyclist red-light-jumping whataboutery and comparing third-party reporting to the Stasi.[326] This must have prompted Celia Walden to write that ambiguous column the next day, asking if Britain would be turned into a nation of snitches, as I mentioned at the beginning of this book.[327] The *Times* drilled the story the following week, trying to reach police officials.[328]

Andy Cox reiterated that if we've "got the mindset that a member of the public might report me, I think that is a significant deterrent". Commander Kyle Gordon, the lead on road policing for police chiefs, confirmed the start of research into achieving a national reporting system. Joshua Harris, director of campaigns at Brake, did not hide his annoyance that the process was taking so long: "The laws of our roads are only as strong as their enforcement." Edmund Kind, president of the AA, invoked a significant reduction in police patrols, allowing serious criminals to go undetected. The paper praised Avon and Somerset Police for their proactive approach and many others for adapting the NextBase Dash Cam Safety Portal. However, it pointed out that even the Metropolitan Police had started promoting reporting 18 months prior (thanks to Andy Cox). Many forces still fail to provide basic facilities (e.g. Police for Scotland up to the time of writing this book).

Summer 2020 ended, and the media seemed to start forgetting about Mike, his strip by the Serpentine and third-party reporting, up to September when former WBO middleweight and super-middleweight champion Chis Eubank jumped a red light in the same part of Hyde Park where Richie was filmed. Mike approached Eubank, who seemed to be using his hand-held device, and challenged him; in response, the former boxer shouted that he was a police officer and told Mike to go away. It turned out that he was indeed a certified law enforcement marshal in Louisiana due to his fame. He didn't accept the initial offer and met with van Erp in Bromley Magistrates Court, where, after pleading guilty, he received three points and £280 in fines, court costs and fees.[329] The event did not give him good press, as papers jumped on his claims to be law enforcement: "Eubank claimed to be a police officer before skipping red light," the *Telegraph* headline roared:[330] "'GO AWAY!' Chris Eubank tells vigilante cyclist he's a COP when caught using phone at wheel of £370k car – before jumping red light."[331] The *Daily Mail* trivialised him for picking a fight in the "wrong sort of ring".[332]

By this time, Mike's fame had reached unprecedented levels and put him in the headlines again. Not far from both previous high-profile incidents, Mike recorded a former Chelsea boss, Frank Lampard, allegedly talking on the phone, clutching a cup of coffee and controlling the steering wheel of his Mercedes.[333] But this time, the celebrity beefed up his defence, hiring a solicitor, Nick "Mr Loophole" Freeman, famed for getting high-profile clients, including David Beckham, off traffic prosecutions.[334] Other famous clients of his were Sir Alex Ferguson (driving on a hard shoulder to avoid traffic), Ronnie O'Sullivan (failing to provide a urine sample when suspected of drunk driving) and, surprise, surprise, Jeremy Clarkson (82mph in a 50mph zone).[335] As expected, the story took over the headlines, especially with the case adjourned after the first hearing.[336] And as expected, titles like *Sun* failed to see the problem with drivers and went to criticise Mike. The *Sun* notably showed a gutter level of the journalist by calling him "Twerp". "There's only one menace to society here – and it isn't the sportsmen or Guy," Clemmie Moodie wrote.[337]

The former Chelsea player went scot-free, but not by a court ruling. The Crown Prosecution Service (CPS) dropped the charge after concluding there was insufficient evidence to provide a realistic prospect of conviction.[338] In other words, they surrendered without picking a fight. In an interview for Road.cc Mike confessed, "A couple of coppers have said the justice system is broken, and they are binning cases left and right to reduce the massive backlog."[339]

There might have been a silver lining to the story, though. Freeman highlighted the flaw in the legislation (most likely commentary on the Barreto case) that made illegal only the use of phones for an "interactive purpose" at that time. As the *Telegraph* reminded us, Freeman successfully made the same argument in 2009, defending comedian Jimmy Carr, arguing he used his iPhone to dictate an idea for a joke while driving.[340] I've heard Carr live and can admit that the situation possibly inspired other gags, so it seems he remembered it.

The growing fame and attention from outside the cycling Twitter (not X yet) and YouTube community wasn't always hostile. *Guardian* columnist Peter Walker wrote an extensive piece empathetically showing his story[341] (I'll come back to it in the next chapter), and in the pages of the *Daily Mail*, Kathryn Knight published a well balanced and objective, in-depth review of his story.[342] Within the one hour they spent together in Hyde Park, they clocked "too many offences to count", including a situation Mike coined a name for: the "WhatsApp gap":

"We spot a lady in a blue BMW with her head down, oblivious to the large space that has opened up in the queue ahead of her. Mike draws up alongside her to find she is busy sending emails, meeting what he calls the 'gold standard' test for prosecution, which currently requires proof of interaction communication with a phone."

Knight wasn't the only journalist to meet him in person rather than spitting at him behind his back. Amy Sharpe from the *Sunday Mirror* donned her helmet and bike as well.[343] "We saw scores on phones, with some emailing, messaging, and even watching TikTok videos." Within a minute, they spot the first one. There is an Audi driver watching videos, a Range Rover taking photos, and another scrolling a playlist and sending messages. Many parents typing while driving kids. Knight points out that Mike has been attacked, trolled, and even threatened with death by some drivers.

And we did not have to wait long for things to get far scarier.

Figure 15 Gandalf Corner

Heavy traffic usually comes from the north, down towards Park Square East and the A501 (leading to the A40 westbound). There are two pedestrian aisles with dashed areas, one on the north side of the junction and the second on the west. A common situation in that place is that impatient drivers will, illegally and dangerously, be on the wrong side of the aisle, against the traffic flow, and sharply turn into the Outer Circle. In doing so, they would go head-on with cyclists going north, and cut in front of vehicles leaving the Outer Circle, where the hedge limits their visibility. Before we add pedestrians, who are bullied off the space designed for them to cross, it's a no-brainer that anyone doing that not only breaks the law but puts others in danger.

Figure 16 Source YouTube Cycling Mikey

As Mike used to commute through the area and experience the situation first-hand, he decided to take action (2019-2020). When he saw a driver about to go in the wrong lane, he entered the road and pointed them to go back. It worked on most occasions. But a lady driving a Volvo SUV drives into him at low speed, trying to push him off the road. She does it regardless of being unable to drive off the junction as a BMW is already blocked by her head-on and a Mercedes is turning from the Outer Circle. In the end, she backs off. After the court ruling, she received five penalty points, a £1,500 fine, £100 costs and a £150 victim surcharge (money for a global fund, not for the victim, Mike).[344] In the description of his video, he reminds us of Mark Rober's video "Snakes and Turtles",[345] which gives a convincing argument for a link between psychopathy and driving an SUV. The event seems to back it to the hilt. And it isn't the only one. His playlist is full of similar occurrences where drivers' entitlement takes over common sense and decency. In one of them, a pair of doctors in another Volvo SUV prefer to argue and bully Mike for minutes on end, to receive four points and a total of £350 charge.[346] I doubt it made good press for the brand that's known for its safety features.

The unspeakable

Figure 17 Source YouTube Cycling Mikey

Mike's luck finally ran out, again at the hands of a wealthy and powerful counterpart, Paul Lyon-Maris, a talent agent representing Oscar-winners such as Catherine Zeta-Jones, Colin Firth and Sir Ian McKellen (my favourite), alongside Daniel Craig, Gillian Anderson and Sir Michael Gambon.[347] The driver allegedly drove at van Erp and carried him for 20 yards on the bonnet of his Range Rover because he had "an appointment at 8:30 a.m.". It was 8:25. The prosecutor, James Dean, according to a detailed report by the *Daily Mail*, stated in the court, "He drove into an individual standing in front of him and caused him to fall on the bonnet, then continued to drive him a short distance and executed a manoeuvre by turning right whilst Mr van Erp was still clinging on to the bonnet ... You may think it would be particularly unlikely that Mr van Erp, despite his commitment to stopping people driving in breach of the rules of the road, would have thrown himself onto that car. The defendant became enraged ... The defendant simply lost his temper and did an act no reasonable driver would've done. He had options. He could have reversed back into the queue, which he may have found quite humiliating ... He claims he was looking for a parking space when, in fact, he was in a rush to get to a physiotherapy appointment and felt entitled, in these circumstances, to break the law then escalate that offence in the way that he did." The agent was charged with dangerous driving and common assault.[348]

To everyone's surprise, the court found Lyon-Maris not guilty, and the media rhetoric sharply shifted in the agent's favour. The *Telegraph* stated that Mike had "jumped" on the bonnet.[349] "I did not move forward. He jumped onto the bonnet, moved back and jumped on again," the defendant said, and his lawyer said it was a van Erp tactic[350]. In emails from the readers, the *Mail* pumped yet again jumping-red-lights-by-cyclists whataboutery.[351]

I wanted to rewatch the video.[352] September 2021, Regents Park. Mike stands on the aisle behind a lamppost. The queue of traffic southbound has no end. In the 15th second, you see the black car indicating to turn right. Before it reaches the dashed area before the aisle, Mike enters the road and stops (00:19). It seems like the Range Rover accelerates to sharply stop (bouncing in front of a pedestrian, 00:21). In my view, this alone would be an offence against the pedestrian that is crossing the road. The driver pushes on, and you see the whole grille and part of the bonnet already hidden behind the video margins (00:22). There is a sharp exchange, and it's difficult to say who's moving. Still, the perception is that Mike's upper body must have been already further than the bumper. At 00:32, you see the car moving relative to the curb and Mike falling. By then, the driver should get out to see if all was fine, even if it wasn't their fault, right? Then we see the footage from the other camera. You can see Mike being pushed over.

Figure 18 Source YouTube Cycling Mikey

The unspeakable

Now imagine the same scenario with a knife or a firearm. We know that a car has the destructive potential of a small explosive device. Let's downgrade it. Not even a baseball bat; let's make it a protest sign. If someone pushed someone over in that manner, they would get convicted of assault. If it were a blade, that would be a jail term. Take aside whether Mike was right or wrong. If he jumped on the bonnet or not. The mere fact of the driver moving with a pedestrian on the crossing seems bonkers and dangerous. But it presents how far we have normalised using a motor vehicle as a weapon. If Sherrilyn Speid was found guilty of dangerous driving at Stop Oil protesters with her Range Rover,[353] which she had the moral spine to admit, why did the same not happen in this case? How is it different from the aforementioned lady in the Volvo? It seems the typical pattern in third-party reporting in London is that if there is no collision, there is a result; if there is a collision, there are no resources.

Figure 19 Twitter

However, the case seemed to be the final straw, and Mike's activity at the corner decreased.

I saw people criticising Mike for "ambushing" drivers on the Hyde Park stretch or at Gandalf Corner. And it seems that compared to other places where he filmed their events, those locations are calmer and more accessible. Both places were his places of work and daily commute, and drivers using phones there were most likely to use them when moving at higher speeds. Most of his videos aren't as scary as Traffic Droid's fight for primary position with aggressive cabbies, or Gaz being cut up by unobservant drivers. I could risk saying that drivers in Minis have pushed me more times than any others on purpose.

Okay, I'd admit that stepping out on Gandalf Corner seems to have a bit of the Ulan cockiness. Still, I would be a massive hypocrite picking on it after almost breaking X with my stand-off with a van driver on Campden Hill Road in Kensington.

All of that doesn't invalidate Mike's input. He is usually careful – perhaps more than most of us. Yet his calmness and strong commitment to the case made people talk about both issues (phone use and dangerous junction-cutting). By reporting distracted drivers, not only did he save countless lives, but by placing his face in the pages of newspapers and the TV, he helped shape the law and public awareness. The fact that he's a synonym for the third-party reporter means something.

I couldn't resist drilling into all that in person. And what better place to do it than at the Serpentine?

The unspeakable

Snakes and Turtles

Coen, 59, was killed on his birthday while riding his motorbike, by a drunk driver in Harare, Zimbabwe.[354] No one would think that the British media would, in the other hemisphere, bring up the death of this loving and dedicated father multiple times. His son Mike was 19 at that time.[355] He had begged him earlier that day to go gliding.[356] They spent loads of time together. Coen taught Mike how to ride a bike, fix punctures, ride a motorbike, and drive a car. But instead of celebrating that day, Mike had to face the wreck of the motorbike and a blanket covering his dad's body after being called by a local shopkeeper.

Losing a parent at that age leaves a mark. I know it myself far too well. But it's not fair to make that event the sole reason why, decades later, Coen's son became a symbol of cyclists' resistance to road crime. While it laid the foundations in the young Dutchman's mind, the lad grew up with his own set of values, wit, lessons learned and cheeky sense of humour.

Peter Walker's piece in the *Guardian* was the first deep dive into the person behind the Cycling Mikey handle and, to this day, remains one of the most touching – even more so, once one has the honour to spend time in Mike's company. In his magical Dutch way, he can turn from extremely serious and factual to cheerful, jocular, and dead serious again. He can be proud of being one of thousands of people working alongside police forces, but gets annoyed by too much focus on himself. "… This has led to headlines, occasional TV appearances, and has made him the semi-reluctant public face of a new era of ride crime enforcement," wrote Walker, "one in which police forces are being encouraged to accept online complaints about offences, backed by video footage." While staying professional, Peter doesn't hide his affection for the cyclist. He has a massive legacy of supporting active travel in the capital and the rest of the country. But he doesn't avoid topics that continue to land Mike bits of salty criticism.

If you look at Mike as a content creator, there is something to be jealous about. At the time, he had 65,000 subscribers, and he confessed to Walker that it gave him a modest side income. At the time of writing these pages, the number has doubled. Van Erp has been picked on many times by anonymous critics and sometimes by other dashcam cyclists. The biggest fallacy in such an attitude is not understanding the levels of effort leading to his message's impact on the public. Like Traffic Droid, Sherry, and many others, he dedicated almost two decades to public service, fighting the red tape, motor-centric propaganda and victim-blaming. He also spent countless hours doing the reporting itself.

In 2019, I reported 301 drivers myself. Those were mainly close passes, but a lot of phones as well. Quite possibly I beat Mike that year. But in 2023, he bypassed that number by a large margin. I could never go back to that level, as it's draining, time-consuming, and stressful, and, with limited feedback on the results, massively demotivating. Then, after the report is done, footage must be stored somewhere, then edited, and after the prosecution proceedings are done, it can be uploaded.

Does it make any impact? Hell yes! You can find many drivers who don't know that they should give way to pedestrians when turning from or into a road (rules 170 and H2), or give way to a bus leaving a bus stop (rule 223), or that it's illegal to keep your engine idling when parked (rule 123). Even traffic wardens pretend not to know the last one. But you will find a handful of people who haven't heard about Cycling Mikey. Despite him being all over the media, many people don't know what he looks like or his real name. But almost every headcam cyclist has heard the question from motorists: "Are you Cycling Mikey?"

"Do you have enemies? That's simply the fate of anyone who has done anything worthwhile or launched any new idea. It's a necessary fog that clings to anything that shines. Fame must have enemies, as light must have gnats. Don't worry about it; just have contempt. Keep your mind serene as you keep your life clear." Victor Hugo

"I just like to think that with the power of one, I'm trying to change a little bit of road safety," Mike confessed in one article. "Most people who cycle realise that bad driving is largely tolerated by society. It's not considered a really serious thing. Yet it's claiming 1,800 people's lives a year in the UK, and 27,000 are seriously injured. That's a quite serious toll, isn't it? ... I started filming because I felt a little powerless."

We sat together on a lovely yet windy summer day in Hyde Park. Mike knows the place well and greets various vendors occasionally. No surprise. It's the place where the papers found him when he was known for teaching skating. His body language dictates his strong position while keeping utter respect for his counterpart. He's an inch from being almost intimidating yet is highly familiar, like he's your older schoolmate. He is ready to pick on you, but in good faith. In the way he's dressed, moves and talks, he's very casual.

"My main motivator is the way the drivers treat cyclists in the UK," he answers when quizzed on the topic, "Here, particularly in central London, it's not a problem really, but when you go further out, into Kent, it's really tough. That's what started me with running cameras, because people never believe how badly you're treated. Like when you phone the company, then there's, 'Our driver said you were in the middle of the road, you were swerving all over the place.'" He couldn't pin down any specific event that was the final nail. "Just too many close passes. I saw too many drivers on the phone."

But even when off the bike, Mike feels the pressure from the motorists. "My second one [motivation] was crossing with my own kids before, and now with Ibrahim. Of course, with him you must take more care than I do even with my own kids, because he's not mine. He has a special need, and I'm working. I really feel like I must do a risk assessment and watch the cars and what's going on."

We try to dig into how the media portrays him and what he thinks about some accusing him of spoiling the cyclist's image. "There is a generalised hate for cyclists in the UK media. It's insane. Why would you hate someone because they cycle? I don't even match the lycra MAMIL stuff." Indeed, he may be a middle-aged man, but usually dons casual clothing and a cap instead of a helmet. "It's largely due to the tabloids," he continued, giving a discreet wink. "It's loads of age, and people are using it. I noticed how Mr Loophole

The unspeakable

(Freeman) tagged into the cycle of hatred to get extra click-bait and publicity. He doesn't care about cycles either way, I don't think. He's doing that purely for publicity in a very smart but also cynical and bad-for-society way. As for me, I don't mind too much, simply because it's still traction when someone likes or hates me. They're still learning about us."

In all fairness, I intentionally did not approach Freeman as I saw him as a lawyer doing his job and representing the views and interests of his clients. I have occasionally heard not-to-repeat accounts of him lending a helping hand to various individuals pro bono publico. But it got me thinking. Indeed, pedalling hate towards cyclists became a trademark of many public personalities far before Mike was heard about. Clarkson, Liddle, Littleton, Cristo, Jeremy Kyle and Mike Graham keep repeating long-debunked myths and othering on their platforms. But still. Where does the demand for hate come from? Why does demolishing public property earn some the title Blade Runners (criminals destroying ANPR cameras), but reporting road offenders lands one the name "snitch"?

"That comes mostly from young men who are probably not very good drivers. They feel I should be part of their group, and you shouldn't report members of your own group, which is basically a criminal group of road pirates. Football is a very common thing, possibly because it attracts those who tend to be more tribal." I got a taste of that a few months later. Pointing out how drivers put pedestrians in danger in Kensington got me an influx of young lads with football references around their profiles and 1.5M views in two days.

"It's a bit like how psychopaths like to buy SUVs. That doesn't make all people who buy SUVs psychopaths." Mike is referring to the "Snakes and Turtles" film. "It basically looked at which demographics will run over snakes and turtles, and that led to who were the most psychopathic. And the SUV owners were the most common demographic intentionally shooting out of their lane and running over an animal." I remember that argument from his previous interviews. Even if he wasn't right, the research clearly shows that

SUVs are more dangerous by their simple existence. Every 10cm increase in a vehicle's front-end height causes a 22% increase in pedestrians' fatality risk.[357]

"I don't want this to consume my life. I have hobbies, and I have family. I limit how much time I spend on this," Mike said in Peter's article.

A controversial TalkTV radio presenter, Cristo Foufas, became famed for criticising anything remotely connected to active travel. On many occasions, his erratic rants, aimed at stirring up the public to bump up his figures, ended up levelled by authoritative commentary. "Mike is such a desperate and weird character. Imagine being so sad as to spend hours at a time at a junction hoping to film inside people's cars. Odd and perhaps even sinister, to say the least," he moaned on Twitter,[358] only to hear from Surrey Police Roads Policing in response, "Wouldn't it be great if we had enough cops to do the same? Unfortunately, we don't, so Mikey is providing a really effective element of road safety. The only people who would find this concerning are Road users committing offences"[359] – Mic drop.

The unspeakable

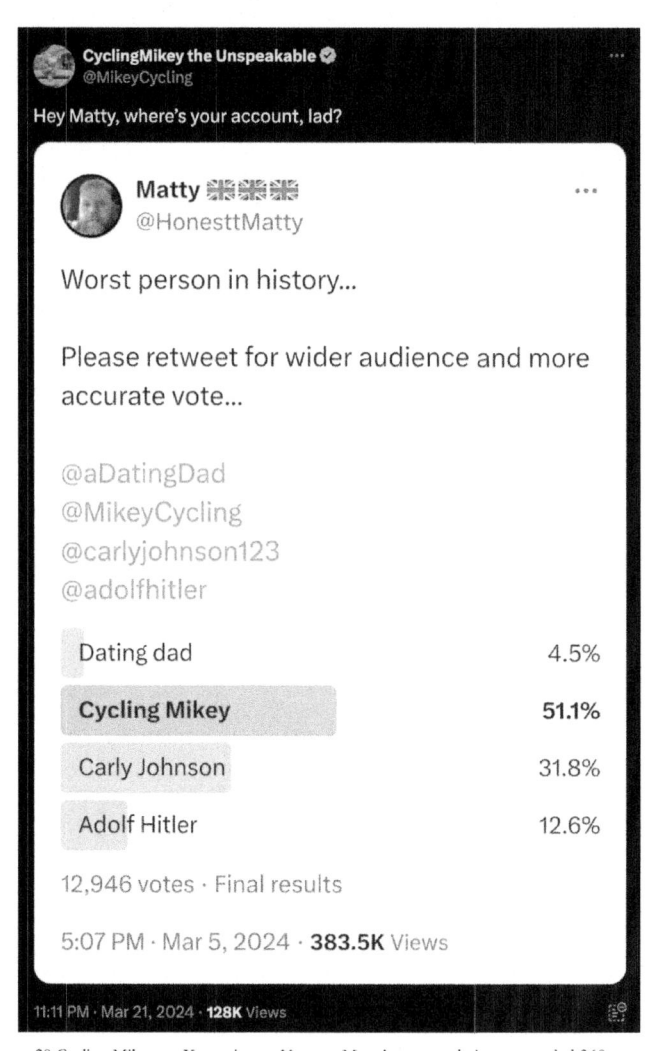

> **CyclingMikey the Unspeakable** ✓
> @MikeyCycling
>
> Hey Matty, where's your account, lad?
>
> > **Matty** 🇬🇧🇬🇧🇬🇧
> > @HonesttMatty
> >
> > Worst person in history...
> >
> > Please retweet for wider audience and more accurate vote...
> >
> > @aDatingDad
> > @MikeyCycling
> > @carlyjohnson123
> > @adolfhitler
> >
> > | | |
> > |---|---:|
> > | Dating dad | 4.5% |
> > | **Cycling Mikey** | **51.1%** |
> > | Carly Johnson | 31.8% |
> > | Adolf Hitler | 12.6% |
> >
> > 12,946 votes · Final results
> >
> > 5:07 PM · Mar 5, 2024 · **383.5K** Views
>
> 11:11 PM · Mar 21, 2024 · **128K** Views

Figure 20 Cycling Mikey on X reacting to Honestt Matty's account being suspended 360

The language

Kate Hopkins, Jeremy Clarkson, Richard Littleton[361] and Joey Barton[362] are only some high-profile names pedalling hate towards cyclists, especially those with cameras. The latter faced legal action for calling Jeremy Vine a *nonce* and opened a crowdfunding campaign that, when writing, struggled to collect funds for his defence.[363]

Across the press, the more conservative the outlet is, the more likely it is to use derogatory language and spin towards cyclists, especially those who resort to third-party reporting. However, left-leaning titles also have a history of clickbaiting, using defamatory language, including the *Independent*.[364] The *Mail* and *Evening Standard* have tended to get more balanced over the years. As mentioned, the former has slid towards more favourable coverage over time, while the latter has employed more negativity.[365] The *Telegraph* kept up an almost constantly hostile rhetoric.

The *Spectator* keeps pushing on their social platforms what seems an evergreen tirade about the "caseless self-pity of cyclists,"[366] full of cliché stereotypes and false historical references about who has "colonised" public space. Jack Wallis Simmons, while admitting being in the "brotherhood of lycra",[367] made a regular appearance in the paper with more and more ridiculous takes on cyclists and reporting.[368] But even under this title, you could find some refreshing takes like "Stop demonising cyclists" by Alec Marsh.[369]

The language

Figure 21 Cover of the *Evening Standard*

The *Evening Standard*, while still conservative, is known for its balanced take on transport, from many features by Ross Lydall to the brilliant Katie Strick campaigning for drivers using the Dutch reach.[370] With a click-bait-worthy cover, Robbie Griffiths painted another fair image of Mike van Erp, Jeremy Vine and others.[371] Yet even in such a company, a false note had to strike. "I am an anti-cyclist cyclist," stated Head of Design, Ped Millchamp. Then he went on a random trope without any substance about "owning the road", "snitching", and "red light jumping".[372]

We live in exciting times. On the one hand, we can read about police going too far when it comes to prosecuting hate speech online;[373] on the other, the same media rolls out regular portions of hate, prejudice, or ignorance towards cyclists. No other group or characteristic can and are so keenly and regularly dehumanised, trivialised, blamed and harassed as cyclists. The drivers go scot-free as against the guidance about road crash reporting;[374] most outlets seem to live by the rule: don't mention the driver.

That language is reflected in society. Sometimes, it takes the form of silly ranting, but it can occasionally turn into violence. On January 8th 2023, Harry Downer drove dangerously out of a nearby lane before stopping in front of a group of cyclists. Then he started shouting racial slurs before reversing, hitting them, damaging their bikes, and injuring them. Then he fled the scene, to return moments later to continue his rant. During the trial, he pleaded guilty to conspiracy to steal motor vehicles. Still, in the end, he received only two years in prison, suspended for two years, 300 hours of unpaid work, a 30-day Rehabilitation Activity Requirement, and an electronic tag curfew for six months.[375]

A few weeks after that incident, Sarah Torgerson closely overtook Justin Wigoder. After a short argument, she rammed him, breaking his spine. She received a two-year sentence suspended for two years.[376]

Talking heads on TV love to call out those who don't wear hi-viz or helmets, but according to a study by Nour S. Kelly and Alexander P. Landry, cyclists wearing safety attire, particularly high-visibility vests, are dehumanised more than cyclists without it. This has been found to lead to hostile and aggressive behaviour.[377]

In cooperation with the More Than a Cyclist campaign, Filmmaker Will Pope released a touching video, "Bloody Cyclists". It shows an imaginary interview with male and female bikers killed by dangerous drivers. It made a massive impression in the cycling community but was ignored at large. The original video had just over three and a half thousand views on YouTube at the time of writing.[378] It did not fit the viral formula of othering.

The language issue is not limited to name-calling. It's crucial when it comes to reporting as well. While the standards for reporting road collisions[379] are long established, most titles still fail to mention the driver or call RTCs "crashes" and use "accident" instead. "Accident" suggests the randomness and

The language

unavoidability of the event when, in most cases, it is entirely avoidable. That is why the word "accident" occurs in this book only in quotes from sources or the interviews.

Axolotol explained it perfectly: "I don't like to say bus, taxi, or car. It's always a driver because they are in control. That's why language is so important. When I'm putting anything out, especially on YouTube or Twitter, I always try to say that 'the driver did something'. It's never the car; it's never the bus. It's not the vehicle causing the problem. People are often saying cyclists vs cars, but it's not. It's just stupid people."

"It's like a crash vs an accident," I interrupted.

"Exactly. I never use accident because it's never an accident. It's always somebody messed up.

"I don't consider myself a cyclist. It's the same as if somebody who takes the bus to work doesn't consider himself a busser. Someone who drives a car to work doesn't consider themselves a motorist."

I didn't want to dwell too long on the language topic. But in the context of third-party reporting, it is important as a trigger that encourages many drivers to behave dangerously and gives them a feeling of impunity. Secondly, it shows how motorists are scared to be put in the "problem group"; they want to deflect the blame onto the cyclists. It is great material for another book. Here, it could be a bit of a side-track.

But life has dragged me once again onto this subject. As I mentioned in "Fix the justice system", the tragic death of Hilda Griffiths triggered an avalanche of hatred and division. I'm not here to debate the guilt of Brian Fitzgerald, against whom charges were dropped. Nor do I condone using the Regents Park for speed training. I know loads of motorists break the 20mph speed limit there, but that's not the point.

The collision was quickly facilitated by MP Iain Duncan Smith to produce a fast-drafted change to the law introducing the offence of causing death by dangerous, careless or inconsiderate cycling.[380] It was a historic victory for Matthew Brigs, who had campaigned for such legislation since his wife Kim's death in 2016. As I said before, there is nothing wrong in it – furthermore, the introduction of such a law removes one more argument from anti-cycling rhetoric.

The real issue came with the way the media handled the event. The term "Killer Cyclist" was pedalled by almost everyone: the *Evening Standard*,[381] the *Daily Mail*,[382] LBC[383]. The *Telegraph* went so far as to accuse cyclists of doing 52mph in London,[384] which was ridiculed by everyone, including Chris Boardman: "I don't normally get involved in calling out headlines but it's just getting bonkers. If this was directed at a gender, race or religion, it would be rightly called out as the hate speech it is. Mums, dads, sons and daughters being labelled as killers. It's just got to stop."[385] *MailOnline* published a chart showing two vertical axes: one with a scale up to 800 for all casualties caused by cyclists, and up to six for fatalities. The chart could read that in some years there were 800 fatalities when there were six or less.[386] The motoring editor I proved wrong about the hypothecated "road tax" went on all week tweeting and commenting about dangerous cyclists and apparent #whataboutery. Yet he did not post anything about any motorist causing harm. Scanning through his profile, I couldn't find any time he did it recently. Jeremy Kyle and Mike Graham, on TalkTV, discussed the topic with an absurd level of cynism, making faces and mocking anyone commuting on bike. Graham stated that cyclists "should be locked up, even if they haven't committed any crime".[387]

The language

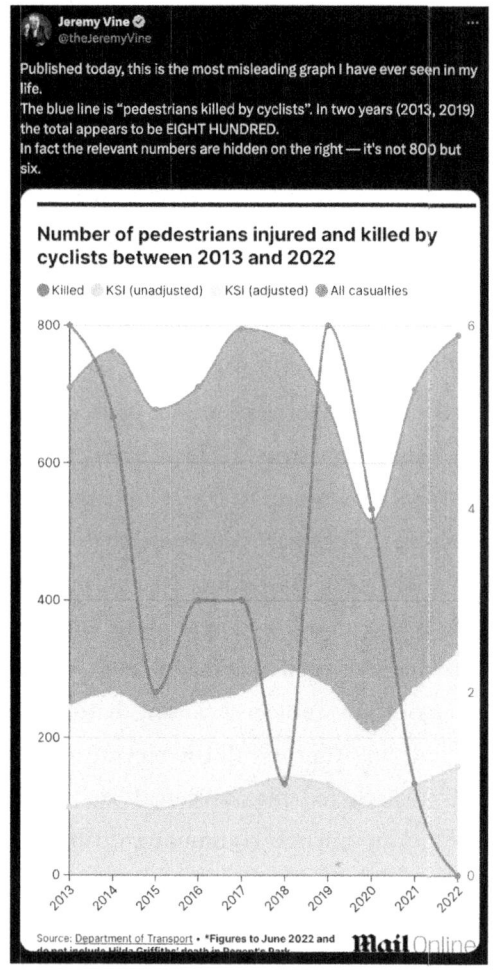

> **Jeremy Vine** ✓
> @theJeremyVine
>
> Published today, this is the most misleading graph I have ever seen in my life.
> The blue line is "pedestrians killed by cyclists". In two years (2013, 2019) the total appears to be EIGHT HUNDRED.
> In fact the relevant numbers are hidden on the right — it's not 800 but six.
>
> **Number of pedestrians injured and killed by cyclists between 2013 and 2022**
>
> ● Killed ○ KSI (unadjusted) KSI (adjusted) ● All casualties
>
> [graph]
>
> Source: Department of Transport • *Figures to June 2022 and do not include Hilda Griffiths' death in Regent's Park* **Mail** Online

Figure 22 Jeremy Vine on X

The rhetoric did not go down well with Matthew Briggs, who wrote on X: "This prob won't get noticed but is important. I have huge respect for people like Chris Boardman, Carlton Reid, Peter Walker, Cycling UK. They have always been decent to me and me to them. We may disagree on things but I will always be respectful even in a robust debate. Any road death is an absolute tragedy. I know the awful consequences. My point has always been that motor-related deaths have clear paths to prosecution. If it's felt that they are not done so adequately, that's a valid but different debate to my call for new laws. We

ALL share those imperfect roads. We are ALL pedestrians at some point. And we owe it to ALL that we conduct ourselves on the roads with care, consideration and awareness. That has never been anti-cycling."[388]

Did the blood-thirsty coverage help Matthew's case? Probably. The same as for MPs who felt the potential to gain some political currency. That isn't a problem. The issue is that amount of brutal, overblown and aggressive language from the media outlets armed many mentally unstable people with ammunition. Abuse from anonymous accounts on social media rocketed. And the feeling was that it had spilt onto the streets as well. The week the story peaked, I had three accounts of when a driver behaved dangerously near me and later tried to escalate the situation by stopping, reversing, blocking my way or provoking me to fight. In multiple accounts, we heard about people actively attacking cyclists.[389] Even the police lost their common sense: the Royal Parks Police posted a photo of a vehicle they named an illegal e-bike. Legally, an electrically propelled bike is called an e-motorbike, even when it has pedals. Many users picked it up and started to ask the force about their ignorance of drivers continuously breaking the speed limit in the same location. In direct response, the force cynically reposted an *Evening Standard* article about Brian Fitzgerald.[390]

The damage done by the press is large and we are still to see how it unfolds. I have been contacted for comment by several outlets and learned that, similarly to the High Street Kensington case, there are a significant amount of staff in various media companies who are distressed by the coverage and its potential effect on their safety.

I posted several honest reactions, and all of them resonated greatly: "I'd like to thank all journalists who jumped on the bandwagon of deflecting road danger from drivers onto the cyclist. Each close pass ends up with the driver trying to escalate. If I don't post for a longer period, call St Georges's."[391] That tweet has had 109 likes as of the evening I write this. The follow-up has 158, and it's still growing. "For context. That lad stopped afterwards, blocked my way, wanted to escalate, and said he 'doesn't have to give me any space' and 'he had to go close as there was traffic ahead' … 101 on how to incriminate yourself."[392]

A few days later, when I posted about this book being available to pre-order, one of the first comments was: "You vile little cunt, you're literally cancer cycling around London streets you self-obsessed little nonce," with a picture of a jumping cartoon dog and the caption "Kill yourself".[393]

The language some use as "banter" or "click-bait" more often materialises as a real threat. Remember that.

Behind the wall

David Brennan looked very touched when he remembered this: "The first demonstration, we expected up to 300 to turn up. And 3000 turned up, was very emotional." He was speaking about Pedal on Parliament, which he co-founded.

"Getting the Scottish government to agree to set up an online reporting system became of one of my highlights. However, this lowlight/highlight is a good demonstration of my approach. When something bad happens, rather than just accept that it has happened, see if you can use that bad thing in a positive way. Yes, I was assaulted. Yes, I was charged with a breach of the peace. I fought it, though, and won, and then, with the help of Cycling UK Scotland, we used this as a catalyst, putting pressure on politicians and the police to introduce the online reporting system."

To this day, Scotland has no system for third-party reporting, even though, theoretically, it can access one used in the rest of the Union at no cost.

"The biggest problem in Scotland was always inconsistency on top of the difficulty of how the system works. Police are coming to your house, you have to talk to them, you have no clue who's going to come in. I've had police just completely dismiss everything I was saying. I've been to a police station where I was told that it was illegal for me to be using a helmet camera. But then you also get officers who are absolutely brilliant. But the problem is you never know who you're going to get. It's like picking from that box of chocolates."

Despite the decades of fight, David persisted: "I had a chat with a local chief inspector, and he talked a nice game – We gonna do all this, we gonna look to build a system – but that has never gone anywhere. It was only when Cycling UK Scotland got involved and pushed their campaign that things started actually changing and politicians paid attention. They pushed for the system to come in. But obviously, there are technical issues."

The challenges are more political and legal. When I sat down with Deacon Thurston, he shared his findings from his research: "You don't need a DVD anymore. USB is enough, but that's only because the officers have been helpful. The police still have to burn a disk to provide it to the Procurator Fiscal. Something worth clarifying is that Scotland has a different legal system. The Road Traffic Act is UK-wide, but the process by which people are prosecuted is very different in Scotland. One of the key things, I think, is corroboration. Police officers always do everything in pairs. You never get a single police officer. Every time I report a driver, two police officers come to my house. One of them sits there doing nothing, while the other one takes my statement and goes through the full process. And the process by which the police submit reports in evidence to the Procurator Fiscal ultimately decides whether they prosecute somebody or not. It would need to be changed for third-party automation to work."

In other words, as in Northern Ireland, the police cannot send any conditional offer like FPN or retraining to offenders, and each case must go through the courts. The fact that officers cannot operate alone and must meet face to face with the witness is an obvious limitation and strain on resources. "In one of my meetings I got with a local police officer, he took me around, and they show me the rota of how many officers were covering traffic in West Scotland, which is a large area, and there were about four officers. That's the part of the problem," David recollected. "You have eight of them in total, but then you have a couple of them on holiday and a couple of them in court. Then they had two cars for the whole of the West Scotland. The standard police can do that stuff as well; they don't always know the rules. The reality is if you're a driver using a phone or speeding, the chances of you being caught are minuscule. And that's common knowledge. Everybody parks on double yellow lines because there are no traffic wardens. Some people won't park there because they know it's wrong. But there will be some who will just say, I don't care. And you'll always have that percentage of society with such an attitude. You'd always need to have some stick to hit them with, but it has to be used properly. That's where there would be a benefit of a system where people can upload video footage. So, effectively, the public becomes the eyes and the ears to cover extra officers that are lost."

In September 2023, Police Scotland released a rather bizarre update named "Proportionate Response to Crime piloted in the North East". It starts with a promise to "inform the people of decisions more quickly". Rather quickly, the response becomes clearer. "An example could be a theft from a garden; if there are no proportionate lines of enquiry such as CCTV or eyewitness evidence, then we may inform the caller that the report will be filed and no further action taken."[394] Many took that update as a downgrade of the service. "Concerned that this is the reasoning behind the lack of online reporting system and my recent 'police phone call' response to a close pass …" David Brennan wrote on X.[395]

Behind the wall

Is there Hope?

In spring 2024, the *Daily Mail*'s John James joined Jeremy Vine on a ride through London. He experienced the attitude of some motorists, the distraction caused by their phones and selfish parking practices. It became clear to him why keeping the primary road position kept them safer, while he gathered why the driver behind him might feel frustrated. "The crucial thing that's happened is they've bought a car because they've seen an advert of it doing 100mph on the side of the mountain, and now they're doing 7mph." In a bit of a picky style, John provided a very fair and objective image of the situation and Vine's actions.[396] Such narratives come more and more often, showing a positive shift. And he wasn't first. His college Alex Mason donned a headcam while beating Darren Boyle in a Mercedes-Benz vs a bike ride through the LTNs.[397] Not much later, the travel editor Ted Thornhill released his commute headcam footage elaborating on the safety of capital roads.[398]

In an interview for Cycling UK, Andy Cox reiterated the value of third-party reporting: "I personally believe in roads policing, and know it plays an integral role in saving lives and tackling crime. But the police can't solve road danger alone ... Police cannot be everywhere all the time, but the public can. When considering the mindset of the driver, enabling the public to report road crime via journeycam is a 'game changer' for road safety. The driver may believe that no police or speed cameras are present but will know the driver in the vehicle next to them is equally able to help enforce the law. This is a real deterrent and has huge benefits to enforcement and crash investigations."[399]

Third-party reporting is not going away. But it's far from perfect as well. I am still on the fence after speaking to so many great people. Most of us would like to avoid the need for it. We offer solutions like infrastructure and reducing motor vehicle usage in the cities. But without significant changes to policing and the legal system, what we are doing will remain a plaster on a deep wound. It's delegation of responsibility, which possibly shouldn't need to happen in the first place. To understand how deep it went into our society, I will mention

Is there Hope?

again the books *Traffication* and *Dark PR*. We are victims of an uncontrolled car industry. Is it likely to change soon? In the UK? I doubt. But I have hope.

I see more and more Londoners taking to bikes. Fewer young people are getting driving licences. Slowly, positive influences from Paris, Amsterdam and Copenhagen spill into our minds. The main problem I experience professionally is the need for more space in overcrowded bike storage.

And even if all of this is just a silly dream, I hope that my tiny contribution will help to prevent tragedies. If it does, we are collectively making our world better and safer. Nazan Fennel dedicated her life to campaigning against drivers distracted by their phones. She did it because her daughter was killed by one.[400] She was hit by a slow-moving truck while she cycled over a crossing on her way home from school. Her name was Hope. She gave us purpose so no parent has to endure the same horror as Nazan.

The video I uploaded in 2022, showing a Mini driver nearly hitting a lady while moving slowly and the driver was on the phone, was shared over 250 times and had a quarter of a million impressions. The situation there is not far different from the one that happened to Hope. Only thanks to the pedestrian's carefulness and my warning did it not end tragically. Now it's used to educate others. That is what it is for.

You may have mixed feelings about the individuals I have mentioned here, but you can't deny they made a difference. They deserve recognition. Mike van Erp can ruffle some feathers, but he made people talk about the danger. Traffic Droid can offend some, but he raised the alarm. Dave Sherry can come across as a bit cocky, but he saved lives. Gaz could look too confident, but he literally forced safer infrastructure to be built. Anne, the Cycling Granny, empowered countless women to stand against road violence. Jeremy Vine and other media professionals influenced the law to protect us all. Andy Cox and Mark Hodson changed the policing. Together with their colleagues, they must be remembered and recognised. And I hope Mark will finally get his bottle.

There is nothing more to say for now. And yet the story is far from done. I sit typing the last sentences and prepare the manuscript to be reviewed. I am happy that this small journey is over. It was supposed to be one year, but it took another six months to complete due to many other factors. I am happy. The goal is achieved. Then I got a message from my college. Not long ago, I showed him footage of a high-profile individual I saw browsing social media while driving his red sports car through Chelsea. He was eager to get that live, but I wanted to wait for the result. I thought he had returned to me to ask again if we could publish it. Instead, he wrote: "I had a crash the other day. I need a helmet cam!"

This story is far from over.

Is there Hope?

Acknowledgements

My warmest thanks should go to my family, who showed enormous support and patience throughout my journey into third-party reporting and writing this book. My wife helped me to keep my feet on the ground and avoid the worst pitfalls of that path. My children made me think about safety and their peace of mind.

Besides them, I can only avoid some of the guests who helped me write this story. Jeremy Vine's quick answer to my email boosted my spirit. David Brennan and his family welcomed me into his home. John Richardson, usually avoiding the limelight, for giving me a credit of trust. Dave Sherry, who was honest with the subtlety of a sledgehammer. Lewis D, aka Traffic Droid, opened his softer part to me. Ian Price, Mark Hodson and Andy Cox helped me understand the police's point of view. Freedom of Information departments of all forces in the UK for providing detailed data. Metropolitan TORS team and Andy Stephens, who guided me over the years. James and Axolotol reached out to me with their stories. Anne, aka CycleGranny, is the warmest star in our hearts. Tina and Rebecca guided me through the experience of female cyclists and cycling instructors and Rachel Aldred who helped me find them. Finally, Mike van Erp draws the most significant attention of those for and against third-party reporting.

Many others helped me deliver this story: Martin Ouvry, who corrected my Ponglish to English, and Daniel ShenSmith, who offered me his criticism and professional opinions. CycleGaz's research was essential in the early days. Grant Ennis, Carlont Reid, and Peter Walker shared some of their secrets and tricks as writers. VNS, WilliamNB, CykelTony, AZB, GothOnABrompton, Drew, 2WheeledWolf, and many others always supported me. Simon MacMichael's article in RoadCC has put me in the headlines.

I can't forget the support I received from people at my work. I'm forever grateful to Oleg, who supported and defended me; Neil and Liz, who helped me build this project professionally and avoid conflicts—tone of cycling to the

Acknowledgements

office colleagues who got my back when needed; and Richard and the rest of my team, who are to me like a family.

Gus Hurley's criticism made me find a critical error in the manuscript, and all the haters and trolls on X/Twitter increased my reach.

I'd love to thank all Kickstarter backers: Norman Oxtoby, Jane Leigh, Mark Turner, Tom, Grant Ennis, Heather Dewick, Vikash, David Brennan, David Wynn, Anne Ramsey, Paul Sielski, Jonathan Jacobs, James Johnston, The Creative Fund by BackerKit.

Figures

Figure 1 Me and David in the summer of 2023..35

Figure 2 Will Norman's tweet showing the benefits of one of the changes originating from Cynthia Barlow's campaigns. 52

Figure 3 Source Traffic Droid – Lewis D. set-up..58

Figure 4 One of the first Vine tweets from near misses.............................70

Figure 5 Typical situation while crossing High Street Kensington.............92

Figure 6 David Brennan's tweet about a close pass report in 2023. 99

Figure 7 Source Mark Hodson 104

Figure 8 Source Mark Hodson on Twitter 105

Figure 9 One of the first tweets with a link to the online upload portal from the City of London`Police...114

Figure 10 One of the first tweets with link to online upload portal from Enfield MPS 114

Figure 11 James May on X..119

Figure 12 Surrey RoadSafe X account about their usage of helmet mounted cameras 136

Figure 13 Anne with number plates on her bike 145

Figure 14 Me with my first headcam setup. 158

Figure 15 Gandalf Corner 174

Figure 16 Source YouTube Cycling Mikey..175

Figure 17 Source YouTube Cycling Mikey..176

Figure 18 Source YouTube Cycling Mikey..177

Figure 19 Twitter..178

Figure 20 Cycling Mikey on X reacting to Honestt Matty's account being suspended 186

Figure 21 Cover of the *Evening Standard*...188

Figure 22 Jeremy Vine on X 192

Figures

Index

100 Women in Cycling list, 148
1991, 41
1999, 41
2_Wheeled_Wolf, 80
2006, 26, 27, 28, 167
2007, 28, 37, 163
2008, 37, 41
2009, 57
2010, 49, 97, 98, 159
2011, 42, 49, 51, 68
2012, 27, 42, 49, 69, 101, 106
2014, 41, 72, 103, 119, 135
2015, 28, 72, 75
2016, 75, 82, 97, 98, 107, 109, 113, 117, 127, 139, 188
2017, 19, 98, 109, 113
2018, 20, 41, 62, 98, 111, 148
2019, 19, 23, 33, 38, 46, 62, 92, 98, 99, 113, 137, 167, 173, 179
2020, 15, 18, 31, 83, 89, 90, 98, 99, 117, 119, 120, 167, 169, 173
2021, 15, 19, 38, 63, 99, 119, 121, 127, 175
2022, 33, 54, 98, 115, 118, 121, 122, 126, 197
2023, 23, 46, 94, 97, 99, 115, 161, 179, 186, 194
2024, 18, 147, 153, 196
20mph, 53, 72, 84, 102, 107, 118, 124, 146, 187
2rocship, 43
30mph, 52, 121, 126
4ChordsNoNet. *See* James Richardson
996, 63
A1(M), 127
A205, 159

A24, 48, 79, 86
A40, 172
A5, 57
A501, 172
AA, 169
accident, 58, 59, 139, 186, 187
Action Cameras, 31
Active Travel, 89
Actual Body Harm, 62, 75
Adam Tranter, 119
Adil Iqbal, 127
Advanced Stop Line, 144
Aerial Video Systems, 25
Akaso, 26
Alec Marsh, 184
Alex Benfield, 17
Alex Jane McVitty, 52
Alex Mason, 196
Alexander P. Landry, 186
AlexGreenBank, 37
Amy Sharpe, 171
Andrew Bennet, 28
Andrew Neater, 70
Andy Cole, 38
Andy Cox, 72, 97, 113, 124, 132, 158, 169, 196, 197
Anna Allatt, 148
Anne Ramsay, 143, 197
ANPR, 181
Anthony Robson, 37
Audi, 71, 171
Auriol Grey, 86, 117
avid cyclist, 21
Avon and Somerset, 139
Avon and Somerset Police, 124, 169
Axon, 111

Index

ban, 15, 19, 20, 38, 90, 121, 126, 127, 128, 161, 167
Bank, 72, 86
Barreto, 96, 170
Battersea Bridge, 89
Bazk666, 42
BBC, 17, 51, 52, 55, 61, 82, 83, 84, 148
BBC Crimewatch, 75
BBC Inside Out East, 61
BBC Look North, 82
BBC Radio 2, 70, 71, 82
Bborp, 37
Belfast, 143, 144, 147
Better Streets for Kensington and Chelsea, 89, 93
BigBlokeOnABike, 43
Bigsharnm, 43
bike nonce, 17, 20
Birmingham Crown Court, 128
Black Belt Barrister. *See* Daniel ShenSmith
Blackfriars Crown Court, 127
Blade Runners, 181
blade-runners, 21
Bloody Cyclists, 186
Blue Light - Emergency Response, 122
BMW, 20, 58, 71, 127, 171, 173
Bob Sinclair, 25
bobby-on-the-beat, 16
Boris Bikes, 41
Boris Johnson, 41, 42, 83, 92
Brake, 169
Brian Fitzgerald, 118, 187, 190
Brig Ford, 106
BristolTraffic, 37
British Horse Society, 111
Bromley, 167
Brompton, 80
Bullycabs, 59
Cab Davidson, 37

Calvin Buckley, 128
Cambridge, 37
Cambridgeshire Constabulary, 98
Campden Hill Road, 177
Cannon Ci-10, 25
Cantankeroussquonk, 37
Carla Francome, 146, 148
Carlton Reid, 189
CBikeLondon, 123
CBS News, 164
CD-ROM, 38, 58, 139
Celia Walden, 15, 169
Celia Ward, 86, 117
Central London, 57, 89, 91
Channel 4, 56
Channel 4 Complainers, 134
Channel 5, 62, 84
Cheam, 67, 68
Cheshire Police, 99
Chief police officers, 41
ChilliTech, 25, 26
Chilterns, 158
Chis Eubank, 169
Chiswick, 84, 87
Chris, 161
Chris Boardman, 82, 106, 118, 188, 189
Church Street, 91
City, 72, 98
City of London, 72, 83, 113
City of London Police, 114, 123
Civil Law, 96, 156, 157
Clapham, 132
Clapham Common, 159
Clemmie Moodie, 170
Cleveland Police, 99
Cllr Joanna Biddolph, 84
Cllr Katherine Miles, 122
Clyde Tunnel, 27, 30
Colliers Wood, 79
Common Law, 96, 156

CommutingWithCamera, 37
Complainers, 57
Connor Chapman, 127
CPS. *See* Crown Prosecution Serivce
CPS - Court Prosecution Service, 20
Cristo Faufas, 181, 182
CritterCam, 25
Crown Prosecution Service, 111, 120, 131, 170
Croydon Cyclist, 27
CS3, 48
CS7, 48
CS9, 81
CTC National Standard Cycle Training, 149
Cycle Granny. *See* Anne Ramsay
Cycle Highways, 41
Cycle Sisters, 88
cycle zealot, 20
CycleGaz, 43, 49, 97, 177, 197
CycleOptic, 43
Cycling In A Skirt, 149
Cycling Mikey. *See* Mike Van Erp
Cycling Plus, 27
Cycling Proficiency, 68
Cycling Sisters, 148
Cycling UK, 19, 148, 189, 192, 196
Cycliq, 26
Cyclists
 Scourge of our roads?, 62
Cynthia Barlow, 52, 103
D.J. Kendal, 71
Daily Mail, 54, 61, 62, 68, 72, 75, 77, 89, 90, 115, 168, 170, 171, 174, 175, 184, 188, 196
Daily Mirror, 75
Daniel ShenSmitch, 122
Daniel ShenSmith, 18, 118
Danny Boyle, 72

Dark PR, 42, 83, 197
Darren Boyle, 196
Dave Sherry, 61, 179
David Beckham, 38, 167, 170
David Brennan, 20, 27, 28, 29, 53, 63, 97, 163, 192, 194
David Danglish, 127
David Jamieson, 105
Deacon Thurston, 33, 192
Dehumanising, 21
Department of Transport, 105, 117
Derbyshire Police, 98
Devon and Cornawall Police, 98
Diplomatic Police, 91
Diplomatic unit, 17
disabled, 63, 64, 80, 92, 148, 153
District Judge Timothy King, 77
Donnchadh McCarthy, 72
Dorset Police, 98
Dr Graham Hole, 151
Dr Tessa Dunlop, 168
Drift, 26
Dunstable, 57
Durham, 127
Durnham Police, 99
DVD, 111, 192
Dwight Yorke, 38
Edgeware, 57
Edignbough, 37
Edmund Kind, 169
Elaine Sullivan, 127
Elisabeth, 153
Ellie Edwards, 127
Elstree, 57
Encliff Park, 152
Epping, 62, 64
Eric Berne, 134
Erin Gill, 41
Essex, 59, 76, 80, 98
Essex Police, 59, 80, 121, 122
ethnic minorities, 21, 148

Index

Evening Standard, 13, 48, 70, 76, 92, 167, 184, 185, 188, 190
Evening, Standard, 51
evidence, 25
Evil Cycling Lobby, 12
exceptional hardship, 38
Exceptional hardship, 19
Exposure Joystick, 74
FairFuelUk, 83
Fiesta, 134
Fiona Russell, 31
First, 30
Fix Our Broken Justice System, 127
Fixed Penalty Notice, 121, 156, 161, 193
Florin Oprea, 127
FOI. *See* Freedom of Information Request
Frank Lampard, 170
Frankie Hough, 127, 128
Freedom of Information Request, 16, 99
freeloader, 51
Fringe, 87
Fulham Football Club, 79
Gandalf Corner, 176, 177
Garmin, 25, 26, 103
Gazelle, 167
GB News, 63
GDPR, 124
Gemma Dobson, 82
Geoffrey Dean, 126
George Monbiot, 127
Geri Halliwell, 38
Give Cyclists Room, 30
Glasgow, 32
Glasgow Southern General Hospital, 29
Gloucestershire Police, 99
Google Trends, 84

GoPro, 25, 26, 61, 94, 156
GoSafe, 109
Grand Union Canal, 164
Grant Ennis, 42, 83
grass, 17
Greater London, 113
Greater Manchester Police, 98
Greenford, 42
Greg Marshall, 25
Grey Hound, 67
GrowingVegetable, 43
Guardian, 13, 31, 41, 75, 87, 163, 171, 178
Guy Ritchie, 15, 167, 168
Guy Street, 87
Ham and High, 58
Hammersmith, 86, 89
Hammersmith Magistrates' Court, 77
Hampshire and Isle of Wight Constabulary, 98
Hampshire Police, 122, 124
Harrie Larrington-Spencer, 148
Harry Bennett, 126
Harry Downer, 186
Hasselblad 500c, 25
helmet, 21
Herefordshire, 149
Hertfordshire Police, 98, 122
HGV, 62, 72, 86, 103, 121, 144, 146
High Court, 94
High Street Kensington, 190
Highgate, 58
Highway Code, 16, 18, 19, 38, 54, 64, 82, 96, 123, 141, 144
Highway Code 123, 16, 179
Highway Code 170, 18, 179
Highway Code 180, 18
Highway Code 223, 179
Highway Code H2, 18, 179
Hilda Griffiths, 118, 187

Hi-Viz, 12, 42, 48, 62, 152, 186
HM Treasury, 12
Hohn Slinger, 168
Holland Park, 90
Home Office, 41
Hornton Street, 75, 78
Howard Cox, 83
Humberside Police, 99
Hyde Park, 72, 169, 171, 176, 180
Hyde Park, 167
Ian Austin, 54
Ian Glovers, 62
Ibrahim, 163, 180
Independent, 54
Insta360, 25, 26
Ion Onut, 127
Isleworth Crown Court, 77
ITV, 61, 103
ITV This Morning, 61
Iuckcan, 42
Jack Wallis Simmons, 184
Jackie Steward, 25
Jaj991, 161
James Dean, 174
James May, 118, 119
James Middleton, 128
Janina Gehlau, 72
Jay Foreman, 68, 150
Jeremy Clarkson, 17, 70, 71, 73, 76, 77, 78, 170, 181, 184
Jeremy Kyle, 61, 181, 188
Jeremy Vaughan, 109
Jeremy Vine, 11, 17, 51, 61, 67, 68, 69, 70, 71, 72, 73, 75, 76, 77, 78, 79, 80, 81, 82, 83, 85, 86, 87, 89, 91, 92, 93, 94, 113, 115, 134, 164, 184, 185, 189, 196, 197
Jeremy Vine Show, 168
Jesse Norman, 82
Jessica, 149, 150, 151, 152
Jim Davidson, 38

Jimmy Carr, 170
Jimmy Hill, 79
Jo Rigby, 148
Joey Barton, 184
John Brazil, 127
John James, 196
John Richardson, 43, 45
Josh Pettitt, 58
Joshua Harris, 169
Julie Dinsdale, 127
Justin Wigoder, 186
Kamar Omar, 148
Kate Bailey, 54
Kate Fox, 15
Kathryn Knight, 61, 62, 171
Katie Hopkins, 17
Katie Price, 38
Katie Strick, 185
Ken Livingston, 41
Kensginton Park, 167
Kensington, 18
Kensington Gardens, 163
Kensington High Street, 69, 79, 90, 92, 94, 162
Kensington Olympia, 89
Kent Police, 98
Kerry Blakeman, 104
Killer Cyclist, 188
Kim Briggs, 117, 128
King Street, 86
King's Life Guard, 163
KiwiCycling, 161
Kyle Gordon, 169
Lancashire Police, 98
Lancaster Gate, 141
Lance Flavell, 128
Laura Thomas, 62
Lauren O'Brien, 94
Leeds, 37
LeedsCyclist, 37
Leicestershire Police, 98

Index

Lewis D, 51, 55, 59, 61, 75, 146, 157, 164, 177, 179, 197
LGBTQ+, 21, 148
Lincolnshire Police, 99
Liverpool Crown Court, 128
London, 15, 19, 20, 32, 37, 41, 48, 49, 57, 58, 64, 68, 69, 72, 73, 76, 78, 81, 83, 85, 87, 88, 93, 94, 98, 103, 114, 117, 121, 132, 140, 146, 148, 154, 158, 163, 168, 176, 180, 188, 191, 196
London Assembly Transport Committee, 81
London Cycle Network, 41
London Cycling Campaign, 82
London Cycling Campaing, 153
Low Traffic Neighbourhood, 83, 196
lycra lout, 20
M66, 127
Mac Bennet, 23
Magistrates Court, 79
Magistrates' Court, 77
Magnatom. *See* David Brennan
Mail on Sunday, 68, 77, 90, 91
MailOnline, 48, 75, 188
MAMIL, 160, 180
Mark Hodson, 97, 101, 104, 105, 113, 114, 118, 122, 124, 133, 135, 151, 197
Mark Schulze, 25
Martyn Gall, 128
Matthew Brigs, 187
Melissa McKelligot, 127
Mercedes, 159, 170, 173, 196
Mercedes-Benz, 159, 196
MET. *See* Metropolitan Police
Metro, 30, 75, 76, 92, 167
Metropolitan Police, 16, 18, 37, 45, 46, 47, 49, 55, 58, 60, 63, 72, 91, 96, 97, 98, 113, 114, 123, 124, 130, 137, 158, 162, 168, 169
Metropolitan Police Traffic Offence Reporting, 46
Metropolitan Police Traffic Offences, 63, 123, 132
MG11, 63
Mike Graham, 181, 188
Mike van Erp, 29, 42, 134, 146, 164, 175, 178, 179, 183, 197
Mike Van Erp, 15
Mikey Bush, 167
Mikey Turf, 167
Mini, 78, 177, 197
Mirror, 167, 171
Mitcham, 68
Monmouth, 76
Morden, 68
More Than a Cyclist, 186
MOT, 94
Mr Loophole, 170, *See* Nick Freeman
MrCellopane99, 37
MrGrumpyCyclist, 42
MRI, 62
Mrs Lee, 71
MyCycleClips, 37
Nazan Fennel, 148, 197
New Kings Road, 89
NextBase, 25, 169
NFA. *See* No Further Action
NHS, 82, 108, 149
Nicholas "*Nick*" Woodman, 25
Nick B, 76
Nick Freeman, 82, 91, 170
Nick Freeman, 180
Nigel Havers, 90
Nikon, 25
NIP. *See* Notice of Intended Prosecution
No Further Action, 53, 55, 123

212

nonce, 17
North Wales Police, 99, 109, 113
North Yorkshire Police, 122
Northamptonshire Police, 99, 113
Northern Ireland, 33, 38, 144, 148, 193
Northumbria Police, 99
Norwich Magistrates Court, 128
Notice of Intended Prosecution, 110, 120, 126, 132, 156, 162
Nottinghamshire Police, 99
Nour S. Kelly, 186
Ombudsman, 145
OnTheRoadUK2008, 37
Operation Close pass, 105
Operation Close Pass, 106, 107, 134
Operation Snap, 98, 109, 124
OpSnap, 109, *See* Operation Snap
Oregon Scientific, 30
othering, 21
Outer Circle, 172, 173
Oval, 49
Oxford Street, 86
parent-adult-child model, 134
Park Square East, 172
Parliamentary Cycling Group, 54
Pass-Pixie, 150
Paul F. Donald, 39, 83
Paul Jones, 37
Paul Lyon-Maris, 174
Paul McNeil, 31
Paul Mullen, 127
pavement cycling, 19, 41
pavement parking, 20
Pavement parking, 20, 120
PC Ian Heathy, 82
Ped Millchamp, 185
Pedal on Parliament, 29, 192
Ped-Al Qaeda, 31
Peel, 16
penalty points, 18
Penticle, 27
Peter Hitchens, 61, 71, 77
Peter Levy, 82
Peter Walker, 13, 171, 178, 189
Peter Williams, 128
Poland, 15, 156, 158
Police for Scotland, 169
Police of Scotland, 194
Police Service for Northern Ireland, 99, 143
Policing by Consent, 16
PompeyCycle, 42
Prenton, 71
primary position, 54, 56, 145, 177, 196
prison slang, 17
Queen's Way, 123
RAC, 19
Radio Times, 73
RadWagon1, 43
Ralpha Phil, 124
Range Rover, 70, 94, 117, 123, 171, 174, 175, 176
rat, 17
Rebecca Morris, 127
red light jumping, 21
Redvee, 43
Regent Street, 59
Regents Park, 118, 175, 187
Richard Littleton, 181, 184
Richard Spillet, 61
Road Casualty Reduction Partnership, 109
Road Crash Investigation Bureau, 120
Road Harm Reduction Team, 106
Road Safe, 121, 122
road tax, 12, 52, 71, 77, 117, 188
Road Traffic Act, 105, 193

Index

Road Traffic Collision, 102, 106, 107, 186
road.cc, 93, 161, 170
RoadPeace, 32, 119, 127, 128
RoadSafe, 59, 63, 135
Robbie Griffiths, 185
Robert Goodwill, 41
Robin P. Clarke, 41
Rod Liddle, 71, 75, 181
RogerHotUK, 37
Ronnie O'Sullivan, 170
Rory McCarron, 122
Ross Lydall, 13, 72, 185
Royal Albert Hall, 89
Royal Borough of Kensington and Chelsea, 68, 69, 75, 79, 83, 84, 86, 89, 90, 91, 92, 93, 162, 177, 181
Royal Borough of Kensington and Chelsea Youth Council, 89
Royal College of Music London, 89
Royal Geography Society, 89
Ruth Mayorcas, 148
Sam Creighton, 72
Sania Shabbir, 128
Sarah Berry, 148
Sarah Torgerson, 186
Sarah Vine, 75
Scotland, 17, 20, 31, 33, 34, 38, 97, 192, 193
Scourge, 62
SD card, 110
Senedd, 84
Serpentine, 167, 169, 177
Sgt Ian Price, 109
ShamRockSoup, 123
Shanique Syrena Pearson, 75, 76, 77, 79, 81, 87
Shaun McDonald, 38
Sheffield, 149
Shelby Sadler, 54
Sherrilyn Speid, 176
Sigrid, 128
Silvio Diego, 38, 43
Sir Alex Ferguson, 38, 170
sir Iain Duncan Smith, 187
sir Ian Duncan Smith, 118
Smart, 94
SMIDSY. *See* Sorry Mate I Didn't See You
snitch, 17, 21
Sorry Mate I Didn't See You, 37
South Circular, 132, 159
South Wales Police, 109
South Yorkshire Police, 99
Southwest London, 45
Speed Awareness Course, 132
speeding, 19, 38, 72, 120, 124, 126, 127, 144, 164, 167, 170, 193
Speeding Demon, 72
Square Mile, 72
squealer, 17
Staffordshire Police, 98
Stagecoach, 37
Stasi, 17, 169
Stay Wider of the Rider, 82
Stephen Hudon, 113
Stephen Hudson, 101
Steve Coogan, 38
Stevenage, 17, 149, 150
Stop Oil, 176
Stuart Baker, 106
STV, 31
Sun, 170
Sunday Times, 61, 67, 71, 109, 115
Surrey Police, 82, 99, 122, 182
Susannah Constantine, 83
Sussex, 76
Sussex Police, 99
SUV, 28, 89, 119, 159, 164, 165, 173, 181
sw19cam, 49

SW19Cam, 43
TalkTV, 61, 182, 188
Tapped Crusader, 31
taxi, 37, 53, 56, 59, 72, 79, 89, 121, 141, 144, 146, 187
Technalogic, 26
Ted Thornhill, 196
Telegraph, 15, 48, 72, 75, 170, 175, 184, 188
Teresa Healy, 109
TFL. *See* Transport For London
Thames Vale Police, 122
Thames Valley Police, 98, 121, 122, 158
Thames Water, 90
the Sun, 19, 31, 32, 83
The Sun, 31, 75, 76
thefireuk, 49
TheFireUK, 43
Thinkware, 25
Times, 70, 75, 163, 168
Tina, 149, 150, 152
Toby Wilsdon, 76
TORS. *See* Metropolitan Police Traffic Offence Reporting
Traffic Droid, 55, *See* Lewis
Trafficaiton, 168
Traffication, 38, 83, 197
Transport Charities, 42
Transport for London, 56
Transport For London, 56, 59, 70, 114, 121
Travis Nelson, 128
Trevor Boardman, 71
TuneAfterTune, 37
Twerp, 170
Twitter, 27
TwoHat, 37
Ultra Low Emission Zone, 118
University of Edinburgh, 158

USB, 193
VanGuard, 122
Vantrue, 25
VeloEvol, 42
Victor Manuel Ben-Rodriguez, 72
Victoria Pendleton, 70
vigilante, 20
VisionZero, 113
Volkswagen Golf, 137, 156
Volvo, 139, 173, 176
VOSA, 49
vulnerable, 21, 38, 47, 82, 86, 87, 103, 107, 108, 109, 111, 125, 145, 148, 156
Wales, 84, 98, 109, 124
Wallington, 68
Wandsworth Council, 123
War on Britain's Roads, 52
Warminster, 71
Warwickshire, 103
Warwickshire Police, 98
West London, 89
West Mercia Police, 98
West Midlands Police, 99, 101, 104, 105, 106, 113, 134, 161
West Yorkshire Police, 99
WestCountryTim, 42
WhatsApp, 171
Wheelie Kay, 80
Wigan, 71
Will Pope, 186
Wiltshire Police, 98
Wimbledon, 19, 46, 89, 117
women, 21
Women Freedom Ride, 153
Women's Freedom Ride, 153
Yangtse55, 42
Ying Tao, 72
YouTube, 27

Endnotes

1 Quote attributed either to Jospeh Stalin or Kurt Tucholsky, see https://quoteinvestigator.com/2010/05/21/death-statistic/

2 Freedom of Information response FOI2023/08001, HM Treasury, May 31st, 2023

3 Hypothecated - fenced, dedicated for

4 Ritchie's film is memorable for the wrong reasons, Celia Walden, Daily Telegraph, July 28th, 2020, page 20

5 Known as Cycling Mikey, @MikeyCycling on Twitter/X

6 Road traffic collisions statistics for 2021 released by Polish Police, Wypadki drogowe - raporty roczne - Statystyka - Portal polskiej Policji (policja.pl), https://statystyka.policja.pl/st/ruch-drogowy/76562,Wypadki-drogowe-raporty-roczne.html

7 Reported road casualties Great Britain, annual report: 2021 - GOV.UK (www.gov.uk), https://www.gov.uk/government/statistics/reported-road-casualties-great-britain-annual-report-2021/reported-road-casualties-great-britain-annual-report-2021

8 Watching the English: The Hidden Rules of English Behavior, Kate Fox, January 7th, 2014, ISBN 9781857886160

9 The quote was attributed to Sir Robert Peel, Primer Minister of United Kingdom 1834-1835, 1841-1845, Home Secretary 1822-1827, 1828-1830

10 The Abolition of Liberty, Peter Hitchens, page 22, Atlantic Books, 2004, ISBN 9781782397731

11 The name *bobby* possibly originated from Peel's first name - Robert

12 General rules, techniques and advice for all drivers and riders, Highway Code, https://www.gov.uk/guidance/the-highway-code/general-rules-techniques-and-advice-for-all-drivers-and-riders-103-to-158

13 The Road Vehicles (Construction and Use) Regulations 1986 – Stopping of engine when stationary, https://www.legislation.gov.uk/uksi/1986/1078/regulation/98/made

14 The Road Vehicles (Construction and Use) Regulations 1986 – Leaving motor vehicles unattended, https://www.legislation.gov.uk/uksi/1986/1078/regulation/107/made

15 Volunteer, unpaid police officers

16 Bike sales down? Good. Sick of the two-wheeled Stasi, Jeremy Clackson, The Sun, March 25th, 2023, page 15

17 Ex-BBC presenter who was jailed for stalking appears in court again, PA Media, Guardian, Jun 1st, 2023, https://www.theguardian.com/uk-news/2023/jun/01/ex-bbc-presenter-jailed-stalking-appears-in-court-again-alex-belfield

18 Katie Hopkins @KTHopkins, Twitter, Jan 23rd, 2024, "A visit to #AlexBelfield in prison. Sentenced to 5 & half years for the new 'crime' of words, spoken online. The British 'Justice'

System is corrupt to the core. Thank you to the wonderful staff @HMPFiveWells for all your kindness. #bikenonce", https://twitter.com/KTHopkins/status/1749893056143269965

[19] Which, for me as a person who learned on the right, makes more sense

[20] Why does driving make us so angry?, Henry Manance, iNews, January 29th, 2022

[21] That would be "unwise", BlackBeltBarrister on YouTube, January 12th, 2024, https://www.youtube.com/watch?v=EIZ4YvTsV84

[22] PhoneKills @PhoneKills, Twitter, January 12th, 2024, "Re-uploading video showing whole story (without reg numbers), the place and the problem @RBKC needs to address. Please also watch this video by @dshensmith that rightly criticise me [LINK] Feel free to comment and criticise. 1.5M views, 610 comments, 136 shares, 617 likes and 33 bookmarks proves you wanted to share your views on it. cc @theJeremyVine", https://twitter.com/phonekills/status/1745885565608734738/video/1

[23] You should give way to pedestrians crossing or waiting to cross the road into or from which you turn

[24] Wait until there is a safe gap, watch for pedestrians

[25] Court exemption allows driver with 68 points on their licence to legally drive on the road, RAC, August 14th, 2020, https://www.rac.co.uk/drive/news/motoring-news/exemption-allows-driver-with-68-points-on-their-licence/

[26] Put the brakes on Britain's worst driver 33, is still on the road despite racking 78 points in just four years, Phoebe Cooke, the Sun, October 22nd, 2019, https://www.thesun.co.uk/motors/10186835/britain-worst-driver-penalty-points/

[27] "Exceptional Hardship" loophole lets one in five drivers escape ban, Sam Jones, Cycling.uk, December 13th, 2021, https://www.cyclinguk.org/press-release/exceptional-hardship-loophole-lets-one-five-drivers-escape-ban-0

[28] I can't afford to lose my licence! More than 35,000 motorists which 12 points avoided bans since 2017 by claiming 'exceptional hardship' if disqualified, Rob Hull, ThisIsMoney.co.uk, December 14th, 2021, https://www.thisismoney.co.uk/money/cars/article-10304829/More-35-000-motorists-12-points-avoided-bans-2017.html

[29] Number of hit-and-run collisions in London hit record high with offence 'almost normalised', Ross Lydall, Evening Standard, January 17th, 2024, https://www.standard.co.uk/news/london/hit-run-police-crash-driving-offences-motorists-london-b1132867.html

[30] Woman arrested over Wimbledon crash that killed two schoolgirls released under investigation, Lydia Chantler-Hicks, Evening Standard, February 1st, 2024, https://www.standard.co.uk/news/london/wimbledon-school-crash-the-study-prep-driver-arrest-selena-lau-nuria-sajjad-met-police-b1136332.html

[31] We will explore that further in the chapter: "Fix the justice system"

[32] Ben Fogle says delivery drivers hurtle around blind bends at 60mph on rural road that his family walk along, as he calls for speed limit to be slashed after his own brush with death, Melody Fletcher, MailOnline, April 21st, 2024, https://www.dailymail.co.uk/femail/article-13332931/Ben-Fogle-describes-nearly-died-rural-road-close-home-family-regularly-walks-calls-lowering-60mph-limit-narrow-country-lanes.html

Endnotes

[33] Nearly half of all drivers admit to speeding on country roads, Shane O'Dogoghue, The Sunday Times Driving.co.uk, February 15th, 2023, https://www.driving.co.uk/news/nearly-half-of-all-drivers-admit-to-speeding-on-country-roads

[34] Home Secretary Suella Braverman "asked civil servants to help her cover up speeding ticket": Mandarins "refused requests to get her a private speed awareness course so she could dodge public shame" - as Labour accuse her of ministerial code breach, Glen Owen, MailOnline, May 20th, 2023, https://www.dailymail.co.uk/news/article-12106227/Suella-Braverman-asked-civil-servants-help-avoid-speeding-fine-private-driving-course.html

[35] Laws forcing pedestrians to cross only in specified places

[36] Father killed in hit-and-run horror, Chris Gregory, Basingstoke Gazette, November 17th, 2008, https://www.basingstokegazette.co.uk/news/3853593.father-killed-in-hit-and-run-horror/

[37] Pedestrians pavement deaths, RoadPace, April 14th, 2021, https://www.roadpeace.org/pedestrian-pavement-deaths-2/

[38] vigilante - Cambridge Dictionary, https://dictionary.cambridge.org/dictionary/english/vigilante

[39] Ulez Blade Runners strike again: Campaigners fighting hated CCTV enforcing Sadiq Khan's £12.50-a-day eco tax attack another camera - and replace it with a Christmas tree, Dan Grennan, MailOnline, January 12th, 2024, https://www.dailymail.co.uk/news/article-12955045/Ulez-blade-runners-strike-Campaigners-against-hated-CCTV-enforcing-Sadiq-Khans-12-50-day-eco-tax-attack-camera-replace-Christmas-tree.html

[40] Harrison Ford, 79, still looks every bit the action man as he dons clinging cycling jersey and bib on bike ride in LA, Justin Enriquez, MailOnline, December 27th, 2021, https://www.dailymail.co.uk/tvshowbiz/article-10348643/Harrison-Ford-79-dons-clinging-cycling-jersey-bib-bike-ride-LA.html

[41] I will repeat it throughout this book

[42] PhoneKills, Twitter, January 6th, 2023, "Loads of drivers on phones. Won't be able to report all captured. But the guy who later parked on zigzags and suggested he can stab me for sure (custom MG 2022 plates)", https://twitter.com/phonekills/status/1611378934007881728

[43] Mac Bennett, Twitter, January 6th, 2023, "Do you have a job and/or a life ? Genuinely curious", https://twitter.com/MacaulayB95/status/1611417204687523841

[44] I was into journalism in high school.

45 History and evolution of action cameras, Zach, Pelvy, November 4th, 2020, https://pevly.com/action-camera-history/

[46] Currently known as X

[47] Video Camera Cyclists, CroydonCyclist, https://www.croydoncyclist.co.uk/video-camera-cyclists/

[48] Clyde Tunnel, Magnatom, YouTube, June 29th, 2006, https://www.youtube.com/watch?v=iGlgk6QdIfE

[49] David Brennan. Magnatom nickname resulted as a typo. He meant to create username Magnetom, which was kind of Siemens MRI scanner type.

[50] French recumbent ride, Panticle, July 10th, 2006, YouTube, https://www.youtube.com/watch?v=_aZvchUqgLs

[51] Commute to work – new helmet cam, Andrew Bennett, YouTube, August 27th, 2006, https://www.youtube.com/watch?v=ZgXb__nE2eE

[52] Often referred as AndyB

[53] Almost doored, Andrew Bennett, YouTube, October 6th, 2006, https://www.youtube.com/watch?v=65SMrl__744

[54] Bus v's camera, Magnatom, YouTube, February 6th, 2007, https://www.youtube.com/watch?v=T4S1bJTHL9E

[55] Females' chart hit, Victoria Bone, Daily Mirror, October 28th, 2004, Scottish Edition.

[56] Safety comes First for the YouTube doc, Stephen Deal, Metro, Glasgow Edition, November 9th, 2007, page 24

[57] Tapped Crusader, Exclusive, Alan Carson, March 25th, 2008, the Sun, Scottish Edition, page 7

[58] Saddle by me, Robert McAulay, the Sun, Scotland Edition, March 26th, 2008, page 29

[59] Cyclists drive me round the bend. Opinion, John Smeaton, the Sun, Scottish Edition, March 27th, 2008, page 39

[60] G2: Ethical Living: Two wheels, Fiona Russel, the Guardian, July 27th, 2008, page 20

[61] Crash, TuneAfterTune, YouTube, November 29th, 2007, https://www.youtube.com/watch?v=chfYMHIfBzk

[62] Assaulted MK16KWW, Magnatom, YouTube, December 2nd, 2019, https://www.youtube.com/watch?v=xYp2BBEVO28

[63] Bus moves across cyclist, Paul Jones, YouTube, February 21st, 2007, https://www.youtube.com/watch?v=tY1MZyCQqHk

[64] Idiot's day out on the buses pt1, TiNuts, YouTube, April 10th, 2007, https://www.youtube.com/watch?v=7fNVfchL4QQ

[65] Interesting stop, alexgreenbank, YouTube, May 15th, 2007, https://www.youtube.com/watch?v=ADpmutOfyrc

[66] Idiot jeep driver, Cab Davidson, YouTube, July 8th, 2007, https://www.youtube.com/watch?v=tJkIlORUtLs

[67] G899FFX 1990 Mitsubishi Colt, TuneAfterTune, YouTube, November 27th, 2007, https://www.youtube.com/watch?v=WM2y58pnZdk

[68] .the invisible cyclist, Anthony Robson, YouTube, January 4th, 2008, https://www.youtube.com/watch?v=lkztOLwEzfw

[69] London bus – cut up, ontheroaduk2008, YouTube, February 20th, 2008, https://www.youtube.com/watch?v=1634sH3ol0Q

Endnotes

[70] Close overtake – twice, mrcellophane99, YouTube, April 13th, 2008, https://www.youtube.com/watch?v=u-LBoBRRAuw

[71] Another close First Leeds bus encounter, leedscyclist, YouTube, April 29th, 2008, https://www.youtube.com/watch?v=fkhAfqtIPx8

[72] SMIDSY – Sorry mate, I didn't see you. A situation when a driver joins the road as if the cyclist wasn't there

[73] Blind man driving, gadgetmind, YouTube, May 20th, 2008, https://www.youtube.com/watch?v=v4riajyEM6s

[74] Drivers going through on red 31-07-08, mycycleclips, YouTube, August 2nd, 2008, https://www.youtube.com/watch?v=9EXmPaY5gYg

[75] Con-SIDERably more important than yew!, cantankeroussquonk, YouTube, August 28th, 2008, https://www.youtube.com/watch?v=BbefjcaHdzE

[76] U Turn, CommutingWithCamera, YouTube, September 2nd, 2008, https://www.youtube.com/watch?v=TjBpCZm47xI

[77] SMIDSY, twohat, YouTube, October 3rd, 2008, https://www.youtube.com/watch?v=1Jh6csRVQ4s

[78] Dangerous cycle lane design, rogerhotuk, YouTube, December 1st, 2008, https://www.youtube.com/watch?v=nl1lUY5wZjg

[79] Close shave, bbborp, YouTube, December 8th, 2008, https://www.youtube.com/watch?v=fYVRbpAlpnk

[80] Don't park there, BristolTraffic, YouTube, December 12th, 2008, https://www.youtube.com/watch?v=56bl0nkNYtM

[81] Stopped by police for no right turn except cyclists, Shaun McDonald, YouTube, February 6th, 2011, https://www.youtube.com/watch?v=f3SAWS9lp50

[82] London Cyclist Stopped by Police! (Funny Stuff!), Silvio Diego, September 16th, 2014, https://www.youtube.com/watch?v=YHMLMKE1tOk

[83] I'm too famous to be banned, speeder Cole tells a court, Jaya Narain, Daily Mail, December 7th, 1999, page 23

[84] 100mph footballer saved by defender, Andrew Loundon, Daily Mail, July 12th, 2001, page 33

[85] Golden balls-up, Stephen Moyes, the Sun, December 5th, 2019, page 5

[86] Driving the celebrity banned list, Jamie Merril, Independent, July 17th 2012, p. 27

[87] Articles about her driving with the ban keep coming back on the time of writing

[88] Banned Katie behind wheel, Amir Razavi, the Sun, March 18th, 2021, p. 7

[89] Traffication, how cars destroy nature & what we can do about it, Paul F. Donald, Pelagic Publishing, 2013, ISBN 978-1-78427-444-3

[90] Why cyclists sometimes opt for the pavement, Erin Gill, the Guardian, May 15th, 2011, https://www.theguardian.com/commentisfree/2011/may/15/cyclists-pavement-fine

[91] Paving the way for cyclists, Robin P. Clarke, Mosley, Birmingham, letter to the Guardian, May 20th, 1991, page 20

[92] Pedestrians Pavement Deaths, RoadPease.org, April 14th, 2021, https://www.roadpeace.org/pedestrian-pavement-deaths-2/

[93] Yes, I mentioned it already, and will again

[94] Transport minister: Responsible cyclists CAN ride on the pavement, Simon MacMichael, January 15th, 2014, Road.cc, https://road.cc/content/news/108119-transport-minister-responsible-cyclists-can-ride-pavement

[95] Transport charities call for £100m fund to put cycling on safer track, Philip Pank, the Times, February 6th, 2012, page 7

[96] 2012 was the year of cycling. Now we need a revolution, Jackie Ashely, Guardian, December 30th 2012, https://www.theguardian.com/commentisfree/2012/dec/30/cycling-bikes-wiggins-environment-transport

[97] Driver Knock down cyclist in Greenford West London, iukcan, YouTube, April 27th, 2012, https://www.youtube.com/watch?v=6qycF0raqpg

[98] Knocked off the road by a car, Silvio Diego, YouTube, December 12th, 2012, https://www.youtube.com/watch?v=OCBHS9edGPw

[99] Locanda Ottomezzo - if you come in the afternoon, it has the best pizza in Kensington

[100] I will explore that event later

[101] London's Most Dangerous Junctions Mapped, London Cycling Campaign, November 7th, 2023, https://lcc.org.uk/news/londons-dangerous-junctions-2023/

[102] Hair-raising moment cyclists are thrown off bikes in central London cycle-superhighway pile-up, Francesca Gillett, Evening Standard, October 12th, 2016, https://www.standard.co.uk/news/london/hairraising-moment-cyclists-are-thrown-off-bikes-in-central-london-pileup-crash-a3367621.html

[103] Horrific cycling crash shows danger of overtaking on 'at capacity' superhighways, Guy Kelly, Telegraph, October 13rd, 2016, https://www.telegraph.co.uk/health-fitness/body/horrific-cycling-crash-shows-danger-of-overtaking-on-capacity-su/

[104] Rider's risky overtake causes calamitous crash sending cyclists sprawling across the floor on a congested superhighway track, Francis Scott, MailOnline, October 12th 2016, https://www.dailymail.co.uk/news/article-3834940/Rider-s-risky-overtake-causes-calamitous-crash-sending-cyclists-sprawling-floor-congested-superhighway-track.html

[105] an accusation that is used against more known headcam cyclists

[106] RTC 16.12.10 Result, CycleGaz, YouTube, October 18th, 2012, https://www.youtube.com/watch?v=VXoqQSmvPBg

[107] W474WGJ – Result, CycleGaz, YouTube, December 11th, 2012, https://www.youtube.com/watch?v=_dI6-_RgmSI

[108] RX11AXP B&T @Work – Result, CycleGaz, YouTube, May 1st, 2013, https://www.youtube.com/watch?v=l-ujuJXNq3w

Endnotes

[109] Cyclist's crusade to film danger drivers, Simon Freeman, Evening Standard, September 22nd 2011, https://www.standard.co.uk/hp/front/cyclist-s-crusade-to-film-danger-drivers-6446044.html

[110] Cycling Mikey started to hand the out recently

[111] Media Reporting Guidelines for Road Collisions, RCRG, https://www.rc-rg.com/guidelines

[112] The psychology of why cyclists enrage car drivers, Tom Stafford, BBC, February 12th, 2012, https://www.bbc.com/future/article/20130212-why-you-really-hate-cyclists

[113] BBV War on Britain's Roads, aired December 5th, 2012

[114] Will Norman, Twitter, October 24th, 2023, "In 2019 London launched the world's first Direct Vision Standard (DVS) to reduce 'blind spots' and make HGVs safer. The number of fatal collisions where vision is a contributing factor has fallen by 75% (2018-2023).", https://twitter.com/willnorman/status/1716739866350825755

[115] Above the speed limit or slow as 5mph, becoming a proverbial Schrödinger cyclist

[116] NFA – No Further Action

[117] Motorists post death threats to 'arrogant' TV cyclist, Keith Gladdis, DailyMail, December 8th 2012, p31

[118] Helmet camera cyclist shrugs off death threats, Ross Lydall, December 7th 2012, Evening Standard, page 9

[119] Who dares films. Helmet-mounted HD cameras are capable of recording riders' face-on thrills, which is why extreme sports fans love them, Will Coldwell, Independent April 12th 2012, page 31

[120] Complainers S01 E01, May 2014, Channel 4

[121] Transport For London

[122] Vigilante cyclist patrosl Highgate to expose dangerous drivers, Josh Pettitt, September 24th, 20211, https://www.hamhigh.co.uk/news/21385934.vigilante-cyclist-patrols-highgate-expose-dangerous-drivers/

[123] Metropolitan Police Force policing roads at that time

[124] 'Britain's most hated cyclist' catches out unsafe motorists, Georgie Keate, The Times, February 6th, 2015, page 4

[125] Police want your dashcam videos of reckless drivers, Jonathan Leake; Hannah Summers, the Sunday Times, January 15th, 2014, page 8

[126] Dashboard sleuths trap texting drivers, George Arbuthnott, the Sunday Times, September 21st 2014, page 17

[127] Drivers on the phone beware: The bicycling vigilante is after you!, Kathryn Knight, the Daily Mail, October 6th, 2014, page 27

[128] Years later, she returned with a widely appreciated portrayal of Mike van Erp.

[129] Hero with a helmet camera, Peter Hitchens, the Mail on Sunday, October 12th, 2014, page 31

[130] With 50 claimed convictions, is this the UK's top reporter of dodgy driving?, John Stevenson, road.cc, February 3rd, 2015, https://road.cc/content/news/141911-50-claimed-convictions-uks-top-reporter-dodgy-driving

[131] Rise of cycle cams debated on This Morning, Alex Bowden, June 26th, 2015, https://road.cc/content/news/155375-rise-cycle-cams-debated-morning

[132] Nick Freeman vs Dave Sherry - The Great Cycling Debate, Jeremy Kyle Live, TalkTV, Nick Freeman, YouTube, August 24th, 2022, https://www.youtube.com/watch?v=YtVQlNWbBc0

[133] The vigilante cyclsist: Man uses heltmet-cam to film rogue motorists on his commute to work and helps police get more than SEVENTY motoring convictions (but his job is a London bus driver), Richard Spillett, MailOnline, February 5th, 2015, https://www.dailymail.co.uk/news/article-2940879/Vigilante-cyclist-uses-three-cameras-film-rogue-motorists.html

[134] Actual Body Harm

[135] The guilty habit that could turn you into a killer, Kathryn Knight, the Daily Mail, August 18th, 2016, page 53

[136] Increase in penalty points and fixed penalty for using hand held mobile phone while driving, Sentencing Council, https://www.sentencingcouncil.org.uk/updates/magistrates-court/item/increase-in-penalty-points-and-fixed-penalty-for-using-a-hand-held-mobile-phone-while-driving/

[137] Resentment, raw emotion and the lessons of history, Adam Sweeting, the i, July 10th, 2019, page 35

[138] Lorry driver's dangerous overtaking manoeuvre that almost killed cyclist, Georgia Diebelius, Metro, February 7th, 2018, https://metro.co.uk/2018/02/07/cyclist-catches-moment-lorry-driver-knocked-off-bike-7293944/

[139] Dave Sherry says lorry driver who hit him left the country and won't face justice, Alex Bowden, March 16th, 2018, https://road.cc/content/news/238786-dave-sherry-says-lorry-driver-who-hit-him-left-country-and-wont-face-justice

[140] Dave Sherry shares his experiences of being knocked off his bike by an uninsured driver, GB News, October 7th, 2021, https://www.youtube.com/watch?v=gZzMrDJ8L8M

[141] A non-police witness statement

[142] Collision form

[143] Time and place Tim Vine – Cheam brings out the child in me and helps me see the funny side, Caroline Scott, the Sunday Times, August 1st 2012, page 3

[144] What happened to London's trams, Jay Foreman, Youtube, December 4th, 2018, https://www.youtube.com/watch?v=Ji3C_PjJonM

[145] Scrap cycle lanes, Nigel, and I'll swap my bike for a Chelsea tractor. Let's see if that stops jams!, Jeremy Vine, Mail on Sunday, November 29th, 2020, page 24

[146] Jeremy Vine, Twitter, January 24th, 2013, "The van doesn't indicate - feints to turn left - then sweeps round to the right. How do I deal with this on my bicycle?

Endnotes

http://youtu.be/1dO2R4cagh8,
https://twitter.com/theJeremyVine/status/294402788161617920

[147] Jeremy Vine, Twitter, April 22nd, 2013, "Cycling in London is so bracing. Watch the grey car:" , https://twitter.com/theJeremyVine/status/326416729666359296

[148] Why do so many drivers want to KILL ME? – Death threats. Near-misses. A run-in with Clarkson. Now Radio 2 host and (very scared) cyclists JEREMY VINE asks …, Jeremy Vine, The Daily Mail, January 13th, 2014, page 15

[149] A menace to cyclists, cars, even low flying aircraft, Jeremy Clarkson, The Sunday Times, December 1st, 2013, page 27

[150] Reported road casualties in Great Britain: younger driver factsheet, 2021, National Statistics, November 24th, 2022, https://www.gov.uk/government/statistics/reported-road-casualties-great-britain-older-and-younger-driver-factsheets-2021/reported-road-casualties-in-great-britain-younger-driver-factsheet-2021

[151] Cyclists still being sold short, Andrew Neater, Evening Standard, January 15th, 2014, page 15

[152] Debate: Should drivers be kinder to cyclists?, the Daily Mail, January 16th, 2014, page 61

[153] Jeremy vs Jeremy, Rod Liddle, the Sunday Times, January 19th, 2014, page 31

[154] Points, the Sunday Times - Driving, January 26th, 2014, page 6

[155] Caught on camera, Paul Gallagher, The Independent on Sunday, February 2nd, 2014, page 11

[156] As a later court ruling enforced, the Royal Parks are the only place in the UK where non-motor vehicles are subject to the speed limits. That includes Richmond Park and Bushy Park

[157] Radio 2 presenter stopped by police for cycling at 16mph in Hyde Park – Speeding Vine, Robin de Peyer, Evening Standard, November 20th, 2014, page 6

[158] Speeding Vine! BBC start stopped … for cycling at 16mph, Sam Creighton, the Daily Mail, November 21st, 2014, page 3

[159] Speed demon: Vine gets a talking to for pedalling at 16mph at Hyde Park, Danny Boyle, Martin Evans, the Daily Telegraph, November 21st, 2014, page 5

[160] Letter, 20mph speed limit would save lives, Dounnachdh McCarthy, Evening Standard, December 4th, 2014, page 75

[161] Around the time of Jeremy's first videos online

[162] Cycling death rate would shut a hospital – BBC presenter Vine 'outraged' by toll of tipper truck facilities, Ross Lydall, Sophia Sleigh, Evening Standard, June 30th, 2015, p13

[163] City Hall anger as Square Mile bosses block cycle routes, Ross Lydall, Evening Standard, July 13th, 2015, page 13

[164] Hight Street Kensington, RBKC

[165] Vine tells of wife's fears over his cycling in London, Sean Morrison, Evening Standard, October 2nd, 2018, page 8

[166] VIGILANTE CYCLIST: I'M HATED BUT I'VE NAILED 70 DRIVERS, Sam Blewett, Metro, February 6th, 2015, page 23

[167] Shamed motorists who fell foul of the cycling vigilante, Andrew Levy, the Daily Mail, February 6th, 2015, page 13

[168] 'Britain's most hated cyclist' catches out unsafe motorists, Geogie Keate, The Times, February 6th, 2015, page 4

[169] Actual body harm

[170] The vigilante cyclist: Man uses helmet-cam to film rogue motorists on his commute to work and helps police get more than SEVENTY motoring convictions (but his job is a London BUS driver), Richard Spillett, February 5th, 2015, MailOnline, https://www.dailymail.co.uk/news/article-2940879/Vigilante-cyclist-uses-three-cameras-film-rogue-motorists.html

[171] Jeremy Vine, cycling scourge of drivers, to head new Crimewatch, Patrick Foster, Daily Telegraph, August 5th, 2016, page 9

[172] Offence on its own as per rule 112 of the Highway Code and Legislation – The Road Vehicles (Construction and Use) Regularions 1986, Use of audible warning instruments, https://www.legislation.gov.uk/uksi/1986/1078/regulation/99/made

[173] I will knock you out! – BBC's Jeremy Vine films woman driver's shocking road rage after he rode bike in front of her car", Tim Lamden, Daily Mail, August 31st 2016, page 9

[174] Jeremy Vine films road rage row, Leon Watson, Daily Telegraph, August 31st, 2016, page 9

[175] I'll knock you out … Radio 2 star Vine films `bike rage`, Fiona Parker, Metro, August 31st, 2016, page 9

[176] Road rage driver threatens TV host, Kaya Burgess, The Times, August 31st, 2016, page 11

[177] Vine road rage scare, Sam Christie, August 31st, 2016, The Sun, page 18

[178] Road rage woman tells Jeremy Vine: I will knock you out 1 Jeremy rides his – Broadcaster's video nasty, Mark Jefferies, The Daily Mirror, August 31st, 2016, page 13

[179] BBC presenter posts clip of road-rage attack, Haroon Siddique, The Guardian, August 31st, 2016, page 11

[180] Middle-aged cyclists: a confession, Sarah Vine, Daily Mail, August 31st, 2016, page 15

[181] A vicious cycle, Jez, the Sun, September 1st, 2016, page 13

[182] Despite both being cyclists, Jeremy …, Sarah Vine, Daily Mail, November 11th, 2020, page 19

[183] Vine's right, cycling is unsafe … so leave your bike at home, Jeremy Clarkson, The Sun, September 3rd, 2016, page 13

[184] Why do cyclists make car drivers boil with rage, Rosamund Urwin, Evening Standard, September 1st, 2016, page 15

[185] Letters, Dangerous drivers should be banned, Metro, September 1st, 2016, page 16

Endnotes

[186] Telly's Vine rode like a cyclopath – exclusive: driver hits back 'road rage' vid row, Jonathan Reilly, the Sun, September 4th, 2016, page 21

[187] Driver arrested for threat to `knock out` BBC presenter Vine, Sophia Sleigh, Evening Standard, September 5th, 2016, page 22

[188] Student charged over Vine `cycle rage` row – TV presenter gives film of incident to the police, Ross Lyndall, October 13th, 2016, page 7

[189] We drivers don't mind cyclists ... if they can behave, Jeremy Clarkson, the Sun, October 15th, 2016, page 29

[190] He's racist! Jeremy Vine `gun` claim was because I am black, Rebecca Camber, Daily Mail, January 14th, 2017, page 5

[191] Driver guilty of road rage against Jeremy Vine, Tristan Kirk, Evening Standard, February 1st, 2017, page 2

[192] Vine road rage woman: I've suffered online, Danny Boyle, February 2nd, 2017, Daily Telegraph, page 7

[193] Facing jail, driver in Jeremy Vine road rage clash with as string of previous convictions, Arthur Martin, Daily Mail, February 2nd, 2017, page 21

[194] Hurrah for the broadcaster Jeremy, Peter Hitchens, Mail on Sunday, February 5th, 2017, page 29

[195] My bike terror, by Vine – Raging driver jailed, Lauren Probert, the Sun, April 19th, 2017, page 26

[196] What I Learnt, What My Listeners Say - And Why We Should Take Notice, Jeremy Vine, Weidenfeld & Nicolson, September 7th, 2017, ISBN 1474604927

[197] Vine sorry that road rage woman went to prison, Hannah Stephenson, The I, August 30th, 2017, page 13

[198] Cycling and pedestrians, Cheery, Cycling UK, https://www.cyclinguk.org/briefing/cycling-and-pedestrians

[199] Why do so many drivers want to KILL ME? – Death threats. Near-misses. A run-in with Clarkson. Now Radio 2 host and (very scared) cyclists JEREMY VINE asks ..., Jeremy Vine, The Daily Mail, January 13th, 2014, page 15

[200] Jeremy Vine, Twitter, December 4th, 2017, "Oh hello", https://twitter.com/theJeremyVine/status/937720049204424704

[201] Jeremy Vine, Twitter, October 5th, 2023, "Where in Bus Driver School do they teach drivers to sit their left wheels in the cycle lane? Do they spend a full morning practising this?" https://twitter.com/theJeremyVine/status/1709884053644587070

[202] Reckless cyclist nearly dies after barging through level crossing, Danie O'Mahony, Matt Watts, Evening Standard, May 12th, 2017, page 11

[203] Jeremy Vine lambasted for backing wheelie cyclist who hit car, Tom Ball, The Times, August 17th, 2019, page 13

[204] Jeremy Vine, Twitter, December 19th, 2017, "Just read about @2_Wheeled_Wolf – became disabled, started cycling to help his body mend, then this happened. Waiting to hear what @EssexPoliceUK are doing about the attacker", https://twitter.com/theJeremyVine/status/943053553064652800

[205] Jeremy Vine confronts driver after being knocked off bike in 'unbelievable' accident, Josie Copson, Metro, September 13th, 2023, https://metro.co.uk/2023/09/13/jeremy-vine-run-over-van-cycling-19493266/

[206] Vine: Alter road layout to protect cyclists, Daily Mirror, February 20th, 2017, page 9

[207] Jeremy Vine warns cyclists need protection from `maniac` drivers, Nicholas Hellen, Mark Hookham, March 25th, 2018, page 7

[208] Brownlee brothers back new `Stay Wider of the Rider` campaign, Ross Lydall, Evening Standard, July 4th, 2018, page 3

[209] Tory tweet announcing new road safety laws branded `shameful` by angry cyclists, Tom Batchelor, PA, Independent, August 18th, 2018, page 16

[210] Police sorry for officer `taking p----` over assault, Daily Telegraph, June 17th, 2019, page 2

[211] East Yorkshire and Lincolnshire.

[212] BBC East Yorkshire, Twitter, May 27th, 2020, "We talked about Hull being a cycling city tonight, great to hear the passion of cyclist and presenter @theJeremyVine. Here's some of the interview from earlier", https://twitter.com/looknorthBBC/status/1265730821761236993

[213] Cyclists? I'd kill the lot of them, says fashion guru, The Times, July 20th, 2020, page 5

[214] Never mind the bollards, Tim Lewis, The Observer, November 2st, 2020, page 11

[215] `Anti-car` Beeb is bias row, Jonathan Reilly, the Sun, January 7th, 2021, page 12

[216] Council says it 'did not manipluate data' after cycling campaigners accussed it of ignoring advice in order to controversially shelve bike lane, Adwitiya Pal, road.cc, May 3rd, 2023, https://road.cc/content/news/kensington-council-ignored-advice-and-manipulated-data-300933

[217] 20mph petition: 'No evidence of duplication or tempering', Senedd say, ITV, September 22nd, 2023, https://www.itv.com/news/wales/2023-09-22/no-evidence-of-duplication-or-tampering-of-20mph-senedd-petition

[218] Jeremy Vine: 'At the BBC you can have values but you can't have views – that's how I operate', Stephen Moss, Guardian, June 1st, 2020, https://www.theguardian.com/media/2020/jun/01/jeremy-vine-at-the-bbc-you-can-have-values-but-you-cant-have-views-thats-how-i-operate

[219] Vine breached impartiality rule with tweets backing LTNs, Will Bolton, Daily Telegraph, August 31st, 2022, page 9

[220] Chiswick councillor Joanna Biddolph suspended, Bridget Osborne, The Chiswick Calendar, March 23rd, 2024, https://chiswickcalendar.co.uk/chiswick-councillor-joanna-biddolph-suspended/

[221] Vine romance with my London village, Mark Anstead, Mail on Sunday, January 21st, 2007, page 15

Endnotes

[222] Pedestrian jailed for manslaughter after causing cyclist to fall in front of car, Rachel Hall, Guardian, March 2nd, 2023, https://www.theguardian.com/uk-news/2023/mar/02/pedestrian-jailed-manslaughter-cyclist-fall-car-huntingdon

[223] BBC presenter posts clip of road-rage attack, Haroon Siddique, The Guardian, August 31st, 2016, page 11

[224] Tell the council you want safe, protected cycle lanes on Kensington High Street and Fulham Road, BetterStreets4KC, https://betterstreets4kc.org.uk/campaigns/high-street-kensington/

[225] Jeremy Vine, Twitter, May 15th, 2022, "Just cycled through the 1980s disaster that is Kensington High Street, and suddenly wondered: is it about to change for the better? @willnorman", https://twitter.com/theJeremyVine/status/1261320643645227008

[226] Written evidence submitted by the Daily Mail and General Trust plc (ATR0094), September 2018, https://committees.parliament.uk/writtenevidence/96636/html/

[227] Nigel Havers takes B-test, Mirror Reporter, February 17th, 1990, Daily Mirror, page 5

[228] Havers' drink-driving moans fail to impress, The Courier and Advertiser, April 1st, 1991, page 6

[229] A walk along the high street was as simple pleasure. Now it's a fume choked Bedlam, Nigel Havers, Mail on Sunday, November, 22th, 2020, page 19

[230] The FairFuel petition mentioned before

[231] Councils start to rip up bike lanes, Michael Powell, Abul Taher, Mail On Sunday, November 29th 2020, page 24

[232] Chelsea Tractor is a term used to describe an SUV, Range Rovers in particular

[233] Scrap cycle lanes, Nigel, and I'll swap my bike for a Chelsea tractor. Let's see if that stops jams!, Jeremy Vine, Mail On Sunday, November 11th, 2020, page 24

[234] Boris Johnson's cycling tsar rang council to beg them NOT to rip up hated Kensington High Street bike lane and promised his 'ballistic' boss would ride down it for a photo opportunity, Abul Taher, James Heale, Micheal Powell, Henry Martin, Mail On Sunday, MailOnline, December 6th, 2020, https://www.dailymail.co.uk/news/article-9022941/Boris-Johnsons-cycling-tsar-told-council-NOT-rip-hated-Kensington-High-Street-bike-lane.html

[235] Sielay, Twitter, December 2nd, 2020, "This is my PRIVATE stand on it. I'm not imposing or suggesting official position of any institution. Anyhow in the current situation as my personal safety is at stake I voice my concerns", https://twitter.com/sielay/status/1334053068984496128

[236] MailOnline employee calls on council to keep Kensington High Street cycle lanes, saying "it made our journey safter", Simon MacMichael, road.cc, December 2nd, 2020, https://road.cc/content/news/mailonline-employee-urges-kensington-chelsea-keep-lanes-279171

[237] Campaigners lose High Court case against council over "premature" cycle lane removal, Ryan Mallon, road.cc, March 15th, 2023, https://road.cc/content/news/high-court-dismisses-kensington-high-street-cycle-lane-case-299939

[238] Work to being on pernament cycle lanes for Kensington High Street, Miriam Burrell, Evening Standard, August 1st, 2023, https://www.standard.co.uk/news/london/permanent-cycle-lanes-kensington-high-street-fulham-road-chelsea-council-b1095677.html

[239] Lauren, Twitter, September 30th, 2023, "This is the reality of cycling in a city like London.

My partner & I don't go anywhere without our GoPros, we realised pretty quickly after moving to the city that they are our best protection when dealing with the state of some drivers on the roads.", https://twitter.com/laurencyclist/status/1708235305348669487

[240] Lauren, Twitter, October 4th, 2023, "What is holding up all this traffic I hear you ask? Take a wild gues :I Clue, it isn't a cycle lane…", https://twitter.com/laurencyclist/status/1709646524395778465

[241] Approved Judgement between Director of Public Prosecutions and Ramsey Barreto, July 31st, 2019, https://www.judiciary.uk/wp-content/uploads/2019/07/19-07-31-DPP-v-Barreto-Ref.-CO2702019-Judgment.pdf

[242] New Highway Code rules trigger huge rise in fixed pentalites issued to motorists, Rob Hull, ThisIsMoney, January 31st, 2024, https://www.thisismoney.co.uk/money/cars/article-13028131/New-Highway-Code-rules-trigger-huge-rise-fixed-penalties-issued-motorists.html

[243] David Brennan, Twitter, March 2nd, 2024, "It has now been reported. To highlight just how variable policing is in Scotland on this occasion I've been offered an 'officer phone call' in the first instance. I've had police officers attend, I've had to attend a police station, but this is a first for an 'officer call'...", https://twitter.com/magnatom/status/1763971061849170300

[244] Mark Hodson, Twitter, October 15th, 2023, "Just a reminder that having the right people, in the right place, at the right time, with the right skill set & motivation addressing the "problem group" can hugely reduce demand, saving lives & £millions… It was a busy stressful year, the first of the RHPT, but very successful", https://twitter.com/markandcharlie/status/1713580122748461295

[245] Road Traffic Act 1988, Section 165, https://www.legislation.gov.uk/ukpga/1988/52/section/165

[246] Carol Boardman death driver jailed for 30 weeks, Steven Morris, Guardian, January 31st, 2019, https://www.theguardian.com/uk-news/2019/jan/31/carol-boardman-death-driver-jailed-for-30-weeks

[247] Policing the road from our front seats, Gaeme Lennox, Sunday Times Ireland, August 8th 2017, page 28

[248] Preferred conferencing software by the UK police but hated by engineers like me

[249] Evidence which confirms or supports a statement, theory, or finding, confirmation

[250] The time I was stopped by the Police for cycling legally on the road, sw19cam, YouTube, July 13th, 2018, https://www.youtube.com/watch?v=gbCWDSWFmyM

[251] Data for Traffic Offence allegations from June 2022 to May 2023, Metropolitan Police, 01/FOI/22/028011, https://www.met.police.uk/foi-ai/metropolitan-police/disclosure-2023/july-2023/data-traffic-offence-allegations-june2022-may2023/

Endnotes

252 The cost of road traffic accidents, 23th November, 2017, Hugh James, https://www.hughjames.com/blog/the-cost-of-road-traffic-accidents

253 Reported road casualties Great Britain, annual report: 2022, National Statistics, September 28th, 2023, https://www.gov.uk/government/statistics/reported-road-casualties-great-britain-annual-report-2022/reported-road-casualties-great-britain-annual-report-2022

254 Op Drive Insured is back for 2023, MIB, https://www.mib.org.uk/op-drive-insured/

255 Proper name is VRN – vehicle registration number

256 No charges brought against Regent's Park cyclist after high-speed crash in which persioner was killed while crossing road, Simon MacMichael, road.cc, May 6th, 2024, https://road.cc/content/news/no-charges-cyclist-after-crash-which-oap-was-killed-308209

257 The raise of deadly cyclists: Chilling number of pedestrians mowed down by reckless riders as Sir Ian Duncan Smith plans to close shocking legal loophole that allows bike users to speed with impunity Darren Boyle, MailoOnline, May 12th, 2024, https://www.dailymail.co.uk/news/article-13396307/The-rise-deadly-cyclists-Chilling-number-pedestrians-mowed-reckless-riders-Sir-Iain-Duncan-Smith-plans-close-shocking-legal-loophole-allows-bike-users-speed-impunity.html

258 Marh Hodson, Twitter, May 5th, 2024, "Why would you run a pain gang type scenario in a park with a 20mph limit ...you wouldn't run one in a 20mph residential area.Poor prosecution, the actual decision to be there cycling in that manner is what they should of concentrated on,the due care started before the collision", https://twitter.com/markandcharlie/status/1787095863283581175

259 Speeding Cyclist Kills Pedestrian – What's the law? @roadcc, BlackBeltBarrister, YouTube, May 14th, 2024, https://www.youtube.com/watch?v=T3PJOujwEiU

260 'There are more people killed by lightning and cows than cyclists', - Chris Boardman on proposed anti-dangerous cycling laws, Adam Becket, Cycling Weekly, May 16th, 2024, https://www.cyclingweekly.com/news/there-are-more-people-killed-by-lightning-and-cows-than-cyclists-chris-boardman-on-proposed-anti-dangerous-cycling-laws

261 The Grand Tour presenter James May says more restrictions for cyclists in London are not needed because most riders can't achieve speeds of 20mph on a bike, Ryan Hooper, MailOnline, May 14th, 2024, https://www.dailymail.co.uk/news/article-13416361/grand-tour-james-restrictions-cyclist-london-not-needed-achieve-speed.html

262 Sir Ian Duncan Smith back 'blade runner' ULEZ vandals: Tory M|P says he is 'happy' for residents of his east London constituency to destroy cameras because they have been 'lied to', Olivia Jones, MailOnline, August 29th, 2023, https://www.dailymail.co.uk/news/article-12458065/Sir-Iain-Smith-ULEZ-vandals-Tory-MP.html

263 James May, Twitter, May 13th, 2024, "When has a cyclists killed somoene but not been identified?", https://twitter.com/MrJamesMay/status/1790094871807627714

264 Machine gun

265 Adam Tranter, Twitter, May 15th, 2024, "Things that the Government could do (and have said they would do), but haven't, instead prioritising the creation of dangerous cycling laws:

- New laws for hit and run offenders, campaigned for by @RoadPeace

- Publishing of England road safety strategy

- Undertake full review of motoring offences and penalties, first promised in 2014

- Transport's Roads policing review: call for evidence began in 13 July 2020 with recommendations due in Spring 2021; to date, no update has been published

- Pavement parking consultation review - closed November 2020. No update has been published

- Allowing death by careless driving sentences to be appealed by families under the unduly lenient sentences scheme

- Establishing the Road Crash Investigation Bureau: promised, then quietly shelved

- Clarify the difference between careless and dangerous driving", https://twitter.com/adamtranter/status/1790824877718475062

[266] Driving Offences, CPS, https://www.cps.gov.uk/crime-info/driving-offences

[267] No points in case of the course, but this form can be used only once in two years

[268] 6 points in first two years after getting the driving license, 12 for other drivers

[269] Essex fines rise for using mobile phone while at the wheel, Sophie England, Basildon Canvey Southend Echo, February 23rd, 2024, https://www.echo-news.co.uk/news/24138556.essex-fines-rise-using-mobile-phone-wheel/

[270] SaferEssexRoads, Twitter, April 25th, 2023, "We accept these if they are reported by cyclists who record it in passing while on their commute but not from those who proactively seek out examples of poor driving.", https://twitter.com/SaferEssexRoads/status/1650800017798471682

[271] Pick and choose Choose Prosecutions - Is it Right?, BlackBeltBarrister, April 26th, 2023 https://www.youtube.com/watch?v=Hh3ehWmDnRY&feature=youtube

[272] Rory McCarron, Twitter, April 25h, 2023, "We accept reports of drink driving but not if you sit outside the local pub in the car park waiting for someone to down 5 pints and get in their car. Think about it…or do you not recognise or appreciate the danger of phone use at the wheel.", https://twitter.com/CyclingLawLDN/status/1650962137034944520

[273] OpSnap Data 2022 for Essex Police https://docs.google.com/spreadsheets/d/1ebwQG69HFWTMAeODVPeKAdFBMZCAPNBs

[274] Near Miss of the Day 806: Driver escapes punishment after reversing at cyclist and running over dog, Simon MacMichael, road.cc, September 9th, 2023, https://road.cc/content/news/nmotd-806-driver-reverses-cyclist-and-runs-over-dog-294737

[275] Fatal Crash on Motorway Calls for Multiuple Response Teams | Motorway Cops FULL EPISODE. | Blue Light, Blue Light – Emergency Response, YouTube, September 29th, 2023, https://www.youtube.com/watch?v=W_hmM9r4bLY&t=3189s

[276] Cllr Katherine S Miles, Twitter, July 16th, 2020, "Stopped by @TVP_Oxford on warneford lane advised not safe #cycling in #oxford with children at rush hour. They were kind but missed the point. #buildbackbetter @tonybrett @bigdamo @OxLivSts @DanyYee

Endnotes

@RosalindRogers @_eleanorvogel",
https://twitter.com/katherinesmiles/status/1283816256655818752

[277] CBikeLondon, Twitter, October 3rd, 2023, "Just had final update from Police about a driver who ran into me (and my then 1 year old onboard) during an inpatient undertake attempt on a narrow residential road, and then proceeded to assault me. "words of advice" is all she's getting.. 1/

On a cargo bike up a hill on narrow residential road. She approaches from behind revving. I refuse to be bullied and don't move over as I'll be getting to an opening momentarily where she can pass safely. She then decides to undertake in the narrow gap. 2/

Hit me from the side. We both stop. No injuries, her car is deeply scratched on the side, I lost a left wheel fender. I take out my phone to take pictures. She says she doesn't 'consent' and assaults me to try get the phone off my hand. I manage to pull it back. 3/

I explain she needs to exchange details with me, she refuses repeatedly. I call 999. During the call she relents and provides details, we part ways. I later find out only my front and rear dashcams were working, but not the helmet camera, so there is no sound.

Months later in the investigation police are understanding and apologetic but make it clear that the evidence is insufficient to progress. So another driver gets off scot free from their actions. But nevermind, since then I'll NEVER get caught out without evidential video again", https://twitter.com/CBikeLondon/thread/1709180639520423990

[278] Shamrocksoup, Twitter, October 3rd, 2023, "I reported one to collisions team last year where a @wandbc-contracted minibus drove headlong into me on a narrow residential street - scraping my elbow.

Despite crystal clear 360 footage, collisions team took NFA on basis driver mightn't have been aware he'd hit me. Inept.", https://twitter.com/ShamrockSoup/status/1709265353719664717

[279] Ralpha (aka Phil), Twitter, November 24th, 2023, "@HantsPolice @HantsPolRoads I gave up submitting as you have zero feedback. Andy's point 1 above is critical to effective and efficient use of your time. It's in your interests to give feedback and yet you don't", https://x.com/2wheelsnot4/status/1728083986319110518

[280] Truth Matters, Will Cycle, June 27th, 2023, https://www.willcycle.com/2023/06/27/truth-matters/

[281] With several exceptions

[282] Sentencing council, Causing death by dangerous driving, https://www.sentencingcouncil.org.uk/offences/crown-court/item/causing-death-by-dangerous-driving/

[283] Adam Tranter, Twitter, November 21st, 2023, "A new nationally representative poll by @YouGov suggests the majority of Brits would support lifetime driving bans for people who cause death by reckless driving.

Driving is a privilege, not a right, but so often killer drivers are able to get their licence back in a few years.", https://twitter.com/adamtranter/status/1727000131336274262

[284] "Arrogant' speeding driver with drugs and alcohol in his system avoids jail for killing cyclist, as prosecutor says incident was 'just below' dangerous driving threshold, Ryan Mallon,

November 1st, 2023, Road.cc, https://road.cc/content/news/speeding-drug-driver-avoids-jail-killing-cyclist-304839

[285] Woman who ploughed into group of Scots cyclsits in horror crash banned from driving, Gordon Currie, Daily Record, October 24th, 2023, https://www.dailyrecord.co.uk/news/scottish-news/woman-who-ploughed-group-scots-31258651

[286] Fix our broken justice system for road crash victims – or Vision Zero will forever be an aspiration, Rebecca Morris, RoadPeace, https://www.roadpeace.org/fix-our-broken-justice-system-for-road-crash-victims-or-vision-zero-will-forever-be-an-aspiration/

[287] Fix our Broken Justice System Victims' Voice guest blog: Frankie Jules-Hough – My soulmate, my peace, my queen, Calvin Buckley, https://www.roadpeace.org/fix-our-broken-justice-system-guest-blog-frankie-jules-hough-my-soulmate-my-peace-my-queen/

[288] If you want to kill someone, use a car, ETA, Vimeo, November 29th, 2019, https://vimeo.com/376388701

[289] Durham A1 crash: Lorry driver was browsing dating sites, BBC, January 11th, 2022, https://www.bbc.co.uk/news/uk-england-tyne-59951710

[290] Cyclist who lost leg in lorry collision criticises driver's £625 fine, Nadia Khomani, Guardian, August 19th, 2016 https://www.theguardian.com/uk-news/2016/aug/19/cyclist-julie-dinsdale-lost-leg-lorry-collision-driver-625-fine

[291] Delivery driver who mounted pavement and killed four-year-old girl cleared of any wrongdoing, Neil Docking, Liverpool Echo, March 22nd, 2017, https://www.liverpoolecho.co.uk/news/liverpool-news/delivery-driver-who-mounted-pavement-12782437

[292] Norwich driver caught back behind wheel FIVE days after ban, Simon Parkin, Eastern Daily Press, October 3rd, 2023, https://martini.edp24.co.uk/news/23831486.norwich-driver-caught-back-behind-wheel-five-days-ban/

[293] Jail for driver distracted by social media apps who killed cyclist and left another seriously injured, Simon MacMichael, road.cc, June 15th, 2023, https://road.cc/content/news/jail-distracted-driver-who-killed-cyclist-301907

[294] Travis and Sigrid, Twitter, October 10th, 2023, "I went to court, the judge was mostly on her phone while the driver harangued me about bad cyclists. Case was dismissed. I tried to file a complaint but was told you can't really do that. Anti-cyclist judges are out there, sadly. You covered it (a bit):", https://twitter.com/sigirides/status/1711791468430446788

[295] https://twitter.com/honorelliott_/status/1711750563249934813

[296] Surrey RoadSafe, Twitter, February 29th, 2024, "Tues, #SPCasualtyReduction Officers worked together on the A281, Guildford. A plain clothed Officer on a bicycle informed uniformed officers when they witnessed offences. In just 2 hours, the cycling officer recorded 23 drivers on their phones & 1 not wearing a seatbelt.

#Fatal5", https://twitter.com/SurreyRS/status/1763311034503164103

[297] Thousands of drivers are prosecuted after angry motorists submit dash cam clips to police, Martin Evans, Telegraph, February 5th, 2021,

Endnotes

https://www.telegraph.co.uk/news/2021/02/05/thousands-drivers-prosecuted-angry-motorists-submit-dash-cam/

[298] CycleGranny – [twitter handle]

[299] The Troubles were an ethno-nationalist conflict in Northern Ireland that lasted for about 30 years from the late 1960s to 1998. Also known internationally as the Northern Ireland conflict, it is sometimes described as an "irregular war" or "low-level war".

[300] Advanced Stop Line, Cycling Embassy of Great Britain, https://www.cycling-embassy.org.uk/dictionary/advanced-stop-line

[301] "Who would want to hurt an older lady cyclist?": Two boys injure cyclist by throwing gold ball at her, Adwitiya Pal, road.cc, January 4th, 2024, https://road.cc/content/news/two-boys-injure-cyclist-throwing-golf-ball-305997

[302] What is stopping women from cycling?, Anna Allatt, BBC News, January 21st, 2018, https://www.bbc.com/news/uk-england-leicestershire-41737483

[303] 100 Women in Cycling 2023, Cycling UK, https://www.cyclinguk.org/100women/2023

[304] According to Pass-Pixie creator Sheffield is one of the top markets for that product

[305] as a cycling instructor

[306] Why drivers should want cycle lanes, Jay Foreman, YouTube, April 19th, 2018, https://www.youtube.com/watch?v=_DNNIB_PdaA

[307] Police operations that support active travel – Mark Hodson, brian deegan, YouTube, December 31st, 2021, https://www.youtube.com/watch?v=OR9WwcV-p1o

[308] Elizabeth, Twitter, January 16th, "Makes me anxious out and about. Some of the cycle paths are isolated and the fear comes if you see a male. Then you go on road and get it from drivers.", https://twitter.com/EbikeBeth/status/1747356361170497661

[309] Women's Feedom, London Cycling Campaign, https://lcc.org.uk/campaigns/womens-freedom/

[310] Cycling to the office makes commuters less likely to be prescribed antidepressants, research finds, Megan Howe, MailOnline, January 15th, 2024, https://www.dailymail.co.uk/health/article-12962641/Cycling-office-commuters-prescribed-antidepressants-research.html

[311] James 2.0, Twitter, September 14th, 2023, "Set up & ready to go. Thanks to the driver who close passed us then ran over & damaged my wheel. You have motivated me to start reporting dangerous drivers & your insurance has funded the cam. If it saves one life it will be worth it. @Bikery1966 @anneramsey740 @MikeyCycling", https://twitter.com/kiwicycling/status/1702244166032339099

[312] Jaj991, Twitter, September 12th, 2023, "Since I tweeted about the new team dealing with #3rdPartyReports at WMP I've been getting feedback from a surprising number of people who were reporting, gave up but have started reporting again and are getting feedback. It's early days but it's looking positive right now.", https://twitter.com/jaj991/status/1701662275549991032

[313] Near Miss of the Day 872: Close passing van driver banned for 12 months and ordered to pay over £700 in costs after narrowly missing cyclist and oncoming motorist, Ryan Mallon,

Road.cc, August 23rd, 2023 https://road.cc/content/news/near-miss-day-872-van-driver-banned-12-months-303419

[314] Charlotte Baker, Twitter, October 19th, 2023, "I recently reported a PHV driver (with clear video) for running a red light on High St Ken 🚦

Chased up as realised I hadn't heard back - and got this response.

It seems @MPSRTPC are struggling to process the sheer amount of bad driving being reported ",

https://twitter.com/charlie_baker23/status/1715000744942670314

[315] Family: Get out more: The Family Challenge: Can inline skating offer exercise-averse Catherine Bennett and her daughter, Frances, a sport they can actually enjoy?, Catherine Benner, the Guardian, August 25th, 2007, page 8

[316] Strap me up before I go-go, Angela Petrusini, The Times, September 19th, 2009, page 3

[317] Tropper praised for going 'above and beyond' in viral video with yourng man with Down's syndrome, Laura Skitt, Forces.net, July 17th, 2023, https://www.forces.net/social-media/trooper-praised-going-above-and-beyond-viral-video-young-man-downs-syndrome

[318] "Cycling Mikey" is every bad London driver's worst nightmaer, Duarte Dias, Ian Less, Tina Kraus, CBS News, April 21st, 2023, https://www.cbsnews.com/news/cycling-mikey-is-every-london-bad-drivers-worst-nightmare/

[319] Lock, stock and a driving ban: Guy Richie filmed texting at wheel by Hyde Park cyclist, Tristan Kirk, Evening Standard, July 23rd, 2020, page 3

[320] Not so wise, Guy, Matthew Young, Daily Mirror, July 24th, 2020, page 14

[321] Driving ban for Ritchie after snatched picture, Metro, July 24th, 2020, page 15

[322] Gotcha, guy!, Emine Sinmaz, Dan Sales, Daily Mail, July 24th, 2020, page 31

[323] Jeremy Vine on 5, Twitter, July 24th, 2020, ""I'd actually like to defend Guy Ritchie here, because I thought he was very well-mannered and polite."

The cyclist who caught the film director texting while driving tells us his side of the story.

@MikeyCycling | @TessaDunlop | @TheJeremyVine | #JeremyVine", https://twitter.com/JeremyVineOn5/status/1286660656750632960

[324] Cycling vigilante - letters to the Editor, the Times, July 25th, 2020, page 28

[325] Two rings don't make a right for pushbike vigilante, Camilla Long, Sunday Times, July 26th, 2020, page 19

[326] Travel money - letters to the Editor, The Times, July 27th, 2020, page 30

[327] Ritchie's film is memorable for the wrong reasons, Celia Walden, Daily Telegraph, July 28th, 2020, page 20

[328] Wanted: volunteer traffic police. Bring own camera, Nicholas Hellen, Sunday Times, August 2nd, 2020, page 10

Endnotes

[329] Activist who caught Guy Ritchie on phone in car nails Eubank for jumping red light, Tristan Kirk, Hohn Dunne, Evening Standard, June 4th, 2021, page 3

[330] Eubank claimed to be police officer before skipping red light, Jack Hardy, Daily Telegraph, June 5th, 2021, page 13

[331] Eubank caught fsormaer boYxing chIampNion GBy Audhia Aoraeha's Cop, Claudio Aoraha, the Sun, June 5th, 2021, page 16

[332] Wrong sort of ring, Chris… boxer caught on phone at wheel of £370k Rolls-Royce, Az Munrallee, Daily Mail, June 5th, 2021, page 31

[333] Lampard drove with coffee in one hand and phone in the other, claims 'vigilante' cyclist, Tristan Kirk, Evening Standard, December 3rd, 2021, page 3

[334] Lampard 'used phone' while driving, Will Bolton, Dailly Telegraph, December 4th, 2021, page 19

[335] Foul! Fury as Lampard escapes scot-free despite being filmed at wheel holding phone and coffee, George Odling, Daily Mail, January 18th, 2022, page 5

[336] Lampard to fight driving charge after cyclist's claim, Ross Kaniuk, The Times, December 4th, 2021, page 8

[337] Pedal but no medal, Clemmie Moodie, The Sun, December 7th, 2021, page 15

[338] 'Mr Loophole' helps Lampard to swerve driving charge, Margaret Davis, the i, January 18th, 2022

[339] Frank Lampard will not face distracted driving charge, Matthew Weaver, The Guardian, January 18th, 2022, page 13

[340] Lampard uses Mr Loophole to beat charge of driving while on phone, Jack Hardy, Daily Telegraph, January 18th, 2022, page 3

[341] 'I felt powerless, so I started filming', Cyclist Mike van Erp's father was killed by a drunk driver. Now he reports motorists for breaking the law. He's even caught some celebrities, he tells Peter Walker, Peter Walker, the Guardian, January 5th, 2022, page 5

[342] Road safety hero or menace on 2 wheels?, Kathryn Knight, Daily Mail, January 22nd, 2022, page 34

[343] On the road with the cycling activist who stops stars in tracks. Dangerous drivers snared by campaigner, Amy Sharpe, Sunday Mirror, January 30th, 2022, page 25

[344] Biggest fine - £1750 at Gandalf Corner - she drives into Mikey - DC65VRP, CyclingMikey, YouTube, September 16th, 2020, https://www.youtube.com/watch?v=1kd8dwR-PUM

[345] Turtles or Snakes- Which do cars hit more? ROADKILL EXPERIMENT, Mark Rober, YouTube, July 19th, 2012, https://www.youtube.com/watch?v=k-Fp7flAWMA

[346] Angry doctors at Gandalf Corner - Results and Timeline, Cycling Mikey, YouTube, March 11th, 2020, https://www.youtube.com/watch?v=PA8ah2dwMxQ

[347] Hollywood agent 'ran over cyclist as he was in a rush', Daily Telegraph Reporter, Daily Telegraph, October 11th, 2022, page 10

[348] Talent agent 'drove 60ft with cycling activist on top of his bonnet', Daily Mail Reporter, Daily Mail, October 11th, 2022, page 15

[349] Man cleared of using car as a weapon to hit cyclist, Daily Telegraph, October 14th, 2022, page 2

[350] On your bike. Video snoop's defeat: 'Cycling vigilante' loses case as jury back driver, Mike Sullivan, The Sun, October 14th, 2022, page 27

[351] Driving me mad - letters, Alan Weatheritt, Ashlington, Northumberland, Daily Mail, October 14th, 2022, page 54

[352] Gandalf Corner: I Get Hit by Paul Lyon-Maris Video 1 - HV04FOX, Cycling Mikey, YouTube, October 13th, 2022, https://www.youtube.com/watch?v=eZMaxLG-Lpk

[353] Mother who moved Insulate Britain protester with Range Rover admits dangerous driving, Emily Atkinson, March 28th, 2022, Independent, https://www.independent.co.uk/news/uk/crime/insulate-britain-protest-range-rover-b2045705.html

[354] On the road with the cycling activist who stops stars in tracks, Amy Sharpe, Sunday Mirror, January 30th, 2022, page 25

[355] Cycling vigilante snatches Guy Ritchie, Neil Johnston, The Times, July 24th, 2020, page 3

[356] 'I felt powerless, so I started filming', Cyclist Mike van Erp's father was killed by a drunk driver. Now he reports motorists for breaking the law. He's even caught some celebrities, he tells Peter Walker, Peter Walker, the Guardian, January 5th, 2022, page 5

[357] Marcel Moran, Twitter, February 26th, 2024, "Terrifying finding from this new study - every 10 cm increase in a vehicle's front-end height causes a 22% increase in pedestrian-fatality risk. https://www.sciencedirect.com/science/article/pii/S2212012224000017", https://twitter.com/marcelemoran/status/1762153758295802333

[358] Cristo, Twitter, tweet removed, https://twitter.com/cristo_radio/status/1453803375276003333

[359] Roads Policing – Surrey Police – UK, Twitter, October 29th, 2021, "Wouldn't it be great if we had enough cops to do the same. Unfortunately we don't, so Mikey is providing a really effective element of Road safety.

The only people who would find this concerning are Road users committing offences.", https://twitter.com/SurreyRoadCops/status/1454046466717196292

[360] Cycling Mikey the Unspeakable, Twitter, March 21st, 2024, "Hey Matty, where's your account, lad?", https://twitter.com/MikeyCycling/status/1770951291994345823

[361] Bike lane Britain … the Great Leap Backwards. Under covor of Covid, officials have turned our city centres into crazy golf courses giving priority to Lycra-clad lunatics on racing bikes, Richard Littleton, Daily Mail, January 22nd, 2022, https://www.dailymail.co.uk/debate/article-10437241/Bike-lane-Britain-Great-Leap-Backwards-writes-RICHARD-LITTLEJOHN.html

[362] Jeremy Vine joins football pundit Eniola Aluko and sues Joey Barton over 'bike nonce' social media jibe, Megan Howe, MailOnline, March 14th, 2024, https://www.dailymail.co.uk/news/article-13194915/Jeremy-Vine-joins-Eniola-Aluko-sues-Joey-Barton-social-media-jibe.html

Endnotes

[363] Championing Justice: Uniting Behind Joey Barton, GoFundMe, March 15rh, 2024, https://www.gofundme.com/f/championing-justice-uniting-behind-joey-barton

[364] pounds 20 fines for `Lycra louts' who pedal on pavement, Randeep Ramesh, Independent, January 14th, 1998, https://www.independent.co.uk/news/pounds-20-fines-for-lycra-louts-who-pedal-on-pavement-1138539.html

[365] City police target 'Lycra lout' cyclists who jump red lights at Bank Junction, Anthony France, Evening Standard, Septebmer 22nd, 2023, https://www.standard.co.uk/news/crime/police-lycra-louts-jumping-red-lights-in-the-square-mile-b1108748.html

[366] The ceaseless self-pity of cyclists, Julie Burchill, the Spectator, January 29th, 2022, https://www.spectator.co.uk/article/the-ceaseless-selfpity-of-cyclists/

[367] The cycling habit most hated by drivers, Jake Williams Simons, the Spectator, May 31st, 2022, https://www.spectator.co.uk/article/the-cycling-habit-that-drivers-hate-the-most/

[368] We don't need riding vigilantes – cyclists already own the roads, Jake Williams Simons, the Spectator, July 16th, 2023, https://www.spectator.co.uk/article/we-dont-need-bike-vigilantes-cyclists-already-own-the-roads/

[369] Stop demonising cyclists, Alec Marsh, March 15th, 2023, https://www.spectator.co.uk/article/stop-demonising-cyclists/

[370] Go Dutch to put brakes on 'car-dooring' and save lives, Katie Strick, Matt Writtle, November 27th, 2019, Evening Standard, https://www.standard.co.uk/comment/comment/go-dutch-to-put-brakes-on-cardooring-and-save-lives-a4298121.html

[371] The rise of the vigilante cyclists targeting London's dangerous drivers, Robbie Griffiths, Evening Standard, March 19th, 2024, https://www.standard.co.uk/lifestyle/jeremy-vine-cycling-mikey-road-safety-cameras-london-cars-drivers-cyclists-b1144841.html

[372] The rise of the vigilante cyclists targeting London's dangerous driversLondon cyclists, stop snitching on car drivers and sort your own behaviour out first, Ped Millichamp, Evening Standard, March 19th, 2024, https://www.standard.co.uk/comment/cycling-london-cycle-lanes-drivers-b1146222.html

[373] "The police crackdown on social media has gone too far", Harry Miller, the Spectator, August 1st 2022, https://www.spectator.co.uk/article/the-police-crackdown-on-social-media-has-gone-too-far/

[374] Media Reporting Guidelines for Road Collisions, RCRG, https://www.rc-rg.com/guidelines

[375] Motorist who racially abused and reversed into group of cyclists in "distressing" attack handed suspended sentence and banned from driving for 20 months, Ryan Mallon, road.cc, December 10th, 2023, https://road.cc/content/news/motorist-racially-abused-and-reversed-cyclists-305589

[376] Motorist avoids jail for deliberately ramming cyclist who questioned close pass, Dan Alexander, October 30th, 2023, https://road.cc/content/news/woman-avoids-jail-deliberately-ramming-cyclist-304777

377 Dehumanization: trends, insights, and challenges, Nour S. Kelly, Alexander P. Landry, January 15th, 2022, https://www.cell.com/trends/cognitive-sciences/abstract/S1364-6613(21)00311-9

378 Bloody Cyclists, morethancyclist, YouTube, November 20th, 2023, https://www.youtube.com/watch?v=ZoD3pLLxwok

379 Media Reporting Guidelines for Road Collisions, RCRG, https://www.rc-rg.com/guidelines

380 UK to introduce new offence of causing death or injury by dangerous cycling, Ben Quinn, Guardian, May 15th, 2024, https://www.theguardian.com/news/article/2024/may/15/uk-to-introduce-new-offence-of-causing-death-or-injury-by-dangerous-cycling

381 'Killer cyclists' crackdown accelerates as MPs back action after deaths in London, Jitendra Joshi, Evening Standard, May 16th, 2024, https://www.standard.co.uk/news/politics/cyclists-crackdown-death-regents-park-strava-b1157850.html

382 Killer cyclists to be treated like dangerous drivers: Reckless riders who cause death or serious injury to pedestrians to face life in prison like motorists who flout law as campaigners hail 'fantastic result', Natasha Anderson, May 15th, 2024, https://www.dailymail.co.uk/news/article-13423009/Killer-cyclists-face-14-year-sentences-new-law-Campaigners-fantastic-result.html

383 Killer cyclists to be treated like dangerous drivers following proposed law changes, Will Conroy, LBC, May 16th, 2024, https://www.lbc.co.uk/news/killer-cyclists-dangerous-drivers-proposed-law-changes-iain-duncan-smith/

384 How cyclists are turning UK roads into death traps, Eleonor Steafel, Ben Butcher, Telegraph, May 16th, 2024, https://www.telegraph.co.uk/news/2024/05/16/competitive-strava-cyclists-turn-uk-roads-into-death-traps/

385 Chris Boardman, Twitter, May 17th, 2024, "I don't normally get involved in calling out headlines but it's just getting bonkers.

If this was directed at a gender, race or religion it would be rightly called out as the hate speech it is. Mums, dads, sons and daughters being labelled as killers. It's just got to stop.", https://x.com/Chris_Boardman/status/1791553647731409403

386 Jeremy Vine, Twitter, May 11th, 2024, "Published today, this is the most misleading graph I have ever seen in my life.

The blue line is "pedestrians killed by cyclists". In two years (2013, 2019) the total appears to be EIGHT HUNDRED.

In fact the relevant numbers are hidden on the right — it's not 800 but six.", https://x.com/theJeremyVine/status/1789348929357619688

387 TalkTV, Twitter, May 16th, 2024, "Mike Graham says cyclists "should be locked up, even if they haven't committed any crime" telling them: "You want to put Lycra shorts on, shave your legs and ride around like you're in the Tour de France." @Iromg", https://x.com/TalkTV/status/1791148926243938308

388 KimBriggsCampaign, Twitter, May 18th, 2024, "This prob wont get noticed but is important. I have huge respect for people like @Chris_Boardman @carltonreid @peterwalker99 @WeAreCyclingUK they have always been very decent to me and me to them. We may disagree on things but I will always be respectful even in robust debate. 1

Endnotes

Any road death is an absolute tragedy. I know the awful consequences. My point has always been that motor related deaths have clear paths to prosecution. If it's felt that they are not done so adequately, that's a valid but different debate to my call for new laws. (2)

We ALL share these imperfect roads. We are ALL pedestrians at some point. And we owe it to ALL that we conduct ourselves on the roads with care, consideration and awareness (3)

This has never been anti cycling. If people attribute that to me, they are misled. It's always been a legal matter. 4

Oh and my politics? Let's just say that my friends think that some of the things thrown at me on here are hilarious. And yes, it was cheeky to say Sovereign and will of the people…but the important point was that this went through un-opposed by all sides of the house. 5

And finally, I've always said that I'll step back once this law is passed. I'm a private person with a life to lead - I just saw something that needed fixing. But after that, this account will close and I'll get on with my life. Have a great day everyone and be kind. 6", https://x.com/BriggsCampaign/status/1791737936758644835

[389] BigDai, Twitter, May 17th, 2024, "I stopped to offer help to two cyclists in Surbiton/Long Ditton. Turns out they were victims of assault by a driver who used his car as a weapon. The first had been close passed, the angry driver then drove at the cyclist, the second tried to stop the driver who aggressively", https://x.com/Bigdai100/status/1791431429986923000

[390] Royal Parks Police, Twitter, May 17th, 2024, https://x.com/MPSRoyal_Parks/status/1791461838363701754

[391] PhoneKills, Twitter, May 16th, 2024, "I'd like to thank all journalists who jumped on the bandwagon of deflecting road danger from drivers onto the cyclist. Each close pass ends up with the driver trying to escalate. If I don't post for a longer period call st George's.", https://x.com/phonekills/status/1791172933034905878

[392] PhoneKills, Twitter, May 17th, 2024, "For context. That lad stopped afterwards, blocked my way, wanted to escalate, and said he "doesn't have to give me any space" and "he had to go close as there was traffic ahead"… 101 on how to incriminate yourself.", https://x.com/phonekills/status/1791400417227608232

[393] PhoneKills, Twitter, May 18th, 2024, "What a lovely person. The profile doesn't let down. Now imagine a person with such a mental state could be allowed to control a two tonne machine with the destructive force of a small explosive device.", https://x.com/phonekills/status/1791934120697778339

[394] Proportionate Response to Crime piloted in the North East, Police Scotland, https://www.scotland.police.uk/what-s-happening/news/2023/september/proportionate-response-to-crime/

[395] David Brennan, Twitter, March 3rd, 2024, "Well this is concerning, I hadn't seen this before. A 'proportionate response to crime…'. Concerned that this is the reasoning behind the lack of online reporting system and my recent 'police phone call' response to a close pass… 🙄", https://twitter.com/magnatom/status/1764346662648938852

[396] Just how dangerous ARE London's roads? Jeremy Vine is a cycling crusader who divides the nation with his one-man war on 'rogue drivers'… Now MailOnline joins the Radio 2 host on his daily commute to find out if the capital really IS a bike death trap, Josh James, MailOnline, March 21st, 2024, https://www.dailymail.co.uk/news/article-13212025/Just-

dangerous-Londons-roads-Jeremy-Vine-cycling-crusader-divides-nation-one-man-war-rogue-drivers-MailOnline-joins-Radio-2-host-daily-commute-capital-really-bike-death-trap.html

[397] Battle of the LTNs: What happened when a driver and a cyclist both took the same one-mile trip across London - when the route was riddled with eco-friendly traffic slowing measures?, Darren Boyle, Alex Mason, ThisIsMoney, MailOnline, February 25th, 2023, https://www.thisismoney.co.uk/money/cars/article-11764273/What-happens-car-bike-face-Londons-LTN-network.html

[398] I'm a cyclist and this helmet-cam footage shows the reality of cycling in London - so after watching it, would YOU dare use pedal power in the capital?, Ted Thornhill, MailOnline, October 4th, 2023, https://www.dailymail.co.uk/travel/article-12589209/Im-cyclist-helmet-cam-footage-shows-reality-cycling-London-watching-dare-use-pedal-power-capital.html

[399] Opinion: DSI Andy Cox on road safety and what must be done, Cycling UK, January 5th, 2024, https://www.cyclinguk.org/blog/opinion-dsi-andy-cox-road-safety-and-what-must-be-done

[400] Thirteen-year-old Hope Fennell was killed by a lorry while cycling home, ITV News, September 12th, 2013, https://www.itv.com/news/central/2013-09-12/thirteen-year-old-hope-fennell-was-killed-by-a-lorry-while-cycling-home-from-school

Printed in Great Britain
by Amazon